Essays in Collective Epistemology

Essays in Collective Epistemology

EDITED BY

Jennifer Lackey

OXFORD
UNIVERSITY PRESS

Great Clarendon Street, Oxford, OX2 6DP,
United Kingdom

Oxford University Press is a department of the University of Oxford.
It furthers the University's objective of excellence in research, scholarship,
and education by publishing worldwide. Oxford is a registered trade mark of
Oxford University Press in the UK and in certain other countries

© the several contributors 2014

The moral rights of the authors have been asserted

First published 2014
First published in paperback 2016

All rights reserved. No part of this publication may be reproduced, stored in
a retrieval system, or transmitted, in any form or by any means, without the
prior permission in writing of Oxford University Press, or as expressly permitted
by law, by licence, or under terms agreed with the appropriate reprographics
rights organization. Enquiries concerning reproduction outside the scope of the
above should be sent to the Rights Department, Oxford University Press, at the
address above

You must not circulate this work in any other form
and you must impose this same condition on any acquirer

Published in the United States of America by Oxford University Press
198 Madison Avenue, New York, NY 10016, United States of America

British Library Cataloguing in Publication Data
Data available

Library of Congress Cataloging in Publication Data
Data available

ISBN 978-0-19-966579-2 (Hbk.)
ISBN 978-0-19-966580-8 (Pbk.)

Links to third party websites are provided by Oxford in good faith and
for information only. Oxford disclaims any responsibility for the materials
contained in any third party website referenced in this work.

Contents

Contributors   vii

    Introduction   1
    Jennifer Lackey

Part I. The Debate between Summativists and Non-Summativists

  1. Social Process Reliabilism: Solving Justification Problems in Collective Epistemology   11
    Alvin I. Goldman

  2. When Is There a Group that Knows? Distributed Cognition, Scientific Knowledge, and the Social Epistemic Subject   42
    Alexander Bird

  3. A Deflationary Account of Group Testimony   64
    Jennifer Lackey

Part II. General Epistemic Concepts in the Collective Domain

  4. How to Tell if a Group Is an Agent   97
    Philip Pettit

  5. The Stoic Epistemic Virtues of Groups   122
    Sarah Wright

  6. Disagreement and Public Controversy   142
    David Christensen

Part III. Individual and Collective Epistemology

  7. Social Roots of Human Knowledge   167
    Ernest Sosa

  8. Belief, Acceptance, and What Happens in Groups: Some Methodological Considerations   189
    Margaret Gilbert and Daniel Pilchman

Part IV. Collective Entities and Formal Epistemology

9. Individual Coherence and Group Coherence 215
   *Rachael Briggs, Fabrizio Cariani, Kenny Easwaran,
   and Branden Fitelson*

10. When to Defer to Supermajority Testimony—and When Not 240
    Christian List

Index 251

Contributors

ALEXANDER BIRD, University of Bristol
RACHAEL BRIGGS, Australian National University
FABRIZIO CARIANI, Northwestern University
DAVID CHRISTENSEN, Brown University
KENNY EASWARAN, University of Southern California
BRANDEN FITELSON, Rutgers University
MARGARET GILBERT, University of California, Irvine
ALVIN I. GOLDMAN, Rutgers University
JENNIFER LACKEY, Northwestern University
CHRISTIAN LIST, London School of Economics
PHILIP PETTIT, Princeton University and Australian National University
DANIEL PILCHMAN, University of California, Irvine
ERNEST SOSA, Rutgers University
SARAH WRIGHT, University of Georgia

Introduction

Jennifer Lackey

Collective entities are the subjects of a variety of epistemic evaluations. For instance, we routinely cite such entities as the source of the knowledge that we possess. I may say, "I found out from the American Kennel Club that the Labrador retriever is the most popular purebred dog in the United States," or "I learned from *Wikipedia* that Abraham Lincoln died on April 15, 1865." The most natural interpretation of these claims is that we can acquire knowledge via *collective testimony*. Collective entities themselves are also often commonly said to believe or know things. For instance, the following was reported in a recent article in *Daily Finance* about Borders lagging behind its competitors with respect to the e-book market: "Armed with data on 38 million customers, Borders *believes* it will easily capture market share" (*Daily Finance*, July 7, 2010, emphasis added). Similarly, a recent story about the Gulf oil spill in *Reuters* writes, "Long before the oil spill in the Gulf of Mexico in 2010, BP (BP.L) *knew* its Macondo well could explode and then lied about how much oil leaked" (*Reuters*, September 30, 2013, emphasis added). The most straightforward reading of these claims countenances the phenomena of *collective belief, collective epistemic justification*, and *collective knowledge*.

Moreover, there are often enormously significant consequences that follow from the presence, or absence, of these phenomena. For instance, if BP did in fact know that a safety device was faulty—one that, if repaired, could have prevented the oil spill in the Gulf of Mexico—then its negligence is significantly greater than if it didn't know this. This, in turn, might make an enormous difference to BP's moral and legal responsibilities. Here is another case: if the Bush Administration justifiedly believed that Iraq did not have weapons of mass destruction, then not only did the Administration lie to the public in saying that it did, but it is also fully culpable for of the hundreds of thousands of lives needlessly lost in the Iraq war.

Despite the widespread occurrence and importance of such epistemic attributions to collective entities, there is surprisingly little philosophical work shedding light on these phenomena, their consequences, and the broader implications that follow for epistemology in general. *Essays in Collective Epistemology* aims to fill this gap in the literature by bringing together new papers in this area by some of the leading figures in social epistemology.

Background and Summaries

One of the central debates in collective epistemology is between summativists and non-summativists. According to summativism, collective phenomena can be understood entirely in terms of individual phenomena. So, for instance, a summative account of justified collective belief holds that a collective entity, E, justifiedly believes that p if and only if some of E's members justifiedly believe that p. A summative account of knowledge maintains that a collective entity, E, knows that p if and only if some of E's members know that p. This view is well positioned to capture some paradigmatic instances of collective epistemic phenomena. For instance, that Northwestern University justifiedly believes that its main campus is located in Evanston, IL can easily be explained by its members justifiedly believing this. That the Catholic Church knows that it does not permit women to be ordained as priests can be accounted for by its members knowing this.

Summativism has come under attack in recent years however, primarily through what are known as *divergence arguments*. Divergence arguments purport to show that there can be a divergence between phenomena at the collective level and the corresponding phenomena at the individual level. So, for instance, a divergence argument against a summative account of justified collective belief holds that a collective entity, E, can justifiedly believe that p, despite the fact that not a single member of E justifiedly believes that p. Similarly, such an argument challenging a summative view of collective knowledge claims that a collective entity, E, can know that p, despite the fact not a single individual member of E knows that p.

These arguments are taken to support non-summativism, according to which collective phenomena are not understood in terms of individual phenomena. Instead, a collective entity, E, is an epistemic subject in its own right, one whose justifiedly believing or knowing that p is over and above, or otherwise distinct from, the individual members of G justifiedly believing or knowing that p. A standard type of case said to support this view with respect to collective justification is as follows:

A jury is deliberating about whether the defendant in a murder trial is innocent or guilty. Each member of the jury is privy to evidence that the defendant was seen fleeing the scene of the crime with blood spatter on his clothes, but it is grounded in hearsay that, though reliable, was ruled as inadmissible by the judge. Given only the admissible evidence, the jury as a group justifiedly believes that the defendant is innocent, but not a single juror justifiedly believes this proposition because it is defeated for each of them as individuals by the relevant reliable hearsay evidence.

Cases of this sort are prevalent in the collective epistemology literature, but Schmitt (1995) provides a particularly detailed version. According to Schmitt, different evidence cases successfully function as divergence arguments only when they involve chartered groups, where "[a] chartered group is one founded to perform a particular action or actions of a certain kind," and "has no life apart from its office" (1995, pp. 272–3). In other words, chartered groups must function only in their offices or risk ceasing to exist. The U.S. Congress, the Sierra Club, and juries are all groups of this sort. Moreover, given the particular charter of a group, it may be governed by special epistemic standards, such as the exclusion of hearsay in a court of law. Because of this,

...a nonlegal group may fail to be justified in a belief because a member possesses countervailing hearsay. A court, on the other hand, would not lose its justification merely because a member possesses countervailing hearsay. And this is because in its legal capacity, the court rightly excludes hearsay, and its legal capacity is the only capacity in which it operates. (Schmitt 1995, p. 274)

Since the jury in the above case is a chartered group, Schmitt argues that its charter prohibits it from considering the hearsay evidence about the defendant fleeing the scene of the crime with blood spatter on his clothes. Without this crucial testimony, the jury justifiedly believes that the defendant is innocent of the murder in question. But since the jurors *qua* individuals are not governed by these special standards of available reasons, they each have a defeater provided by the hearsay evidence for believing in the defendant's innocence. Thus, the non-summativist concludes that the jury justifiedly believes that the defendant is innocent despite the fact that not a single individual member justifiedly holds this belief.

In place of summativism, non-summativists argue that collective epistemic phenomena, such as collective justification, should involve actions at the level of the group. The classic non-summativist view of collective justification is the joint acceptance account, where a group has a reason to believe that p if and only if the members of the group would jointly accept r as the group's reason to believe that p. Thus, the reasons available to a group are determined by their joint acceptance, and the epistemic goodness or badness of these reasons can then, in turn, be fleshed out in terms of standard epistemological theories, such as reliabilism, evidentialism, and so on.

Several chapters in this volume contribute, either directly or indirectly, to the debate between summativists and non-summativists. In "Social Process

Reliabilism: Solving Justification Problems in Collective Epistemology," Alvin I. Goldman offers a new account of justified group belief, which holds that the greater the proportion of members who justifiedly believe that p and the smaller the proportion of members who justifiedly reject that p, the greater the group's level, or grade, of justifiedness in believing that p. In particular, Goldman applies process reliabilism, which he has extensively developed to account for the justified beliefs of individuals, to collective belief and shows how combining this view with aggregation principles can yield a view of justified collective beliefs. Goldman's view is, thus, broadly summativist, since group justifiedness is determined by aggregating the justifiedness of the beliefs of the individual members.

In contrast, Alexander Bird defends a non-summative account of collective knowledge in his "When Is There a Group that Knows? Distributed Cognition, Scientific Knowledge, and the Social Epistemic Subject," a paradigm of which is knowledge attributed to the scientific community. According to Bird, the scientific community is a social subject that can know that p, even if not a single member of the collective entity is even aware that p. In this way, he denies that collective knowledge supervenes on the mental states of individuals. To support this thesis, Bird draws on work on distributed cognition and Durkheimian sociology to, first, characterize when a collection of individuals forms an entity that is more than just the mereological sum of its constituent persons and, second, to provide conditions under which such a subject is said to possess knowledge.

In "A Deflationary Account of Group Testimony," Jennifer Lackey takes up the topic of group testimony as a *source of knowledge* and answers the question: when we acquire knowledge from the testimony of a group, who is the source? Is it an individual or set of individuals or is it somehow the group itself? In answering this question, *reductionists* maintain, on the one hand, that a group's testimony that p is epistemologically reducible to the testimony of some individuals. The standard reductionist theory is the *summative* view, according to which a group testifying that p can be understood in the minimal sense that all or some members of the group would testify that p were the relevant opportunity to arise. On the other hand, *non-reductionists* hold that the testimony of a group is irreducible to that of all or some of its members and, moreover, that in some very important sense, the group itself is the source of the knowledge. According to a *non-summative* view in particular, a group testifying that p cannot be understood in the sense that all or some members of the group would testify that p were the relevant opportunity to arise. In this chapter, Lackey argues that these two distinctions—between reductionism and non-reductionism, and between summativism and non-summativism—are not equivalent. She then develops a *deflationary account of group testimony* according to which a group's testimony *is* reducible to that of one or more individuals, though not necessarily ones who are members of the group in question. Thus the resulting view is both reductionist and non-summative in nature.

Other chapters in this volume focus on more general epistemic concepts and explore how they apply in the collective domain. In "How to Tell if a Group Is an Agent," Philip Pettit takes up the issue in the title of his chapter—how we can tell when a group is a bona fide agent, epistemic or otherwise. He first offers a general account of agency, arguing for distinctions between different modes of agency and of agency-detection. Relying on this material, Pettit argues that only direct or indirect evidence of *interpersonal engagement* provides a warrant for ascribing agency to groups. Thus, he concludes that the only group agents that are generally recognized as such are those of a personal kind and, moreover, that such groups count as real, non-fictional agents.

Sarah Wright shows how a Stoic account of the epistemic virtues can be extended from individuals to groups in her "The Stoic Epistemic Virtues of Groups." She begins with the Stoic distinction between *telos* and *skopos*: with respect to the epistemic virtues in the individual case, a subject's *telos* would be believing well while her *skopos* might be believing the true answer to a particular question. A Stoic account of the epistemic virtues of groups, then, needs to include both components, and Wright provides the framework for explaining how this can happen. In particular, she shows how the Stoic view of epistemic agency clearly has the resources for countenancing group beliefs. Given this, she argues that there are no obstacles to groups either having dispositions to believe well or to aiming at true group beliefs, and thus we can see how groups can have both an epistemic *telos* and an epistemic *skopos*.

In "Disagreement and Public Controversy," David Christensen applies the conciliatory approach that he has developed with respect to disagreements involving individuals to public group controversies in philosophy and politics. According to conciliation, when a subject has strong positive, dispute-independent reasons to think that those who disagree with her are equally well-informed and equally as likely to have reasoned correctly as those who agree with her, then she should significantly reduce her confidence in the disputed proposition, perhaps to the point of withholding belief. Christensen shows not only that complexities arise when a conciliatory approach is taken in the collective domain, but also that group disagreements are more powerful defeaters of rational belief, even when the groups in question are comparable in size and epistemic credentials.

Two of the chapters in this volume examine even broader questions related to collective epistemology. Ernest Sosa considers how far the social extends into individual epistemology in his "Social Roots of Human Knowledge." He begins by examining why it is that that a batter's 15 percent competence and a basketball player's 40 percent three-point percentage are regarded as outstanding while an epistemic ability at these levels is taken to be inadequate to provide knowledge. According to Sosa, the answer is that epistemic competences are relevant not only to the attainment of beliefs for the believer, but also to informing others and thereby enlarging the pool of shared information. In this sense, the social dimension of epistemology imports a requirement of reliability higher than is necessary in other domains, and thus knowledge and belief are constitutively social in an important respect. Sosa then shows how this conclusion bears both on the value that knowledge has and on how the pragmatic can encroach on epistemology.

In "Belief, Acceptance, and What Happens in Groups: Some Methodological Considerations," Margaret Gilbert and Daniel Pilchman examine the relationship between individual and collective epistemology, with a particular focus on the debate between those who grant that groups have beliefs and those who claim that they have only acceptances. Gilbert and Pilchman argue that there is an important methodological constraint that most have failed to appreciate: it should not be assumed that theories and distinctions accepted in individual epistemology will apply straightforwardly to the corresponding phenomena in collective epistemology.

The remaining two chapters in this volume explore issues that arise regarding collective entities in formal epistemology. Rachael Briggs, Fabrizio Cariani, Kenny Easwaran, and Branden Fitelson begin their "Individual Coherence and Group Coherence" by noting that paradoxes of both individual coherence—such as the preface paradox—and of group coherence—such as the doctrinal paradox for judgment aggregation—often assume that deductive consistency is a coherence requirement for both individual and group judgment. In this chapter, they introduce a new coherence requirement for individual belief, and then show how this approach has the resources for resolving traditional paradoxes. Moreover, though their coherence requirement avoids the standard doctrinal paradox, they prove a new impossibility result that reveals that other versions of the doctrinal paradox arise even for their requirement.

In "When to Defer to Supermajority Testimony—and When Not," Christian List takes up the view of Philip Pettit, according to which deferring to majority testimony is not generally rational because it may lead to inconsistent beliefs. In place of deference to majority testimony, Pettit proposes deference to supermajority testimony, which is taken to fare better in this respect. However, this, too, may lead to inconsistency, and so List provides conditions under which deferring to supermajority testimony ensures consistency, and conditions under which it does not. In addition, he introduces the concept of "consistency of degree k," which is weaker than full consistency in that it rules out only "blatant" inconsistencies in an agent's beliefs while allowing less blatant ones. Finally, List shows that though deferring to supermajority testimony often fails to ensure full consistency, it is nonetheless a route to consistency in the weaker sense he developed.

PART I

The Debate between Summativists and Non-Summativists

1

Social Process Reliabilism
Solving Justification Problems in Collective Epistemology

Alvin I. Goldman

1.1. The Epistemology of Collective Subjects

In recent years many philosophers have pursued questions about the nature of groups and group activity, including group action, group intention, group belief, and so forth. Salient contributions to this literature include Bratman (1999); Gilbert (1989, 1994, 2002); Lackey (this volume), List and Pettit (2005, 2011); Pettit (2003); Quinton (1975/76); Schmitt (1994, 2006); Searle (1995); Tollefsen (2007); Tuomela (1992, 2007); and Wray (2010). There is widespread agreement that groups—at least some groups—are the bearers of propositional attitudes. Such attitudes are colloquially ascribed to many groups, and most philosophers who write on the subject endorse the aptness of such ascriptions. Of special interest here is a subclass of propositional attitudes, namely, "*doxastic*" attitudes, including belief, disbelief, suspension of judgment, and degrees of confidence. Courts of law, scientific panels, athletic teams, and institutional bodies of many varieties are described in terms of such attitudes.

A few social epistemologists have worked not only on collective belief *per se* but on its epistemic appraisal. This topic has been treated by Schmitt (1994, 2006), Mathiesen (2006), Bird (2010), and List and Pettit (2011), among others. Here I focus on one narrow question in collective epistemology: the justification question. Justification questions certainly arise from time to time in public discourse. When the Bush Administration claimed that Saddam Hussein possessed weapons of mass destruction, many people questioned whether the Administration was justified in holding this belief (assuming they really believed it).

When it comes to group justification, a natural thought is that such justifiedness must arise from the justified beliefs of its members. This paper therefore devotes considerable attention on the question of *justificational dependence* in general, laying the ground for decisions about justificational dependence of groups on their members. Collective epistemologists generally agree that a group's possession of a belief typically derives (in some fashion) from those of its members. In this paper, however, the focus is not on group *belief* possession but on the justificational status of such beliefs.

It is generally acknowledged that groups come in different varieties, ranging from loose, unstructured assemblages of individuals to highly structured, organized collectivities. The present discussion focuses on more formally structured groups with some kind of unifying organization. Whether the theory also applies to looser, merely "summative" groups is discussed briefly in section 1.10.

1.2. The Metaphysics and Epistemology of Collective Entities

How the beliefs of collective subjects are aligned with beliefs of their members is one question for the theory of group, or collective, subjects. List and Pettit suggest that collective subjects have a qualified supervenience relation to their members. This is a reasonable metaphysical position, by my lights, but it might be preferable to substitute an increasingly popular term of metaphysical art, namely, the *grounding relation* (Fine 1994, Schaffer 2009). The claim might then be that the propositional attitudes of collective subjects are *grounded* in propositional attitudes of their members plus the group's organizational structure. Under either proposal, group agents are seen as distinct from their members (singly or collectively); a result that for example, List and Pettit, embrace.

A full investigation of the relations between groups and their members, however, must distinguish between metaphysical and epistemological matters. For present purposes there are two types of questions in this territory I call "metaphysical". One type is: Do group entities exist at all? What types of groups are there? A second type of question is *psychological*. Do group entities have psychological properties, specifically propositional attitudes? If so, how are a group's attitudes related to those of its members? Both types of questions should be distinguished cleanly from epistemological ones, especially the justification question. My main aim here is to inquire into the determinants of justificational status (J-status) for collective beliefs.

1.3. Collective Psychology vs. Collective Epistemology

Before turning to questions about collective justifiedness, however, let us consider the subject of collective belief. List and Pettit (2011) offer the most systematic treatment of collective belief,[1] and I shall generally follow their treatment. However, I shall not spell out in detail any particular theory of group belief. That is a difficult enough problem in its own right, and I'll have enough on my hands with the theory of justification. Nonetheless, it helps to have a suitable sample of such a theory before us, and I shall use the List-Pettit model for that purpose.[2]

List and Pettit assume that group beliefs are the outputs of a function that takes profiles of individual members' beliefs as inputs and yields collective beliefs as outputs. Such a mapping is a judgment aggregation function, or, as I shall call it, a *belief aggregation function* (BAF). An example of a BAF is the majoritarian rule according to which a group believes proposition P if and only if a majority of group members believe P. Another example is a supermajoritarian rule, in which the group believes P just in case a qualified majority of members do so (e.g., two thirds). Another example is dictatorship, in which the group belief is always the same as that of a fixed member.

The idea of a BAF is initially presented in terms of rules that groups formulate and adhere to when forming beliefs of their own as a function of their members' beliefs. However, the same concept can be applied to groups that have no officially formulated rules to govern their belief-forming methods. Instead, interpersonal mechanisms of psychological influence give rise to patterns describable in terms of such a rule. These types of groups can be subsumed under the BAF framework. List and Pettit call this a "functionally inexplicit organizational structure" (2011: 60). "Organizational structure" also refers to ways by which a group enacts and implements a BAF (List and Pettit 2011: 60). For example, majority voting can be implemented by paper ballots or electronic ones, or by a process of deliberation that leads group members to converge on the attitudes of the majority.

---

[1] List and Pettit (2011) use the term "judgment" rather than "belief." The trouble with "judgment," however, is that its referent is ambiguous as between a speech act and a psychological state. Although speech acts can be evaluated in epistemic terms, as are beliefs, the criteria for speech act evaluation seem quite different than those for belief evaluation. So I shall generally avoid the term "judgment."

[2] I will not be assuming that a group belief in a proposition requires that all members of the group believe it. Thus, my examples will fit with Gilbert's (1989) model. Indeed, although Gilbert uses the language of "group belief", her "joint acceptance" view is best seen as a theory of group action rather than group belief, because "acceptances" in her treatment are verbal expressions (see 1989, p. 306).

Having introduced the idea of an organizational structure, List and Pettit proceed to explain the relation between group attitudes and member attitudes as follows:

> The things a group agent does are clearly determined by the things its members do; they cannot emerge independently. In particular, no group agent can form intentional attitudes without these being determined, in one way or other, by certain contributions of its members, and no group agent can act without one or more of its members acting. (2011: 64)

Despite this, however, they also argue for a degree of autonomy for group agents. Group beliefs do not supervene on member beliefs in a proposition-wise fashion but instead via a looser relation of *holistic* supervenience in which the set of group beliefs across propositions is determined by sets of individual attitudes across all of the same propositions (not each proposition taken singly) (2011: 69). From this they infer that "individual and group attitudes can come apart in surprising ways, thereby establishing a certain autonomy for the group agent" (2011: 69). For present purposes, as indicated earlier, it suffices to say that group minds have the metaphysical relation of being grounded in individual minds. Because grounding is an irreflexive relation, it follows that group minds are non-identical with any individual minds (or sets thereof), and non-identity is all we really need for our epistemological purposes.

1.4. Justification Transmission: Intrapersonal vs. Interpersonal

Before turning to group justification, it will help to highlight certain features of justificational factors in individuals. In the individual domain I shall spotlight some contrasts between *intra*personal and *inter*personal justification relations. It is convenient at this point to formulate the issues in the terminology of "reasons."

Suppose Jones has a good reason, R, for believing P. For example, she already justifiedly believes certain premises that entail P and she recognizes this entailment. Does she therefore have at least prima facie (propositional) justification for believing P? Yes. Special cases aside, possessing good reason(s) R automatically gives Jones such justification for believing P.[3] Now consider a different case. Although Jones lacks reason R, Smith possesses R. Does *Smith's* having reason R automatically give *Jones* prima facie justification for believing P? Of course not! One person's reason, or justification, never transfers automatically to a second person. Granted,

---

[3] I set aside here problems about "transmission failure" of the sorts that preoccupy Crispin Wright (2002, 2003) and others.

Jones might acquire good reason to believe that Smith has a good reason to believe P; she might have this higher-order reason without knowing what Smith's reason is. As Richard Feldman has quipped, "evidence for evidence is evidence." In this new case Jones' evidence is not R, but the (different) fact that Smith has a good reason to believe P. The fact that Jones has this higher-order reason does not imply that this reason emerges *automatically* from Smith's having his first-order reason, namely R.

The foregoing points are perfectly compatible, of course, with the thesis that if Smith has reason R to believe P, he can often easily convey it to Jones via testimony. Hearing Smith assert P and provide the supporting reason R will often give Jones reason to believe P. But such conveyance of reasons does not occur automatically; a testimonial act (plus other suitable conditions) is required. And such a testimonial act will not always suffice, especially if Jones has prior reasons to doubt Smith's credibility.

Granted this point, can a hearer become testimonially justified in believing P if the speaker himself is *un*justified in believing P? In other words, is speaker justifiedness necessary for hearer justifiedness? Lackey (1999, 2008) argues convincingly to the contrary for both knowledge and justification. She offers a varied array of examples to demonstrate the point that speaker justifiedness is neither necessary nor sufficient for hearer knowledge or justifiedness (Lackey 2008: 47–71). Even Schmitt (2006), who defends what he calls the "transindividual basing thesis," presents an example of his own to show the non-necessity of a speaker being justified as a condition of a hearer being justified. Schmitt writes: "I can have a justified belief that there are strawberries in the refrigerator on Tina's testimony even if Tina has no good reason to believe this, if I justifiedly though mistakenly believe that Tina has a good reason to believe this" (2006: 193–4).

Our target questions about *group* justification parallel those we have just been discussing. Are the J-statuses of members' beliefs automatically transmitted to the J-status of a group belief? Does the relation between group and member justifiedness parallel the case of *intra*personal inference, in which the J-statuses of one's own premise beliefs are automatically transferred to one's conclusion beliefs? Or is it more similar to *inter*personal cases, in which no such automatic transmission occurs, and instead testimonial acts are normally required? Let us proceed here with the help of an example.

1.5. Member/Group Justification Transmission? The British Museum Example

What kinds of justification relations obtain between a group's belief in P and its members' beliefs in P? To explore this problem, consider the following example (see Table 1.1). G is a group whose members consist of 100 guards (M_1—M_{100}) at the British Museum. Each of the first 20 guards, M_1-M_{20}, justifiedly believes that guard Albert is planning an inside theft of a famous painting (= A). By deduction from A, each of them infers the (existential) proposition that there is a guard who is planning such a theft (= T). The remaining 80 guards do not believe and are not justified in believing A. Each of the second 20 guards, M_{21}-M_{40}, justifiedly believes that Bernard is planning an inside theft (= B), and deductively infers T from B. The other 80 members do not believe B. Each of a third group of 20 members, M_{41}-M_{60}, justifiedly believes that guard Cecil is planning an inside theft (= C) and deductively infers T from C. The 80 others do not believe C. Thus, 60 members of G (justifiedly) believe T by deduction from some premise he/she justifiedly believes.

What does group G believe (whether justifiedly or unjustifiedly) with respect to these matters? To answer this question we must make some assumptions about G's psychology, especially the BAF by which members' beliefs in various propositions are mapped into G's beliefs. Assume that this BAF is a supermajoritarian operation that proceeds in a proposition-wise fashion. G believes a proposition P if and only if at least 60 percent of its members believe P. Because 60 percent of G's members believe T, it follows that G itself believes T. But no premise or set of premises believed by G jointly entail T. G believes neither A nor B nor C, because each of these propositions is affirmed by only 20 percent of G's members and rejected by the remainder. Further assume that G believes no other suitable premises. So, G believes no premises that deductively imply T; but G does believe T. The upshot is that G believes T; but it is unclear whether its belief in T is justified.

Table 1.1 Individual-Level and Group-Level Beliefs and Some J-Statuses

Individual-Level Beliefs

About the premises	About the conclusion
20 members bel (A) (J'dly)	
20 members bel (B) (J'dly)	
20 members bel (C) (J'dly)	60 members bel (T) (J'dly)
80 members do not bel (A)	40 members do not bel (T)
80 members do not bel (B)	
80 members do not bel (C)	

Group-Level Beliefs

About the premises	About the conclusion
G does not bel (A)	
G does not bel (B)	G believes T.
G does not bel (C)	

There are two ways G's justificational status vis-à-vis T might be approached: in light of *other* beliefs of G and their J-statuses or in light of the *members'* beliefs (vis-à-vis T) and their J-statuses. What emerges if we consider the J-status of G's belief in T in light of its members' beliefs? Recall how the case was described. First, only 20 members of G have justified beliefs in A, 20 have justified beliefs in B, and 20 have justified beliefs in C. There is no obvious route from these J-statuses to G's being justified in believing A, believing B, or believing C. But wait! We also concluded that each of 60 members justifiedly believes T, in virtue of deducing it from either A, B, or C. Moreover, each of the premises on which the sixty members based their respective inferences to T justifiedly believed them. So, sixty members justifiedly believe T.

Let us now assume a sample *justification aggregation function* (JAF), viz., JAF-1:

(JAF-1) If at least sixty percent of G's members justifiedly believe P, G is also justified in believing P.

JAF-1 is not presented as a *correct* JAF, or even a prototype of one.[4] Nonetheless, it is instructive to consider JAF-1 as a sample principle in order to explore the British Museum example and get a feel for member/group aggregation patterns. It will also help us draw a distinction between "vertical" and "horizontal" methods of group justification acquisition. Notice that JAF-1 mirrors the BAF previously postulated for G. There is no necessary connection, however, in the sense that a JAF must always "sanction," or approve of, whatever BAF a given group selects. On the contrary, a given BAF may be one that a suitable JAF would classify as unsuitable for generating justified group beliefs. In particular, I will later propose principles of justifiedness that are linked to reliability, i.e., truth conduciveness, implying

---

[4] For one thing it is possible to produce examples in which JAF-1 would assign positive J-status for group beliefs in each of an inconsistent set of propositions. This might well preclude its acceptability as a correct JAF. Here is such an example provided by David Christensen (personal communication). Continuing with the British Museum example, suppose that each group of guards has done some elementary reasoning and are justified in the results. Assume that the 40 guards in the remaining group (who don't suspect A, B, or C) justifiedly believe that no guard is planning to steal. As before, let proposition T = "At least one guard is planning to steal. "Since T is justifiedly believed by each member of the first three groups of guards, this is a total of 60 guards, so the group justifiedly believes it. Next consider another proposition, "T → (B v C)" (where the arrow represents the material conditional). This proposition is justifiedly believed by the 40 guards who suspect B and C. It is also justifiedly believed by the 40 guards who don't believe that anyone is planning a theft. So it is justifiedly believed by 80 guards. So the group justifiedly believes this as well. Finally, consider a third proposition, "~(B v C)". This is justifiedly believed by the 20 guards who suspect A and by the 40 guards who believe that no one will make a theft. This makes sixty guards, so the group justifiedly believes this third proposition as well. Hence, the group justifiedly believes an inconsistent set of proposition, when JAF-1 is used. This result may well demonstrate the unacceptability of JAF-1. (However, in light of the many impossibility results associated with judgment aggregation principles—see List and Pettit, 2011—we should not reject such principles too hastily, even ones with unattractive properties).

that an acceptable JAF would not authorize just any old BAF. Proper BAFs (ones that can help generate *justified* group beliefs) will have to be ones that meet suitable standards of truth-conducivity. This will become clearer in later sections.[5] For illustrative purposes, however, it is convenient to begin with a "paired" set of BAF and JAF. .

As previously indicated, I do not mean to present here any particular account of group belief, or how such beliefs are formed. On one possible approach groups can select their own BAFs as they see fit. It might be done by some sort of "constitutional" act, as it were. Alternatively, BAFs might be artifacts of socio-psychological forces operative within a group's membership, without requiring any voluntary choice or decision on their part. The core question of interest in this section concerns the *dependence* (or *transmission*) relation between the J-statuses of a group's beliefs and the J-statuses of its members' beliefs. Using the British Museum example, we can pinpoint a core analytical problem about J-dependence relations.

The J-status of G's belief in T may be approached from two different perspectives or dimensions: the *horizontal* dimension and the *vertical* dimension. The horizontal dimension addresses the J-status of G's belief in T solely in terms of other beliefs of G, i.e., *group-level* beliefs. G's belief in T is unjustified in terms of horizontal J-dependence because G cannot infer T by any legitimate means from any justified beliefs *of its own*. The situation is different, however, when we consider G's belief in T by reference to vertical J-dependence, i.e., G's position vis-à-vis its members. Consider the members' beliefs in T and the proportion of them that are justified. As Table 1.1 shows, 60 percent of the members justifiedly believe T. So, given JAF-1, G's belief in T seems to be justified (because 60 percent of G's members justifiedly believe T). We confront, then, something of a dilemma. The verdict delivered by the horizontal dimension and the verdict delivered by the vertical dimensions conflict with one another. Such a conflict cannot be tolerated in a satisfactory theory of group justifiedness. Which dimension should take priority: the horizontal one or the vertical one?

I raise this priority question only to set it aside. It is too large a question to settle in this paper. What I am going to undertake instead is a more modest task. I shall concentrate almost entirely on vertical J-dependence and seek to understand it better. Specifically, I seek to illuminate the crucial interface between member

---

[5] What this implies is that what are called "justification aggregation functions" in the middle sections of the paper are really best viewed as conditional justification aggregation functions. They indicate when a group belief is justified conditional on the J-statuses of the input members' beliefs. The aggregation function or process at the "terminal phase" of a group process of belief formation does not all by itself determine the J-status of the output group belief. A J-status for the group belief is partly a function of the JAF used but also partly a function of the J-statuses of the inputted member beliefs.

justifiedness and group justifiedness as it arises in the problem of justification *aggregation*. Moreover, I shall argue that an existing theory of *individual* justification—namely, *process reliabilism*—can be borrowed from mainstream individual epistemology and applied fruitfully to the present problem, with only a modest number of tweaks or modifications.

1.6. Two Models of J-Dependence between Groups and Their Members

The crucial question here is whether the justification dependence (J-dependence) relation between groups and their members more closely resembles *intrapersonal* J-dependence, where the J-status of a person's own states are often automatically transmitted to her other states, or more closely resembles *interpersonal* J-dependence where, lacking such automatic transmission, J-dependence typically requires acts of testimony. The intrapersonal J-dependence model I have in mind would include (i) automatic (default) transmission of J-status from believed premises to believed conclusion, and (ii) automatic (default) retention of J-status of a memory-preserved belief from one time to another. What I mean by automatic default transmission is that J-status transfer occurs automatically although its force can be defeated if the subject has beliefs or meta-beliefs that undercut the transmission process. Absent such defeaters, a memory-preserved belief continues to have (roughly) the same J-status it had originally; and the J-status of an inferred conclusion is shaped (in part) by the J-statuses of the premise beliefs. (The "in part" qualifier is required by the fact that the strength of the premises/conclusion support relation must also be factored into the equation.)

The second possibility is to interpret the J-dependence relation between groups and their members on the model of the J-dependence relations between testifiers and hearers. This view might be motivated by the List-Pettit view that groups have "minds of their own." This means that group minds are distinct from the minds of any of their members. If so, the intrapersonal model of J-dependence seems dicey and ill-motivated. The only alternative in play, moreover, would seem to be the interpersonal J-dependence relation, in which one person must communicate his reasons to the other and hope that the hearer is suitably positioned (in terms of background beliefs) to accept this testimony justifiedly. As Schmitt's example of Tina illustrates (section 1.4 above), a hearer's justifiedness in believing the content of testimony depends on his *own* justified beliefs and not simply on those of the testifier. It does not automatically inherit the source's justificational state. On which model of J-dependence should the member/group justificational relationship be understood?

Here are several reasons to prefer the *intra*personal model to the *inter*personal model. First, almost all theorists agree that there is a special, intimate relation between groups and their members. A group is in some sense "composed" of its members, and members' beliefs play some sort of "constitutive" role in determining, or grounding, group beliefs. The testifier/hearer model is intuitively inappropriate for the relation between members and group.

A problem confronting the testifier/hearer model concerns the communications that would have to occur between members and group. What communication could support the production of justified belief in the group concerning the requisite justified belief states of the members? If we think about the communication as something like a vote, with each member conveying its belief vis-à-vis the proposition in question, this would fail to provide crucial information about the various members' *justifiedness*. The distribution of members' beliefs alone is uninformative about the J-statuses of those beliefs. If, on the other hand, members must inform the group of their respective *reasons* or *grounds* in addition to the beliefs themselves, the quantity of information transmitted may become prohibitive. (For the group to assimilate.)

In addition, who or what would be the receiver of these communications? What exactly is the group that would "hear" or otherwise register these communicative contents? Is it the entire membership of the group? Would every member have to receive messages from all of the other members with the propositional contents as sketched in the previous paragraph? That would be a massive amount of communication. And it is hard to see how it would be executed by groups of any reasonable size of the sorts to which we often ascribe beliefs. In short, the testifier/hearer model of justification propagation seems hopeless as a realistic model of how this might transpire.

There are weighty reasons, therefore, to prefer the first model, in which a group's J-dependence on its members more closely resembles J-dependence relations for *intra*-personal rather than *inter*personal cognition. This is what I am calling the "transmission" model of J-dependence, and it is what I shall assume in the remainder of this paper. However, the notion of (justificational) transmission must be tweaked a bit from the notion commonly found in the standard epistemological literature. To say that member M's J-status with respect to p is automatically "transmitted" to the group is not to say, or imply, that the group's J-status with respect to p automatically becomes the same as the J-status of M's belief. It only means that M's J-status with respect to p is *one component* of a multi-component *vector* that (vertically) influences the group's J-status with respect to p. Each of the other members of the group may also have J-statuses with respect to p and these will be additional components in the same vector. What interests us is how the entire vector of members' J-statuses affects the group's J-status.

1.7. How Process Reliabilism Explains Aggregative Collective Justifiedness

To this point I have said nothing about what justification consists in, what it takes—in "substantive" (non-epistemic) terms—for an agent's belief to qualify as justified.[6] Next, however, I offer a familiar theory of justification that this author and others have defended in previous writings, i.e., *process reliabilism* (Goldman 1979, 1986, 2008, 2011a, 2011b, 2012; Kornblith, 1980; Lyons 2009, 2011; Comesana 2002, 2009; Goldberg 2010; Schmitt 1984). Process reliabilism is traditionally advanced as an account of individual justification. With only a few tweakings, however, it can be extended to group justifiedness, as the rest of this paper undertakes to show. The paper does not attempt a full-scale account of group justifiedness. Such a theory would have to cover the "horizontal" dimension of justifiedness, and no full treatment of that dimension will be offered here. The paper continues to focus primarily on the distinctive feature of collective cognition, namely, acquisition of group justifiedness from members' justifiedness (with respect to the same proposition).

The core idea of process reliabilism[7] is that a belief is justified just in case it is produced by a reliable belief-forming process—or sequence of processes—in the psychological history of the agent (Goldman, 1979). Exactly *how* reliable processes must be to confer justification is left vague, in virtue of the vagueness of the term "justified" itself. It is assumed that belief-forming processes (process *types*) do not have to be 100 percent reliable. More fully, justification-conferring processes can be either *unconditionally* or *conditionally* reliable. A process is unconditionally reliable just in case its ratio of true beliefs to total beliefs (when operating in the relevant domain[8]) is very high. Unconditional reliability is the appropriate

---

[6] Throughout I confine the discussion to "doxastic" justifiedness rather than "propositional" justifiedness, Presumably the theory on which I shall focus has decent ways to explain propositional justifiedness in terms of doxastic justifiedness. At least so I proposed in Goldman (1979).

[7] Like almost all theories of justifiedness, the distinctive parts of process reliabilism must be supplemented with a component that takes account of defeaters. We will turn to defeaters in due course. To get started, however, the need to handle them will be set aside.

[8] Which is the relevant domain is a question that confronts reliabilism. It might be the actual world (past, present and future), it might be a selected portion of environments in the actual world, or it might be some class of possible worlds more inclusive than the actual world. I don't try to resolve this question here.

standard for belief-*independent* processes, i.e., processes having no belief inputs. Belief-independent processes might include perception and introspection. Belief-dependent processes are ones that take beliefs as inputs to their operation. Such processes would include inference processes and (some kinds of) memory processes. For these processes unconditional reliability is an inappropriate standard. A given inference type might generate a great many false conclusion beliefs because it is often applied to false premise beliefs. This would not demonstrate any defect in the inference type. We can define a notion of conditional reliability, however, that supplies a more appropriate criterion. A process is conditionally reliable only if it has a high ratio of true belief outputs to total belief outputs for those cases in which the inputs to the process are (all) true.

As the phrase "belief-forming process" suggests, the heart of the theory includes the thesis that a belief token's J-status depends on how the token is causally produced, where causal production involves psychological processes. The idea applies most easily to the *doxastic* rather than the *propositional* sense of justifiedness, although it can also be adapted to the latter (Goldman 1979). In the main, the rest of this paper addresses doxastic justifiedness. That beliefs are formed (and retained) via psychological processes is uncontroversial for individuals. Here this idea is generalized to group, or organizational, processes. We have already assumed that groups have psychologies (section 1.2). Group psychologies differ from those of individuals; but we can live with that difference. Since we are already tolerating group beliefs, why not profit (theoretically) by tolerating group belief-forming processes?

A further important feature of process reliabilism is the idea that if a belief is generated by a series of intermediate beliefs—via a sequence of inferences, for example—the final belief is justified only if it is the product of a succession of conditionally reliable processes each of which operates over *justified* input beliefs (see Goldman 1979). That these inputs must be justified, in order for an output belief to be justified, is an important requirement. The original theory assumed that output beliefs are justified only if *all* input beliefs to their processes are justified. In collective epistemology, however, this requirement may need to be relaxed. This is an instance of the inevitable need for tweaking when a theory originally designed for one domain is applied to a different domain.

With this overview of individual process reliabilism in hand, we turn now to the task of formulating and defending *social* (i.e., *collective*) process reliabilism, especially for the special topic of justification aggregation. As previously indicated, we concentrate on the vertical dimension of justification, in which J-statuses of member beliefs play a central role in determining the J-status of an aggregated group belief. To mesh with process reliabilism, this idea must be re-construed in terms of *processes*. The processes in question will take profiles of individual beliefs as inputs and return group beliefs as outputs. We already encountered belief aggregation functions in section 1.5; but these aggregation functions should not be thought of as purely abstract functions. They should be thought of as functions that get implemented by some sort of (explicit or implicit) organizational processes. The J-statuses of group beliefs will then depend on (1) the J-statuses of their member belief inputs and (2) the conditional reliability of the belief aggregation processes used.

For convenience think of the prototypical process as a (secret) balloting process that occurs at a (physical or virtual) meeting of the group. Each member clicks a box on his/her computer screen to input her personal belief on the proposition in question. All ballots are transmitted to the group and aggregated automatically in accordance with the pre-selected aggregation procedure. The group belief so formed is then available for use by the group in ensuing decision-making or actional contexts. Our question, however, concerns the *justificational* status of the group's belief so formed. Although the members input only their beliefs, not the J-statuses of their beliefs (which they themselves may or may not know), each of their beliefs *has* a J-status, and the distribution of their beliefs plus J-statuses is what determines the J-status of the group belief. The group belief's J-status is a product of *transmission* from all of the members' J-statuses.

The process of J-transmission from members to group spans, or crosses, an *agential gap*, a gap between pairs of agents each consisting of an individual agent and a collective agent. Is this a tenable position for process reliabilism? After all, under traditional process reliabilism, all belief-forming processes take place entirely within the head of an individual agent. How can we now countenance a violation of this principle and still remain within the process-reliability tradition?

An analogous kind of "extension" of process reliabilism across agential gaps has been proposed by Sanford Goldberg (2010) for the case of testimony. Goldberg thinks of the process of receiving (and reacting to) testimony as a process that begins in the testifier's head, proceeds across the interpersonal gap via an utterance (or inscription), and culminates in cognitive activity of a receiver. Goldberg argues that this is a fine analogue to a memory process in which a subject's earlier belief is retained in the subject's mind over some temporal interval; and as long as no "defeating" cognitive events occur during this interval, the J-status of the belief remains the same over time. In other words, as I understand him, it is argued that the J-status of the belief is transmitted along with the belief itself. In extending this picture to testimony between persons, he claims to be adhering to the memory analogue.

Goldberg's proposal for testimony-based justification (and/or knowledge) parallels the present proposal for group justification. In testimony the J-status of interest is the J-status of the hearer's belief. Goldberg is saying that the justifiedness of the hearer's testimony-based belief is automatically transmitted from testifier to receiver. I am not persuaded by this kind of move in the case of testimony among individuals. But I am happy to accept it for collective belief. Although members report their beliefs to the group upon voting, the J-statuses of these beliefs are not similarly reported. Nonetheless, their J-statuses are transmitted (along with J-statuses of their co-members) and automatically influence the J-status of the group's resultant doxastic attitude. In assessing the J-status of the group's attitude, we should take into account not only what is the membership's *belief*-profile with respect to the proposition in question but what is its *justification* profile. Why do I accept this transmissional picture in the case of aggregation but not in the case of interpersonal testimony? The crucial difference is that two individuals are completely independent epistemic agents whereas group agents are essentially dependent on their members. The latter dependency is a good reason, by my lights, to acknowledge transmission in the group justification-determining process.

1.8. Collective Justifiedness and Belief-Forming Processes

Collective beliefs' J-statuses can potentially be affected by several kinds of events, states, and processes. These can be studied with the helpful guidance of Figure 1.1. The left side of the diagram depicts individual members (M_1 through M_4) who utilize various belief-forming processes (shown with dashed lines and small arrows) that result in either acceptance or rejection of proposition P.[9] Some of these resulting attitudes are justified, others unjustified. The block arrow in the middle of the diagram depicts a belief-aggregation process that runs from the profile of member attitudes to the group attitude shown on the far right. The J-status of this group belief is partly a function of the members' attitudes and their J-statuses that comprise its inputs and partly a function of the reliability of the process itself, specifically, its conditional reliability.

A key feature of process reliabilism is its *historicity*. Under individual process reliabilism a justification-relevant history of beliefs consists of psychological

---

[9] Although the processes are "individual," this does not preclude their being related to other people. Indeed, the processes might take as inputs the reception of testimonial acts of others, so they could be embedded in larger, deliberative processes. The important point is that these processes, represented by dashed arrows, are not "vertical" processes, which support a mapping from individual doxastic attitudes to group doxastic attitudes. Only the block arrow in Figure 1.1 represents a vertical process.

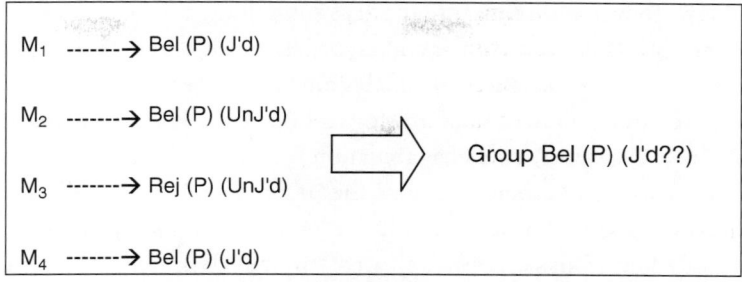

Figure 1.1 Causal Processes that Affect the J-Status of a Collective Belief

events that operate (over variable periods of time) to generate individual beliefs. Traditional epistemology was driven by an attachment to "solipsism of the moment," according to which the justificational status of a subject's believing something at time t is determined exclusively by what holds of the subject *at time t* (especially, his/her mental states at t). By contrast, historical reliabilism says that mental or cognitive events occurring in the subject at times earlier than t can also (indirectly) influence the J-status of a subsequent belief at t. This is why chains of belief-forming processes going back in time can be relevant to a dated belief's J-status. (The historical feature of reliabilism is not fully represented in the diagram. See section 1.9). When we turn to *social* process reliabilism, the relevant histories include both the sequence of individual processes that occur in each group member plus the member/group processes that give rise to group doxastic outputs. The full story would also include ("horizontal") processes occurring within a given group; but we agreed to ignore these horizontal processes for most of our discussion.

Our next task is to be more specific about the nature of the aggregation processes that span the member/group "gap" and how to assess their reliability. In the existing literature on belief (or judgment) aggregation, the standard term used is aggregation *function*. Can we replace the notion of an aggregation function with that of an aggregation *process* and produce a satisfactory theory within the framework of process reliabilism? "Functions" seem to be rather abstract and mathematical; processes are neither. How can one replace the other?

It is profitable here to re-introduce List and Pettit's notion of an "organizational structure" (section 1.3). Organizational structures, it will be recalled, are rules and procedures that groups use to enact and implement a BAF (List & Pettit, 2011: 60). Construed as linguistic entities, rules are not processes. But there are also *exercises* or *applications* of rules and procedures, and these entities might be excellent examples of group belief-forming processes. They help to constitute an organization's "psychology." They may be conceptualized as computational operations of a group mind, operating (*inter alia*) on member belief profiles. Whether explicitly or implicitly, they apply procedures by which group BAFs are implemented.

With these points made, I shall now often talk as if a BAF *is* a belief-forming process (type). Of course, a belief aggregation function will be a *belief-dependent* kind of belief-forming process because the inputs to BAFs are beliefs (or doxastic states) of group members. A crucial step for epistemologists of collective justification is to establish criteria for justificationally desirable BAFs. Since reliabilist social epistemologists are interested in reliable processes, a precise criterion might be thought to require a fixed truth-ratio threshold of justifiedness. However, given the inherent vagueness of the notion of justifiedness the prospect of designating a specific threshold may be folly. Although we initially presuppose a fixed threshold in this section, a more flexible proposal will be made in section 1.9, where *degrees* of justifiedness are introduced. The central aspiration, of course, is to identify the general "shape" of group justifiedness under process reliabilism.

In the original formulation of process reliabilism two key conditions for justifiedness were presented, conditions that loom large for belief-dependent processes in particular. These two conditions can be formulated as follows (cf. Goldman, 1979).

(R1) If belief B is an output of belief-dependent process Π, B is justified only if

(A) all of the belief inputs to this operation of Π are themselves *justified*, and
(B) process-type Π is *conditionally reliable*.
(A process type is conditionally reliable IFF for a selected threshold T (>.50), at least T percent of the cases in which all input beliefs to the process are true are also cases in which the output belief is true.)

Condition (R1) states two necessary conditions for individual justifiedness, applied to outputs of belief-dependent processes. Condition (R1)(A) is a justification *transmission* condition. It says, in effect, that premise beliefs must "contain" justifiedness in order to transmit justifiedness to the conclusion belief. Otherwise, where does the justificational "juice" come from? Moreover, in the case of inference it is plausible that an epistemic agent's conclusion belief is justified only if *all* premise beliefs of the inference are justified for the agent. If we introduce a counterpart condition for collective belief aggregation, we need to consider exactly what that counterpart should be. Similarly, if we are to find a collective-domain parallel for the conditional reliability requirement of condition (R1)(B), we should specify—or at least point in the direction of—a suitable analogue of the conditional reliability requirement in the individual domain. These tasks are addressed in the next section.

1.9. Permuting Process Reliabilism for Collective Epistemology

A straightforward analogue of condition (R1)(A) for cases of group belief based on aggregation, might be $(R1_G)(A)$:

> $(R1_G)(A)$ If a group belief B in P is generated by aggregating a profile of member attitudes vis-à-vis P, belief B is justified only if all members' beliefs in P belonging to that profile are themselves *justified*.

On reflection, however, should it be required that *all* beliefs (in P) by the members be justified? What warrants such a strong requirement? In the case of inferential justification, every premise used in the inference may be essential to drawing the conclusion, at least to make the conclusion highly likely. The falsity of a single premise might substantially lower the likelihood of the conclusion's truth. So we may reasonably hold the conclusion belief to be unjustified if any premise belief lacks justification. But if a group has a large number of members, a large proportion of whom justifiedly believe the target proposition P, is it really necessary that *all* such members believe P justifiedly in order for the group to believe P justifiedly?

For example, suppose that group G has 100 members, of which 60 believe P, 30 reject P, and 10 withhold judgment. Further suppose that under the governing BAF this attitude profile suffices to generate a belief in P by group G. Now suppose that 58 of the 60 members who believe P do so *justifiedly*, whereas none of the 30 P-rejections is justified. How should the *group's* P-belief be assessed in justificational terms? According to condition $(R1_G)(A)$, justifiedness is denied to G's P-belief because not all the members' beliefs in P are justified. This seems grossly over-demanding. Why couldn't some of them be considered "redundant"? Why isn't it sufficient for 58 of the 60 believers to be justified in believing P?

Until now we have been assuming a categorical, or binary, notion of justifiedness. That's how the theory of epistemic justification is usually discussed. A belief is either justified or unjustified and the problem is to specify the conditions for each. On reflection, however, maybe this problem is rather artificial. To the extent that we use the notion of justifiedness, or reasonableness, it is much easier to think of it as a matter of degree, a gradable notion rather than a categorical one. And this gradability approach seems more tractable than the categorical one when we are addressing groups with multiple members. Such groups will rarely display unanimity, and there is no obvious way to set a non-arbitrary threshold that would be essential for a categorical notion. Of course, the categorical notion of justification has been popular because of its presumed utility in defining knowledge ("S knows p only if S is justified in believing P"). But recent epistemologists have been attracted by degrees of justification even in their accounts of knowledge. Contextualists, for example, claim that the level of justification required for knowledge attribution varies with the conversational context (DeRose, 1992, 2009; Cohen, 1986). Within this tradition it is highly desirable to have a story about grades of justifiedness. If this holds for individual justifiedness, it might be even more imperative for group justifiedness, where the expected variation in groups inevitably makes categorical notions more difficult to employ.

I shall not attempt to sketch a full theory of justificational gradability.[10] But a few sample principles are adduced to convey the flavor of what seems appropriate. Here I assume that *members'* doxastic attitudes have categorical J-status, and this assumption will be used in formulating plausible principles of graded J-status for group belief. Here is one such principle (which introduces two factors):

(GJ) If a group belief in P is aggregated based on a profile of member attitudes toward P, then *ceteris paribus* the greater the proportion of members who justifiedly *believe* P and the smaller the proportion of members who justifiedly *reject* P, the greater the group's level, or grade, of justifiedness in believing P.[11]

I further propose that J-status "facts" about the memberships' justificational profile vis-à-vis P are automatically transmitted from that profile vis-à-vis P to the group's J-status level with respect to P. In other words, suppose the group forms a belief in P based on a profile of attitudes held by its members. The group's belief output is a function of its BAF applied to the membership's attitude profile. But the membership's attitude profile per se tells us nothing about the *J-statuses* of these member attitudes, and nothing about the J-status of the group belief. The J-statuses of the members' attitudes will depend on the processes by which they severally arrived at their respective attitudes (and retained them over time). Similarly, the J-status of the group belief will depend on the members' attitude profile and on the J-statuses of those attitudes.

Notice that although the J-status of a group belief *depends* on the J-statuses of its members' beliefs, the group need not be *aware* of the J-statuses of the several members' attitudes. The group belief justificationally "profits" or "suffers" from the J-statuses of its members' attitudes because these statuses are transmitted to the

---

[10] Actually, degrees of justification are very easily handled in process reliabilist terms. Ceteris paribus, the higher the truth-ratio of a belief-forming process, the greater the justifiedness of the beliefs it generates. However, this approach presupposes the correctness of process reliabilism, so doubters of this approach might not be cheered by this account.

[11] This principle and the one that follows both use a categorical notion of justifiedness (with respect to members' beliefs) and a graded notion of justifiedness (with respect to group belief). It is arguable that this is objectionable, and if so new principles would have to be devised that employ graded justifiedness throughout. I leave this task for another day, or for others.

group's J-status.[12] For example, the J-status of the Bush Administration's belief in the existence of WMD (in the hands of the Iraqi government) depended substantially on whether the technical experts who contributed to the Administration's opinion themselves had individual justification.[13]

I turn now to the second necessary condition for the justifiedness (or a relatively high degree of justifiedness) of a group belief formed by belief aggregation. This is the conditional reliability condition appropriate for an aggregation process, which can be stated as follows:

($R2_G$)(B) A group belief G that is generated by the operation of a belief-aggregation process Π is justified only if (and to the degree that) Π has high conditional reliability.

Conditional reliability as a requirement of justifiedness was originally inspired by two thoughts. The first is the guiding theme of process reliabilism, viz., that truth-conduciveness of the process(es) used is a key to the justifiedness of a token belief. For example, beliefs formed by perception (in normal conditions) are usually justified because perceptual processes are generally reliable processes. By contrast, beliefs formed by wishing thinking or idle speculation are unjustified because these kinds of belief-forming methods are generally unreliable. However, if truth-conduciveness is the main motif of process reliabilism, why should a theorist retreat to *conditional* reliability when it comes to belief-dependent processes like inference? The rationale is straightforward. When it comes to inferences (like many other things), "garbage in/garbage out" is an apt motto. If you start with false premises, you cannot expect inference to deliver true conclusions. In short, one cannot reasonably expect an inferential process to yield true beliefs as a general rule if it frequently starts with false premises. The only "fair" test of an inferential process is how often it delivers true conclusion beliefs when it is fed true premise beliefs to start with. This is what a conditional reliability condition requires, in the form it was originally proposed (Goldman 1979). Why shouldn't the same, or a similar, idea apply here? The requirement that an inference process map truths into truths—more precisely, true beliefs into true beliefs—looks like a fair, not unduly demanding condition, yet still a substantial one, which can exclude the

---

[12] Of course, if a group does happen to have a higher-order belief about these features of the membership's justificational profile, such a higher-order belief would influence the J-status of its belief in P. But this does not conflict with the transmission of the membership's J-profile. Transmission does not imply total determination, just default determination.

[13] My treatment of the WMD example assumes throughout that the Bush Administration genuinely believed that the Iraqis had WMD. An alternative possibility, of course, is that they merely pretended to believe it and made public pronouncements accordingly. While historically quite possible, this scenario would eliminate a collective belief for us to evaluate; so I ignore it.

riff-raff among inferential processes. So it seems natural to apply it to the belief aggregation domain as well.

There are some differences, however, between inferential processes and belief aggregation processes. In the inference case a process would commonly start with a number of premise beliefs and end with a *different* conclusion belief (of the same agent). In the case of belief aggregation, by contrast, there is a potentially large number of individual agents with different attitudes toward a specified proposition plus a group agent that adopts one of these attitudes toward the *same* proposition. Achieving true-belief preservation here cannot be a matter of simply conforming to logical connections among propositions. A good BAF must be one that somehow "sees to it" that those group members who believe the truth, or are likely to believe the truth (given the route by which they arrived at their beliefs), have a suitable amount of influence on the group's attitude selection so that the group also believes the truth. This is what will capture the kind of conditional reliability appropriate to the belief aggregation domain. In short, for purposes of a reliabilist theory of justification for belief aggregation, conditional reliability should be interpreted not in terms of a requirement that *all* input beliefs of the members be true, but rather in terms of (enough) input beliefs having a *high probability* (or chance) of being true. As it happens, this might neatly fit the template presented by the Condorcet Jury Theorem.

Majoritarian voting is a widely touted belief aggregation process. Although voting is not the same as believing, it is instructive to consider majoritarian belief aggregation in the context of the well-known Condorcet Jury Theorem (CJT). CJT is often seen as a mathematical rationale for majority decision-making. Here I mean to observe that this rationale can also be interpreted in terms of *conditional reliability*. It nicely illustrates what might qualify as a good belief aggregation process because it approximates what a reasonable conception of conditional reliability might be for the domain of belief aggregation.

Details aside, CJT says that majority voting is a conditionally reliable aggregation procedure in that, *conditional* on voters' having a uniform competence greater than one half (e.g., prob = 0.52) for believing the truth about a target question, a group belief that emerges from a majoritarian aggregation procedure has an even higher probability of yielding the truth. Under a majoritarian aggregation rule, the group's probability of believing the truth swiftly approaches 1.0 as the group size increases. This is the sense in which a majoritarian process of belief aggregation is conditionally reliable.[14] Where the condition of uniform member competence is

---

[14] Moreover, while Condorcet's original theorem assumed a uniform level of competence greater than one-half, this condition can be relaxed. It is sufficient that the average probability of being right among the members is greater than one half and their competences are symmetrically distributed. See Grofman, Owen, and Feld (1983).

satisfied, the majoritarian process reliably leads to a high probability of the group belief's being true.

The reader might wonder why majoritarian aggregation is being credited only with *conditional* reliability. Isn't that an affront to its strength? Readers swept away by the putative "wisdom of the crowd" thesis, for example, might contend that a large group of independent individuals are *unconditionally* disposed to get the truth. Why is this special power of group decision-making being derogated by insistence on the qualifier "conditional"? The reason is simple. Majoritarian belief aggregation is not unconditionally reliable, that is, reliable under all conditions. In fact, it is as much conditionally *anti*-reliable as it is (positively) conditionally reliable. Specifically, if group members are uniformly *in*competent, i.e., have a probability less than half of (independently) believing the truth, the probability of a majority-driven group believing what is true rapidly approaches *zero* as group size increases. This is why it would be excessive to require (as a condition of justifiedness) that a belief aggregation procedure be *un*conditionally reliable. Perhaps no such procedure is even possible. In any case, conditional reliability seems like an eminently appropriate requirement.

However, several addenda and qualifications must be entered here concerning the CJT and its applicability to our problem. First, in addition to the requirement that all members have a probability greater than half of being right, CJT also requires that the members' competences be independent of one another. Second, the original formulation of CJT is restricted to cases where there are only two options on the table. List and Goodin (2001) generalized the theorem so that it applies to cases involving more than two options, but it is still an open question whether this helps us in our problem area. Why should more than two options be a potential sticking point for our problem? Aren't we discussing cases where the truth or falsity of a single proposition is on the table? Doesn't this already restrict our problem to two options, unlike cases where, for example, voters choose from a list of three or more candidates?

No, the mere fact that we are dealing with true-or-false propositions does not eliminate the problem. Our epistemic agents, being doxastic decision makers, confront at least three possible *attitudes* to adopt, not two, viz., belief, disbelief, and suspension of judgment (agnosticism). In the CJT literature it is ordinarily assumed that each option on the table has some chance of being "right" or "correct". But no meaning can be attached to the idea of suspension, or agnosticism, being the "right", "correct", or "true" option. These are among the reasons why the CJT is not a perfect illustration of a conditionally reliable belief aggregation process. It is still a helpful illustration, however.

Of course, the conception of conditional reliability it introduces is not exactly the one introduced in connection with individual process reliabilism. In the original notion of conditional reliability, reliability is conditioned on the *truth* of all premise beliefs. In the CJT case reliability is conditioned on each group member possessing an objective *chance* (greater than half) of being right (plus these chances being held independently of one another). Although these are slightly different conceptions of conditional reliability, they are close enough to be members of the same family. This strikes me as sufficient to view the CJT approach to epistemic goodness as belonging to the same family as that of the conditional reliability approach to individual process reliabilism.

A final tweaking of the process reliabilist theory needs to be undertaken in the context of justified group belief based on aggregation. The need for this tweaking is also reflected in the CJT. One of the most important qualifications included in the CJT (mentioned earlier) is that members' beliefs (or judgments) be independent of one another. For example, if they all form their respective beliefs based on the *same evidence*, their belief-forming processes would not be independent. Hence, one cannot expect the group's likelihood of being right to be "boosted" in the same fashion as it would if all have entirely separate bodies of evidence. This is why CJT is correct only if it is subject to the independence requirement. This factor cannot be ignored in the present process reliabilist approach either.

Isn't this a serious threat, however, to the viability of process reliabilism in this terrain? Isn't it well known that reliabilism and evidentialism are entirely distinct—indeed, opposed—epistemological approaches? How can we contemplate incorporation of an evidentialist component in our theory and still label it "process reliabilism"? In fact, however, a synthesis of reliabilism and evidentialism is not unprecedented. I offered such a synthesis—and a rationale for it—in a recent paper (Goldman 2011b). I also pointed out that viewing states of mind as evidence (or states of evidence possession) is not foreign to the spirit of reliabilism, although it was never mentioned explicitly in early statements of reliabilism.[15] When one considers that belief-forming processes need mental states as *inputs*, and those input states might be viewed as items of evidence or evidence possession, the notion that there is a fundamental gulf or opposition between process-elements and evidential elements evaporates. They can be quite complementary. However, fusing evidential factors and process factors into a unified theory of justifiedness is

---

[15] More generally, belief states of a cognizer may include justified beliefs that represent external states of affairs and thereby constitute states of evidence possession, where the items of evidence possessed are the represented external facts. Comesana (2010) is another proposal by a reliabilist to synthesize reliabilism and evidentialism, although Comesana's rationale for such a synthesis is quite different from mine.

no simple task, and it will not be undertaken here. I flag the importance of evidential elements, however, because they cannot be ignored even within a predominantly process-oriented approach. For a more systematic treatment of evidence in the context of group justifiedness, see Lackey (forthcoming).

It is time to complete the general contours of (aggregation-based) group justifiedness by saying more about the left-most portion of Figure 1.1. This part of the diagram is only suggestive of the larger story. It depicts group members as forming beliefs in P and it labels some of those beliefs as justified and others as unjustified. What determines their J-statuses? In each case there will be a story about the cognitive route by which an individual arrives at his/her belief, some of them a series of reliable belief-forming processes and others a series of processes with mixed reliability. It could be that all or some of the members formed his/her beliefs "individualistically," without interacting with any group members. Other members may have had extended conversations or debates about P with other members before arriving at their current doxastic attitudes. Such activities should be considered parts of a *deliberative* process (among the members), but not parts of the group aggregation procedure that generates a *collective* doxastic attitude. These conversations and individual belief-forming processes are all parts of *pre-aggregation* processes. Thus, the full history of justificationally-relevant activities that culminate in a collective belief (with a particular J-status) is not exhausted either by the process depicted by the block arrow at the center of Figure 1.1 nor by the individual processes depicted at the left of the diagram. The full history would go back even further, requiring more space than the page allows. The full history would be a leftward spreading tree, with (finitely) many additional nodes and branches. This provides a glimpse of the reason that I call process reliabilism a *historical* approach to justifiedness.

1.10. Other Kinds of Reliable Aggregation Process Types

Let us now depart a bit from purely majoritarian aggregation processes and consider related belief aggregation processes discussed by philosophers and political theorists. Many of these approaches also view reliability, or truth conduciveness, as the fundamental epistemic aim. And although they rarely if ever mention *justification* as their targets of analysis, they strike me as kindred spirits to process reliabilism, at least with respect to belief aggregation.

Among the methods proposed for optimal reliable belief aggregation functions are ones involving the deployment of *experts*, who are given more than the customary amount of influence or weight in the aggregation process. In the usual majoritarian schemes, group members are all assigned equal weight in influencing a group choice. In other schemes, however, the system makes special use of experts to boost truth-getting properties of the group.[16] Experts are understood (by definition) to have greater than average truth-getting competence, at least in their areas of expertise (Goldman, 2001). This gives rise to systems in which the membership possesses *heterogeneous* levels of competence as opposed to a *homogeneous* level.

Bradley and Thompson (2012: 68–9) lay out several possible schemes in which even heterogeneous levels of competence across a membership can have epistemically superior properties for a group. What they call "oligarchic" schemes are voting rules that count only the votes of the most reliable members. A second category include schemes in which everyone's vote is counted but weighting rules assign different weights to different voters according to reliability. The oligarchic category includes expert majority rule, whereby a proposition is accepted by the group if it is accepted by a majority of its most reliable members. The weighting-rules category assigns weights to voters as a function of their respective competences or the log of their competences (Grofman et al., 1983). Then the weighted sum of all of the votes determines the group belief. Under certain assumptions, e.g., independence, any of these procedures yields a higher probability of a group belief's being true than a (rival) majority rule and/or an equal-weight system.

Returning to the issue of justifiedness, here is a key question. Suppose that one of these expertise-sensitive systems is adopted by a committee or political unit, and the designated experts really are more reliable than their co-members. Does the use of such a reliability-enhancing system generate greater (prima facie) *justifiedness* of a group belief than a less reliable system? I would say that it does generate greater justifiedness. In the preceding cases, certain facts pertaining to the membership's J-status profile—including the kinds of evidence possessed by assorted members—automatically influences the J-status of the group belief in a proposition P. Analogously, the facts that "ground" the reliability property of the expert-oriented system contribute positively—and automatically—to a positive J-status for the group's belief in P. It is automatic in the sense that the group itself need not have any belief about the correctness of the choice of this or that individual as an expert. Such higher-order beliefs are not needed for the system to be highly reliable and only high reliability is required to influence the J-status of the

---

[16] List and Pettit discuss the deployment of experts under the heading of "epistemic gains from decentralization" (2011: 95–7). Suppose that a group seeks to form a belief on a certain conclusion based on k premises. Instead of inviting each group member to make a judgment about each premise, the group might be partitioned into k sub-groups, one for each premise, whose members specialize on that premise and make a judgment on it alone.

group's belief in P. This is quite consonant with the *externalist* character of process reliabilism.

Of course, if the group has "defeater" beliefs to the effect that some choices of people as (putative) experts are misguided, then such beliefs might lower the J-status of the group's belief in P. But it would not cancel the positive and automatic contribution of the de facto reliability of the weighted voting system. The defeater beliefs just compete with the de facto reliability of the system in influencing the ultima facie justifiedness of the group's P-belief. Finally, in saying that a group would *ceteris paribus* have greater justifiedness in believing P based on a weighted voting scheme than on a (less reliable) equal-weight voting scheme, this pertains only to epistemic justifiedness, not political (or moral) justifiedness. There may be grounds to object to an "episitemracy" on moral or political grounds, but the present question concerns epistemic character only.

1.11. Some Residual Issues

I conclude this essay with remarks on further issues that cannot be addressed in depth but should not be wholly neglected. The general burden of this section is to support the claim that process reliabilism is a fruitful approach to collective epistemology despite certain challenges that need to be met.

The first challenge is the question of whether process reliabilism is applicable to all kinds of groups to which collective beliefs are ascribed. How does it apply, for example, to loose assemblages of individuals that might also be considered "plural subjects"? Are there causal processes that link doxastic profiles of member beliefs to collective beliefs, processes that possess a determinate level of conditional reliability?[17] Consider all the people currently situated in Times Square, New York. It's a hot day and they are all thinking it is hot. So we might describe the assemblage as having a collective belief, "It is hot." Is there an aggregation procedure that *causes* such a plural-subject belief to be held? This seems doubtful.

In this case, however, it is equally doubtful that the Times Square assemblage qualifies as a genuine group, or the subject of a collective belief "It is hot". This is what has been called a merely "summative" ascription to a group (Quinton 1975–6), not a genuine collective attitude. Since there is no group attitude, the question of group justifiedness does not arise.

But suppose the Times Square assemblage "deliberates" with one another, now on another subject. Suppose that a number of them spot a flying entity high up in the sky, and several cry out, "It's an alien spaceship." Others are soon prompted

[17] This problem was pressed upon me by Holly Smith and Frederick Schmitt.

to repeat the cry, "Look, an alien spaceship," and by a process of contagion a large majority of them form the belief that an alien spaceship is approaching. Here the assemblage acquires the character of a unified (or semi-unified) group, and more plausibly has a genuine group belief. But is a *belief aggregation function* used to produce the belief? By assumption this group formulates no formal belief aggregation rule, so how does our theory apply to it?

This kind of problem was already anticipated in section 1.3, where we broadened the notion of a BAF to include "functionally inexplicit organizational structures." As indicated there a BAF does not require a *formula* or formally instituted *procedure* that a group follows. It can instead be a dynamic pattern of interpersonal influence by which beliefs spread from some members to others. This might be considered a variant of the member-group aggregation process that constitutes a BAF for purposes of justification appraisal. And there are certainly causal processes at work there.

Alternatively, the pattern of dynamic interpersonal influence may be conceptualized as a *pre-aggregation* step on the road to group belief. In Figure 1.1 the left side depicts members forming individual beliefs by means of causal processes. These processes might not be wholly internal to the members. There might also be interpersonal processes involving contagion. There still needs to be a group aggregation process, even under this option, but the contagion processes would not comprise the aggregation process. The aggregation process would be some species of metaphysical event—composition or constitution—that generates a group belief without causing it.

Can process reliabilism live with the suggestion that some *links* or *phases* in the total process of group formation are *non-causal* phases? Why not? Why can't process reliabilism concede that in the alien spaceship example, individuals in Times Square communicate with one another and causally persuade a majority of them to believe that an alien spaceship approaches? At this juncture, with the group having formed a suitable "unity" (however that happens), a metaphysical step of *composition* or *constitution* occurs in which the numerous individual beliefs generate a collective belief. Process reliabilism can accept the presence of a non-causal aggregatone link because it is only one link in a series of processes most of which are causal. This leaves ample room to appraise the collective belief by means of the reliability of the historical process that leads to it. Given these various options, process reliabilism need not fret unduly over cases involving collective beliefs by loose assemblages of people. In any event they are only borderline or limiting cases of collective beliefs that are candidates for justificational appraisal. If they are not a perfect fit with the mold of the best candidates for such appraisal, this should be neither a surprise nor a serious concern.

I turn next to a different issue concerning the application of process reliabilism to collective-level epistemology. The focus thus far has been the vertical dimension of group belief formation. What about the horizontal dimension, in which inference or reasoning occurs within a group mind? Presumably, social process reliabilism implies that the J-statuses of collective inferential beliefs are a function of the belief-forming processes that produce them. Is this applicable at the level of collective belief? One question is whether a causal-process model of collective propositional attitudes is really appropriate. A second question is whether—assuming such a model is appropriate—it is the causal processes that are specifically relevant to the J-statuses of the collective beliefs they generate. The second of these questions will be briefly addressed here.

I argue that the J-status of an inferential belief does depend on the properties of the causal process responsible for generating it.[18] I shall use an example of an individual cognizer, but the point readily generalizes to groups—at any rate, groups capable of inference or reasoning. Suppose that Chad justifiably believes two propositions of the form "P or Q" and "not-Q". Suppose further that he uses these beliefs to infer a belief in P. However, he doesn't use the "process" of disjunctive syllogism to draw this inference. Instead, he uses a process that overgeneralizes disjunctive syllogism. It is a psychological propensity of his to view as valid any inference from two premises of the form "P $ Q" and "not-Q" to a conclusion of the form "P", where "$" is replaceable by *any* binary truth-functional connective (disjunction, conjunction, material conditional, etc.). If *this* is the process he uses, intuitively his conclusion belief is not doxastically justified (although somebody else could have used the same premises to arrive at the same conclusion justifiedly). Chad's problem is his use of a flawed belief-forming process. His "dollar-sign" inferential process is not conditionally reliable. Applied to a range of easily constructible examples (with true inputs), its set of outputs would have a rather low truth-ratio. Clearly, it is this conditionally unreliable *process* that explains the unjustifiedness of his belief in P. What else might be driving our intuition here?

Could a group epistemic agent exemplify the same case? Why not? Of course, there must be machinery, whether human, silicon, or what have you, to ground the group's hypothetical mimicking of Chad. But as long as we understand the way it works (which computations are being executed, if you will), we will deem the inference type to be a bad one. And conditional unreliability of the inference pattern is an obvious rationale for dismissing it as defective.

---

[18] The example is drawn from Goldman 2012: 7.

I turn next to memory. Assume that epistemologists like me are right to think that a transmission principle is commonsensically used to impute a J-status to a belief at time t_n that duplicates the content of a belief held earlier, at time t_0. The question is: Is there an underlying *process* assumption that underlies this memory transmission principle? If we were given a case in which no retention *process* is at work, would we respond differently? And might this be detectable in a group agent example?

A good test case would be one in which there are *accidental* content replacements in the same "container". In a group agent case, a relevant scenario would be one in which individuals who represent the group (in important ways) are continually leaving or joining the group in such a fashion that the group never ceases to have a certain belief content represented but there are no causal links between their being so represented; it's just a matter of chance. Intuitively, I suggest, this would not be regarded as memory. What would be missing is an operative process that reliably maintains the content "in place" from moment to moment. This is how we conceptualize memory, I suspect, and the notion of process is central to it.

Here is a final thought in a different vein, concerning the feature of historicity distinctive to process reliabilism. A critic might complain that the historical approach to justification embedded in process reliabilism is unsatisfactory because it includes the cognitive biographies of individual epistemic agents, distinct from the group agent whose J-properties are in question. It is fine to track the J-status of a belief backwards as long as one stays within the target agent whose belief is in question. Going any further back, however, would be going too far! Yet that is precisely what we are proposing for the J-assessment of collective beliefs. We are proposing (in Figure 1.1) that a collective belief's J-status depends in part on the history that takes place within the members but outside the group. This is surely wrong, contends the critic.

I can understand and appreciate this sentiment; occasionally I feel it myself. But "classical" process reliabilism already made room for precisely this ecumenical sentiment. "What Is Justified Belief?" already distinguished between two forms of reliabilism: *historical* and *terminal-phase* reliabilism (Goldman, 2012: 42–3). As the label suggests, terminal-phase reliabilism makes a J-status assessment depend on how well the agent performs given the (evidential) resources available at the *final phase* of belief formation. Historical reliabilism, by contrast, highlights how well the agent proceeds at *all* of the decision points *leading up to* as well as including the final phase. Each approach has some claim to being a satisfactory explication of "justified," where justifiedness is construed broadly as a state that results when one proceeds appropriately given one's evidence, perspective, or starting point. An assessor's choice of a starting point can be flexible, leaving room for both the historical account and the terminal-phase account.[19]

References

Bird, A. (2010). "Social Knowing: The Social Sense of 'Scientific Knowledge.'" *Philosophical Perspectives* 24: 23–56.
Bradley, R. and Thompson, C. (2012). "A (Mainly) Epistemic Case for Multiple-Vote Majority Rule." *Episteme* 9(1): 63–80.
Bratman, M.E. (1999). *Faces of Intention*. Cambridge: Cambridge University Press.
Cohen, S. (1986). "Knowledge and Context." *Journal of Philosophy* 83: 574–83.
Comesana, J. (2002). "The Diagonal and the Demon." *Philosophical Studies* 110: 249–66.
Comesana, J. (2009). "What Lottery Problem for Reliabilism?" *Pacific Philosophical Quarterly* 90(1): 1–20.
Comesana, J. (2010). "Evidentialist Reliabilism." *Nous* 94(4): 571–600.
DeRose, K. (1992). "Contextualism and Knowledge Attributions." *Philosophy and Phenomenological Research* 52: 913–29.
DeRose, K. (2009). *The Case for Contextualism*. Oxford: Oxford University Press.
Fine, K. (1994). "Ontological Dependence." *Proceedings of the Aristotelian Society* 95: 269–90.
Gilbert, M. (1989). *On Social Facts*. Princeton: Princeton University Press.
Gilbert, M. (1994). "Durkheim and Social Facts." In W. Pickering and H. Martins (eds.), *Debating Durkheim* (86–109). London: Routledge.
Gilbert, M. (2002). "Belief and Acceptance as Features of Groups." *Protosociology* 16: 35–69.
Goldberg, S.C. (2010). *Relying on Others*. New York: Oxford University Press.
Goldman, A.I. (1979). "What Is Justified Belief?" In G. Pappas (ed.), *Justification and Knowledge*. Dordrecht: Reidel. Reprinted in Goldman (2012). All page citations for this article refer to the 2012 reprinting.
Goldman, A.I. (1986). *Epistemology and Cognition*. Cambridge, MA: Harvard University Press.
Goldman, A.I. (2001). "Experts: Which Ones Should You Trust?" *Philosophy and Phenomenological Research* 63: 85–109.
Goldman, A.I. (2008). "Immediate Justification and Process Reliabilism." In Q. Smith (ed.), *Epistemology: New Essays* (63–82). New York: Oxford University Press. Reprinted in Goldman (2012).

---

[19] I am greatly indebted to Jennifer Lackey for valuable comments on two earlier versions of this paper, as well as to Holly M. Smith and Fred Schmitt for exceedingly helpful comments during various periods of my research on this material. Predecessors of this paper were presented at the American Philosophical Association (Central Division), College de France (Paris), King's College London, a graduate student discussion group at Rutgers University, a conference in Bled, Slovenia on "Evidence, Reliabilism, and Social Epistemology," the Inter-American Congress of Philosophy in Salvador, Brazil, and a social epistemology workshop at Arche Research Center, University of St. Andrews. Audiences provided helpful comments and suggestions at each of these venues.

Goldman, A.I. (2011a). "Reliabilism." *The Stanford Encyclopedia of Philosophy* (Spring 2011 edition), E.N. Zalta (ed.), http://plato.stanford.edu/entries/reliabilism/. Reprinted in Goldman (2012).

Goldman, A.I. (2011b). "Toward a Synthesis of Reliabilism and Evidentialism." In T. Dougherty (ed.), *Evidentialism and Its Discontents* (254–80). New York: Oxford University Press. Reprinted in Goldman (2012)

Goldman, A.I. (2012). *Reliabilism and Contemporary Epistemology*. New York: Oxford University Press.

Grofman, B., Owen, G., and Feld, S. L. (1983). "Thirteen Theorems in Search of the Truth," *Theory and Decision 15*: 261–78.

Kornblith, H. (1980). "Beyond Foundationalism and the Coherence Theory." *Journal of Philosophy 72*: 597–612.

Lackey, J. (1999). "Testimonial Knowledge and Transmission." *Philosophical Quarterly 49*: 471–90.

Lackey, J. (2008). *Learning from Words: Testimony as a Source of Knowledge*. Oxford: Oxford University Press.

Lackey, J. (this volume). "A Deflationary Account of Group Testimony," in J. Lackey (ed.), *Essays in Collective Epistemology*. Oxford University Press.

Lackey, J. (forthcoming). "What Is Justified Group Belief?"

List, C. and Goodin, R.E. (2001). "Epistemic Democracy: Generalizing the Condorcet Jury Theorem," *Journal of Political Philosophy 9*: 277–306.

List, C. and Pettit, P. (2005). "On the Many as One," *Philosophy and Public Affairs 33*(4): 377–90.

List, C. and Pettit, P. (2011). *Group Agency*. Oxford: Oxford University Press.

Lyons, J.C. (2009). *Perception and Basic Beliefs*. New York: Oxford University Press.

Lyons, J.C. (2013). "Should Reliabilists Be Worried About Demon Worlds?" *Philosophy and Phenomenological Research 86*: 1-40.

Mathiesen, K. (2006). "The Epistemic Features of Group Belief." *Episteme 2*(3): 161–76.

Pettit, P. (2003). "Groups with Minds of their Own." In F.F. Schmitt (ed.), *Socializing Metaphysics* (467–93). New York: Rowman and Littlefield.

Quinton, A. (1975-76). "Social Objects," *Proceedings of the Aristotelian Society 75*: 1–27.

Schaffer, J. (2009). "On What Grounds What." In D. Chalmers, D. Manley, and R. Wasserman (eds.), *Metametaphysics* (347–83). New York: Oxford University Press.

Schmitt, F.F. (1984). "Reliability, Objectivity, and the Background of Justification." *Australasian Journal of Philosophy 62*: 1–15.

Schmitt, F.F. (1994). "The Justification of Group Beliefs." In F.F. Schmitt (ed.), *Socializing Epistemology: The Social Dimension of Knowledge* (257–87). Lanham, MD: Rowman & Littlefield.

Schmitt, F.F. (2006). "Testimonial Justification and Transindividual Reasons." In J. Lackey and E. Sosa (eds), *The Epistemology of Testimony* (193–224). Oxford: Oxford University Press.

Searle, J. (1995). *The Construction of Social Reality*. New York: Free Press.

Sylvan, K.L. (2012). "How to Be a Redundant Realist." *Episteme 9*(3): 271–82.

Tollefsen, D. (2007). "Group Testimony." *Social Epistemology 21*: 299–311.

Tuomela, R. (1992) "Group Beliefs." *Synthese 91*: 295–318.

Tuomela, R. (2007). *The Philosophy of Sociality: The Shared Point of View*. Oxford: Oxford University Press.

Wray, K. B. (ed.) (2010). *Collective Knowledge and Science*, special issue of *Episteme* 7(3): 182–283.

Wright, C. (2002). "Anti-Skeptics Simple and Subtle: Moore and McDowell." *Philosophy and Phenomenological Research* 65: 330–48.

Wright, C. (2003). "Some Reflections on the Acquisition of Warrant by Inference," in S. Nuccetelli (ed.), *New Essays on Semantic Externalism, Skepticism, and Self-Knowledge*. Cambridge, MA: MIT Press.

2

When Is There a Group that Knows?
Distributed Cognition, Scientific Knowledge, and the Social Epistemic Subject

Alexander Bird

Introduction

When is there a 'group', 'collectivity', or 'social system' that knows? That question may be broken down into two more specific questions. The first is the ontological question of the existence of a group: (i) when does a collection of individuals form an entity that is more than just the mereological sum of its constituent persons? The second, epistemological, question concerns the epistemic (and doxastic) states of such a social entity: (ii) given that there is a group of this sort, under what conditions does it know (or believe etc.)? In this paper I address these questions in order to answer a third: (iii) we talk of 'scientific knowledge' in a broad sense, as when we refer to the growth of scientific knowledge'; can we regard this scientific knowledge as an epistemic state of some social entity?

We can find many terms to talk of social entities (as indicated in my opening sentence). I shall disregard any possible differences there may be between their senses. On the assumption (yet to be justified) that there are social entities that can know things, I shall talk of a 'social epistemic subject'. So our third question can be framed as asking whether science involves a social epistemic subject?

My approach will be to compare two conceptions of group knowledge, which I call the *commitment* model and the *distributed* model. The commitment model is the one most favoured by authors endorsing the claim that there are social epistemic subjects. I shall argue, however, that the distributed model offers a better picture of the social epistemology of what I will call 'wider science'. One might conclude from this that (wider) science does not after all involve a social epistemic subject. But I shall argue that there is indeed a social epistemic subject for science. And so we should conclude that satisfying the commitment model is not a necessary condition for the existence of a social epistemic subject. I shall also ask what constitutes the social epistemic subject in the case of wider science.

2.1. Two Models of Social Cognition

2.1.1. *The commitment model*

Collective epistemic activity often takes the following form. A committee is formed in order to make recommendations on a particular question. The committee gathers evidence. It discusses the evidence. By some agreed procedure, it reaches a conclusion and submits its recommendations. What constitutes the existence of the committee in addition to its members? Relevant considerations include the fact that the committee has a purpose, a purpose to which the committee's members are individually committed in their role as members of that committee. The pursuit of that purpose is guided by certain norms, which may be explicit or implicit, to which the members are also committed. And when the committee reaches its conclusion, by the appropriate mechanism, the individual members are committed to that conclusion, *qua* committee members. That commitment may, according to some views, involve public endorsement of the conclusion, even if the individual's private opinion differs.

This committee provides one kind of model for thinking about social epistemic subjects. In this model two related features are prominent: first, the norms governing the committee, and, secondly, the commitment of the individuals to those norms. Opinions may differ about what commitments and norms must be involved. Nonetheless, the picture is clear of what an ideal social epistemic subject is like; it is an epistemic version of a sporting team—a tug-of-war team might be the best analogy—with each participant committed to their collective goal and to an agreed, commonly understood mechanism for reaching that goal. The justification for engaging in this form of group cognition is the thought that two (or more) heads are better than one.[1]

The commitment model of group epistemic and doxastic states is supported by a number of philosophers, including Raimo Tuomela (1992, 2004), Margaret Gilbert (1987, 1989, 2004), and Frederick Schmitt (1994). Philip Pettit (2003) also endorses the commitment model as a necessary but not sufficient condition on

---

[1] Whether that is in fact true is another matter. See Kanai and Banissy (2010).

the existence of a 'social integrate'. With regard to belief, Gilbert (1989: 306) and Schmitt (1994: 262) hold that:

(G) A group G believes that p just in case the members of G jointly accept that p, where the latter happens just in case each member has openly expressed a willingness to let p stand as the view of G, or openly expressed a commitment jointly to accept that p, conditional on a like open expression of commitment by other members of G.

Gilbert (2004) summarises the kind of commitment involved in (G), whereby several individuals come together and commit themselves as a body to something, as *joint commitment*. So (G) says that a group believes that p when its members are jointly committed to believing as a body that p. Assuming that knowing entails believing, then (G) places necessary conditions on group knowledge.[2]

As a consequence of the shared norms and commitments entailed by (G), individuals making up such an epistemic social subject will typically be conscious of and involved in the epistemic work of the committee. If indeed public commitment to the conclusion is required, then we would expect that individuals, in order to be comfortable with such a commitment, will want to know how the conclusion is reached and to be able to influence that conclusion.[3] Even without the requirement of commitment to the conclusion, merely being associated with that conclusion will often be enough to provide the motivation for understanding of and involvement with the decision-making process. Some authors argue that such consciousness is among the norms governing the social epistemic subject.[4]

Since this model has the characteristic that the group's members will be aware of one another as members of the group and aware of the group's modus operandi, we might also call this the *mutual awareness* model, following Pettit (2003).

2.1.2. *The distributed model*

Often we encounter circumstances such as the following. A complex task is information driven. But the information cannot be obtained and processed by any one individual. So several individuals are given roles in gathering different pieces of

---

[2] Gilbert (1987: 192; 2004: 99) regards the commitment in (G) as strong, imposing an obligation on group members not to disavow the group belief p, such that any disavowal may be rebuked by other group members. I am unsure that this is an inevitable feature of the groups that (G) seeks to describe, and I suspect that it varies from case to case. Perhaps group members may still affirm that p is the view of the group even if not of all of them individually. For example a court may come to an opinion that some of the judges openly disagree with in a minority opinion.

[3] This point will have greater force where the commitment has the strength claimed by Gilbert, as mentioned in footnote 2.

[4] I note though that Gilbert does not require that all members of the group always know what views the group espouses collectively. The group may come to a conclusion in the absence of some members, who are nonetheless committed to the group view. They may then ask, 'What do we think about X?'

information while other individuals have the task of coordinating this information and using it to complete the task. A famous example from Edwin Hutchins's (1995a) *Cognition in the Wild* concerns the process of bringing a large ship, the *USS Palau*, safely into port. Several crew members are given different landmarks whose bearings they are required to record and to communicate to a plotter who determines the ship's position and course. Another of Hutchins's (1995b) examples concerns the distribution of tasks between the two pilots (the Pilot Flying, PF, and the Pilot Not Flying, PNF) on a commercial aeroplane, in describing the task of determining the correct airspeeds at the various point of the plane's descent when coming in to land.

The key feature of such examples of the production of knowledge by a group is that the task is broken down into components, which are given to different members of the group. Membership of the group in this case is a matter of having a particular function within the overall system. This kind of group knowledge production is known, following Hutchins, as *distributed cognition*. The distributed cognition approach can be characterized in a number of ways; for current purposes, I propose the following. Distributed cognition identifies a *system* for producing knowledge, and studies how the various components, usually performing distinct sub-tasks, contribute to that overall task.

In typical cases, including those pertinent to social epistemology, the components of interest are usually individual human subjects. There is division of cognitive labour—the different human participants are given distinct cognitive sub-tasks. As Hutchins has emphasized from the outset, almost always in such systems there are non-human vehicles for representing various pieces of information; these must be taken fully into account in articulating how the system achieves its cognitive goals. For example, in the navigational task there are distinct cognitive tasks for the sailors involved, such as taking bearings and plotting the vessel's course. In carrying out those tasks an alidade is used to measure and record the bearings, while the plotter has specially constructed maps and instruments in order to use the bearings to calculate the correct course. In the aeroplane, the PF controls the plane while the PNF operates the aircraft systems and has responsibility for completing the checklists required for each phase of flight. In addition, the pilots are aided by a variety of instruments, not only for recording important information, such as airspeed and aircraft weight, but also for calculating the correct airspeeds for the changing wing configurations (the configurations of flaps and slats that change in order to maintain lift as the aircraft reduces its speed during descent). When the correct airspeeds for the different stages of the descent are determined, these are represented by 'speed bugs', moveable markers around the rim of the airspeed indicator; this is done in advance of the information being required, since the pilots will be too busy to calculate the correct arises in real time; hence the need for a system to represent or 'remember' its correct airspeeds.

2.1.3. Some differences between the two models

Groups engaged in distributed cognition typically do not satisfy the commitment model. It may be correct to say that the *USS Palau* knows (and so believes) that it is heading NNW at 14.2 knots, but that is not something which all the crew members have expressed a joint commitment to accept, not even all those involved in navigation. A midshipman may be on deck taking bearings and contributing to the generation of that knowledge, but that knowledge is not something he is aware of, let alone committed to.

The commitment model leads to questions and puzzles such as Pettit's discursive dilemma (2003). Commitment doesn't guarantee group rationality even if every individual is rational. This is because the opinions of the group's members might be aggregated in a way that leads to a paradoxical outcome.[5] Because distributed cognitive systems employ the division of cognitive labour, rather than aggregation of beliefs, Pettit's discursive dilemma is not an issue for distributed cognitive systems per se.

We may note, however, that a committee, the paradigm of the commitment model, may sometimes show some features of distributed cognition. For example, the committee may form specialist subcommittees or may choose to defer to the expertise of particular members. (By doing so it may also reduce the chances of the discursive dilemma arising.) Even so, a committee will usually bring the distributed knowledge back together to the whole committee so that all can share in the any fruits of distributed cognition. In that way the committee would be atypical of distributed systems, which do not usually share the knowledge produced across the system. The process by which the group comes to know according to the commitment model is not a distributed process—it is a process that is the same for all members of the group, involving them all individually in the same process of cognition.

---

[5] Imagine three subjects, A, B, and C, considering three propositions, p, q, and $p \wedge q$. A holds p to be true but q to be false, and so holds $p \wedge q$ to be false. B holds p to be false but q to be true, and so also holds $p \wedge q$ to be false. C holds both p and q to be true and so holds $p \wedge q$ to be true. Now imagine that A, B, and C have committed themselves in conformity with (G) to deciding which propositions to regard as the beliefs of the group by majority vote. Accordingly they regard p as true (A and C vote in favour), and q as true (B and C vote in favour), and they also regard $p \wedge q$ as false (since A and B both vote for the falsity of $p \wedge q$). Consequently the group beliefs are inconsistent. This is the discursive dilemma and according to Pettit a group only becomes an agent if it adopts a belief aggregation procedure that can avoid the dilemma.

2.2. The Two Models and Science

Does either the commitment model or the distributed model provides a satisfactory model for understanding group knowledge in the sciences? The commitment model is generally regarded by its proponents as a model for group knowledge in general, and so if science can generate group knowledge then the model should encompass science too. Tuomela (2004: 109) implies this when he opens his paper 'Group knowledge analyzed' saying 'One can speak of knowledge in an impersonal sense: It is accepted as knowledge that copper expands when heated...'. Distributed cognition is intended to be an approach with widespread application. Nonetheless, its central examples are cases of a well-defined cognitive task, implemented by a carefully designed system, with sub-tasks assigned to individuals who have some understanding of their role within the larger task. While some group activities within science, such as an experiment carried out by a team in a laboratory, will have these features, it is less clear that science on a larger scale is like this. And so it is a genuine question as to whether the distributed model can be applied to the interactions of scientists on a larger scale.

2.2.1. The commitment model and science

Research teams in science might sometimes satisfy the commitment model. The team discusses the results they have been getting and their significance, possible interpretations, problems with the experiment and so forth. They may reach a view which can be expressed as the conclusion of the group, which may be reported as 'We have discovered that p; we believe that this shows that q'. One would normally expect the team members to avow such conclusions as the view *of their group*, even though some members may have reservations. The larger the research teams the less well they fit the commitment model and the more clearly they exhibit the structure of distributed cognition. Karin Knorr Cetina, in her (1999) *Epistemic Cultures: How the sciences make knowledge*, described the High Energy Physics (HEP) experiments at CERN (the predecessor experiments to those carried out with the Large Hadron Collider). Knorr Cetina points out that the size, complexity, and long duration of the HEP experiments means that expertise cannot be centralized—the research leaders, she says, are not at the top but in the middle. It is neither necessary nor possible for participants in a HEP experiment to share all that they know with other participants, let alone to come together to agree on a common view.[6]

---

[6] Gilbert (2000: 37–49) applies the commitment model to scientific groups in particular; she argues that scientists are committed as groups to certain sets of beliefs. I think that this is quite possibly true for collaborative research teams, but I do not think that larger groups in science show this kind of

We may think of scientific knowledge as being produced and also possessed by groups larger even than the teams at CERN. For there is a social, non-personal sense of 'knows' that is employed in saying that it is known that copper expands when heated (to use Tuomela's example) or that anthropologists know *Homo sapiens* originated in Africa. In such cases the group in question is not the small, organised research team, but a much larger collection of people, whose boundary is not clear and which is not organized (in some cases the 'we' might seem to include everyone). This is what I shall call *wider* science, in contrast to the more local science of a research group. Participants in wider science clearly do not think of themselves as a group of which every member has expressed a willingness to let some p stand as the view of the group and have not openly expressed a joint commitment to accept p conditional on a like open expression of commitment by all other members.

The fact that the wider enterprise of science does not fit the commitment model does not necessarily refute the model's claim to be a general model of group knowledge. For proponents of that view might argue that there is not any group knowledge, beyond the defined research team, in wider science. While Tuomela for one does seem to want to include wider science within the remit of group knowledge, it might be that this is a mistake. And so in a later section I shall argue that we ought to regard wider science as involving a social epistemic subject.

2.2.2. *The distributed model and science*

Prima facie, the wider enterprise of science seems to fit the distributed model rather better. Science does have the key feature of distributed cognition, division of cognitive labour. The HEP experiments exhibit this very clearly; the participating scientists have their own areas of expertise and communicate with others on the basis of what needs to be shared for the local coordination of their parts of the project, what Knorr Cetina calls 'management by content'. While she says that this is something *like* distributed cognition, Ron Giere (2002a) argues, this *is* distributed

---

collective commitment. It is true that shared beliefs are important to a scientific community, but the importance arises less from commitment than from the fact that shared background beliefs (among other things) are a prerequisite for cooperation and mutual understanding, as explained by Kuhn. Those who reject beliefs core to a paradigm will not have reneged on a commitment; but they may find themselves excluded from the community because the basis for effective cooperation no longer exists. Gilbert proposes that her shared commitment explains why old hands are reluctant to buck the consensus: neophytes and outsiders are helpful to scientific change because they are not bound by their joint commitment to that consensus. There are other explanations. Kuhn (1962: 62–5) argues that training with exemplars builds certain cognitive habits that will make alternative views invisible to those entrenched within a scientific community. Furthermore, established scientists may have more invested in a certain way of doing things; threats to the consensus are threats to their expertise and to the basis of their prestige.

cognition. Giere points to the similarities between the HEP case and the USS *Palau* (while recognising that there are also important structural and cultural differences between the two cases).[7]

Scientists build on the work of other scientists. That includes using both the results of their experiments and their theoretical conclusions. In modern science a scientist is almost never able to reproduce all the experimental results upon which her work depends for its epistemic justification. Trust in the scientific work of others is a ubiquitous and nowadays inevitable feature of science (Hardwig 1991). This goes also for theoretical results as well as for the outcomes of experiments. For although it is in principle easier for a scientist to follow and so internalize the reasoning of another scientist, in practice this too is often a matter of trust. Often those who use a scientific result are not themselves working in the field that produced that result. Palaeontologists may date a fossil from the age of the rocks in which it lies. That dating will be supplied by radiometry which depends on theories of radioactive decay. The typical palaeontologist will understand the basic ideas of that theory, but will have to accept from the physicists that the detailed reasoning involved is cogent and well-supported.

Science also displays another feature of distributed cognition, the role played by non-human vehicles of cognition. Hutchins focuses on physical means of representing information—alidades and sextants, cockpit dials and speed cards, and so forth. These are important mediators between components of the distributed cognitive system. These are present in science also—printed and now online journal articles, reference resources, and datasets are the obvious example for wider science, for these are the principal means by which scientific information is communicated between scientists; we may include informal means of communication, letters, emails, and blogs, as well as educational resources, television broadcasts, podcasts, and the like. We ought also to include the non-human means of generating and representing information, which may include experimental equipment, satellites, computers running data analysis software, and even robot scientists. Giere (2002b: 293) argues that visual representations in science can be thought of not merely as aids to cognition but as parts of systems engaged in cognition.[8]

---

[7] Giere says, rightly in my view, that Knorr Cetina's description of an intended contrast to the HEP experiments, a molecular biology laboratory with centralized management, is also a case of distributed cognition. Its structure has some of the management structure of the *Palau* case. In his (2002b) Giere argues persuasively for the conclusion of this section, that science should be seen an instance of distributed cognition. Brown (2009) usefully supplements the case, in particular relating it to approaches in the sociology of science and learning theory.

[8] Giere (2002b: 293–4) also argues that scientific theories and models may be too complex to be fully realized as mental models, and so the models are reconstructed as external representations when needed. A slightly different approach, though one that Giere does not endorse, is to think of the mental as extending beyond the skin, so that external representations can be part of the individual's mind,

There are however differences between wider science and Hutchins's examples of distributed cognition. The structures of the distributed cognitive systems in those cases have been designed to perform specific cognitive functions. The structures of wider science as a whole have not been designed (although some of their components have been). For example, the system of peer-reviewed journals is one that has evolved. That system may in due course be superseded—this is an issue of current debate; if it is superseded that will most likely be determined by what scientists find useful; scientific organizations may play a role in that debate, but there is no central world organization that could decide what will happen. In Hutchins's example of the cockpit of a commercial airliner, the system is designed to meet a specific goal—knowing at each point during the plane's descent what the correct speed and wing configuration should be. While local science may have well-defined goals around which the systems are designed, wider science is not like this.

These differences between science and the paradigm examples of distributed cognition may not immediately show that the distributed model does not apply to science. One might reply that whether a cognitive system is designed or has come about by some other process is not relevant to how it functions. But that would be too quick: how a system came into being may well determine what functions it and its components have—whether something is a bug or a feature depends on design intentions. In order to think of a structure as a cognitive system whose parts have functions we need to assign a (cognitive) goal to science. Given that science is not a designed system, can we do this?

We think that science progresses—over times science gets better in certain respects; for example its scope widens, its precision and accuracy increase, and our understanding deepens. Why do we think of such changes in science as *progressive* (as opposed to merely occurring)? The best explanation of this, I propose, is that we think of science as having a goal: science progresses when it achieves or gets closer to its goal (or goals—there could be more than one). And given what we think of as contributing to the progress of science (new discoveries, theoretical advances etc.), it is plausible that science has a *cognitive* goal. It is my view that the goal of science is the production of knowledge (see Merton 1973: 270) and that science progresses when we accumulate scientific knowledge (Bird 2007). But the more general argument that the progress of science implies a cognitive goal for

---

as proposed by Andy Clark (1997). I shall not pursue this debate here, since I am concerned with the social subjects of cognition rather than individuals. But it is worth noting that Giere and Clark agree that there is a distributed cognitive system of which both the biological animal and the external device are parts.

science is independent of this particular account of the goal and progress. P. D. Magnus (2007) holds that we cannot find a goal for science, and so the characterization of science as distributed cognition is problematic. He notes that the goal of knowledge does not allow for the speculative activity of exploring a hypothesis. He also argues that the aim fails to discriminate between worthwhile and pointless knowledge. Both points can be answered. Some instances of 'exploring a hypothesis' do generate knowledge—for example knowledge of the mathematical or logical relationships between the hypothesis and other hypotheses, models, etc. More importantly, exploring a hypothesis is scientifically worthwhile because it can lead to knowledge—for example by allowing us to see what evidence might refute or confirm the hypothesis. If the aim of science is knowledge, then many activities (such as designing an experiment) will count as scientific because they are conducive to that end even if they do not in themselves achieve that end. Magnus is right that the kind of knowledge that science aims at needs to be circumscribed. He himself points to Kitcher's (1993) notion of significant truth. There are problems, as Magnus says, in saying what exactly 'significant' amounts to (I would suggest that significance is relative to a scientific tradition of a Kuhnian kind). But the existence of such difficulties in articulating precisely the goal of science is not a strong reason for denying that there is such a goal, whereas the commonplace idea that there is such a thing as scientific progress implies that science does have a goal.[9]

So although wider science is not designed, it can have a goal or function, just as evolved organisms and their organs can have goals and functions (this biological analogy is one to which I shall return). Given that science does have a cognitive goal (or goals) we can think of it as a system whose components contribute to that goal. Consequently science meets the characterization of distributed cognition given above.

2.3. Distributed Cognition and the Social Epistemic Subject

We talk as if we are committed to social epistemic states. We use locutions such as 'it is now known that Kepler's conjecture is true', 'we know that smoking causes cancer', 'North Korea knows how to build a nuclear weapon', and so forth. Such locutions are not reducible to claims about individuals (see Gilbert 1989; Bird 2010). For example, it is unlikely that any individual North Korean knows how

---

[9] See also Brown (2009) for a response to Magnus.

to build a nuclear weapon (I give further examples below). Being irreducible, it is the central thesis of this paper that such statements—statements concerning wider science—are made true by the existence of social entities in epistemic states. In this section I shall argue that the distributed model of science helps us see that (i) the subjects of such statements are indeed social entities, because they are composed in a way that gives them an appropriate unity (that collections of individuals generally do not have), and (ii) such social entities have epistemic states.

It is clear that the distributed model provides a better model for understanding wider science than does the commitment model, which is no surprise. But then the two models were developed with different aims. The commitment model aims at articulating what genuine group doxastic and epistemic states are. The distributed model was developed with the aim of understanding how systems with differentiated components can achieve cognitive goals. Since the conditions that the commitment model lays down are so stringent, it is plausible that if there is any group knowledge at all, then the commitment model describes one way it can come about. The explicit commitment of individuals to the group does as much as could possibly be done to ensure that it is a unity. The distributed model does not have this ontological focus. It is true that Hutchins does *talk* of his systems (rather than just the individuals involved) as having cognitive states—one paper is entitled 'How a Cockpit Remembers Its Speeds'. But he does not pretend to give an argument for this ontological commitment. Hence the defender of the commitment model may respond to the forgoing as I indicated above: *The commitment model provides our best account of how there can be a social epistemic subject. Insofar as science or other examples of the distributed model fail to fit the commitment model, we have no reason to suppose that they are cases involving genuine social epistemic subjects (so this challenge asserts). We should therefore see the distributed model as a model of the distributed production of knowledge, not the distributed possession of knowledge.* The challenge is made sharper by the fact that within the (designed) systems that Hutchins discusses, there is typically a node, a human individual, who does possess the crucial information that the system produces and is able to use it for the purposes of the system—the Pilot Flying in the case of the aeroplane cockpit, and the plotter in the case of the ship. So it might well appear to the social epistemologist that distributed cognition really concerns what I have elsewhere called 'individual–social' epistemology, viz. epistemology that is concerned with the epistemic states of individuals as they relate to their social context, rather than with the epistemic states of social epistemic subjects ('social–social' epistemology).

What considerations are relevant to judging that there is an epistemic social subject in the case of distributed cognition, as found in science? In this section I argue that the hypothesized epistemic social subject has sufficient *unity* to be considered to be a genuine entity; this is because division of labour can provide the principle of composition for some social entities. I then argue on functionalist grounds that this entity can have intentional, including epistemic states. I then turn to the objection that the knowledge in question is subjectless; that is we should accept the argument of the second subsection but not the first—this is a case of knowing without a knower.

2.3.1. *The unity of the subject*

For any entity that has parts there must be something that unites those parts. In so saying, I am assuming that composition is restricted. (If it is not, then it is trivial that the components of a putative social epistemic subject form a whole.) For most physical objects that unity is mechanical—the parts will be physically joined to one another. For social entities, the principle of composition will not be like this. We ought to bear in mind that there might be different ways in which individuals can form social entities and that the resulting different kinds of entity may differ in their existence conditions. A set of individuals may form a social entity of ontological kind G but not of some other kind G'. So we may wish to consider that the principle of composition for a social *epistemic* subject ought to be one that plays some part in explaining how that resulting entity can be the possessor of epistemic states.

One concern that we might have in holding that there are any social entities at all, is that the individuality and free-will of human beings is a barrier to their being unified into a supra-individual entity—have not totalitarian leaders promoting social unity sought to suppress individuality and freedom? Some biologists emphasize the unity of a hive of bees or a colony of ants to the extent of arguing that these are the true organisms, not the individual bees and ants. While these insect groups do show distributed cognition, one might think that it is the 'mechanical', genetically hard-wired nature of their co-operation that allows us to think of them as forming a single entity. But the cognitive cooperation of individuals, especially in wider science, is not like that, being subject to the will.

The fact that a social entity's putative existence may be subject to the will of individuals is not sufficient to deny that that such existence is genuine. After all, the continued existence of my body is subject to my will (as is the existence of this mug, that cake, etc.). If there is sufficient strength of will directed towards the unity of the social entity that ought to allow for this objection to be overcome. So it is perhaps no surprise that the commitment model emphasizes commitment so centrally, since that is a demonstration that the individual members all will that their social entity should exist. And this might explain also the significance for Gilbert and Tuomela of the standing to rebuke, for the existence of that standing will reinforce the commitment of the individuals to the group's existence as an epistemic subject.

Individual commitment to the group is one way that the wills of individuals can support the existence of the group. But it is not the only way. The sociologist Émile Durkheim was concerned with the question of what holds societies together. The means by which social cohesion is achieved he called *solidarity*. While the question of the sources of solidarity was for Durkheim a sociological question—how do societies hold together and function effectively rather than break down or fragment?— responses to that question may also be seen as answers to the composition question for social groups. Durkheim (1893) distinguishes between *mechanical* and *organic* solidarity as means by which society can be held together. In societies characterized by mechanical solidarity there is unification through the shared beliefs (experiences, obligations etc.) of individuals. Cohesion is achieved by the individuals in the group valuing their similarities of belief and value, their kinship, and their cooperative practices. In societies characterized by organic solidarity, however, cohesion is achieved not by similarity among individuals but instead by difference. Unification is generated by mutual dependence arising from, above all, the division of labour. Where an economic system operates by division of labour that system's existence does not require commitment of the individual to the system; commitment by the individual to perform his function within the system will suffice. The fruit canner does not need to have any conception of the economic system of which he is a part in order for him to contribute to its existence and operation, so long as he is committed to the grocer to supply his needs and to the grower to take his produce—commitments that self-interest will generate.

So individuals can compose a social unity when they cohere because of the mutual interdependence that arises from the division of labour. While Durkheim thought principally in terms of economic division of labour, we need to consider whether there is an epistemic analogue—solidarity arising from cognitive division of labour—if we are to think of scientists forming epistemic social groups.[10] And indeed, that is exactly what distributed cognition gives us.[11]

---

[10] I do acknowledge that there is an element of mechanical solidarity in many social entities even when organic solidarity predominates, including communities of scientists. The latter may well see themselves as a community in virtue of shared values, goals, and interests.

[11] I argue that distributed cognition is one way of implementing organic solidarity (in epistemic groups). Is there an analogous relationship between entities satisfying commitment model and mechanical solidarity? Collective commitment to shared beliefs does look very much like a form of mechanical solidarity. There may be mechanical solidarity that does not involve commitment, so collective commitment is just one realisation of mechanical solidarity. That said, it should be recognized that mere similarity of belief does not its own constitute mechanical solidarity—it is also required that this fact be mutually recognized and engender a sense of belonging together. Although this falls short

Hutchins's examples of a landing a plane and navigating a ship show division of labour among two or more individuals (and also non-human devices). Those individuals are trained for their particular sub-tasks, and various social, professional norms (and self-interest) ensure that they are reliably performed. Just as there is division of cognitive labour in Hutchins's examples, there is division of cognitive labour in the local science of an experiment or research project. It is true also of wider science, although in this case the division of labour has evolved without a plan being imposed upon the participants. That does not itself detract from unity, for the economic division of labour, generating Durkheim's organic solidarity is likewise an un-designed evolution. No modern science depends for its conclusions just on the intellect and the evidence of the senses of a single scientist nor even of a local team of scientists. The work of other scientists will be drawn upon in the design of equipment used, in auxiliary hypotheses and background knowledge, and in the statistical methods and computer software employed to analyse data. The scientist's conclusions may be worthwhile in themselves but they will frequently be used as evidence or background knowledge in some other scientist's reasoning. So wider science exhibits the division of labour that gives rise to organic solidarity. This is not restricted to fields or sub-fields, for the interdependence of science crosses such boundaries. Wider science is, for the most part, a single entity.

2.3.2. The epistemic subject

I have just argued that there is a principle of composition (other than commitment) that can bind individuals together to form a social entity. This can apply to groups involved in distributed cognition and to science in particular. Given that there is a social entity composed of scientists, we need further to show that such an entity can be the subject of intentional states, in particular epistemic states.

The argument that entities engaged in distributed cognition have epistemic states is a functionalist one. We can identify particular behaviours and states of the system and its parts that are best understood as actions and the intentional states that explain those actions. In Hutchins's cases, those systems are designed to fulfil a function—controlling an aircraft's descent carefully, navigating a ship. So these systems have goals and engage in actions to achieve them. The successful execution of those actions to achieve those goals depends on the systems generating and being able to access certain crucial pieces of information, and as described by distributed cognition, the systems are designed precisely to produce that information and deliver it to those parts of the system that need it. The

---

of collective commitment, it points in that direction in that both require members of groups to have a sense of the group as a group and to know that certain beliefs or intentions are shared by its members.

system's goals and actions are thus supported by an information processing function of the system. If a system has goals and performs actions to achieve them, and has an aspect or subsystem whose function is to provide information that guides those actions, then that function is a cognitive one. The states that the system is in as a result of performing that cognitive function are correspondingly cognitive/epistemic ones. For example, the *Palau* needs to enter Hampton Roads at Naval Station Norfolk (goal). So the ship changes course to 265°. Why? Because the *Palau* has taken its bearings and knows that Hampton Roads lies in a direction 5° south of due west.

Can the functionalist argument be extended from Hutchins's central examples to wider science? Wider science is not a designed system (though it does have designed components). Nonetheless, as has been discussed, the lack of a design does not preclude possession of a function. Functional explanations are common in biology without that being any concession to the intelligent design view; rather, evolutionary accounts of function are required. Above I briefly argued that science has a cognitive goal. This claim is reinforced by the Durkheimian perspective, which sees various social institutions, especially those in societies characterised by organic solidarity, as fulfilling various functions, in a manner analogous to the functions of the various organs in a living being. Societies can have collective goals and engage in collective actions (such as those coordinated by governments); there are institutions that provide the information that allows those goals to be pursued and those actions to succeed; science is one of these institutions and an increasingly important one as the goals and actions become increasingly technologically sophisticated.

To the claim that the group can be an epistemic subject, one might respond that this is unnecessarily inflationary given that we can ascribe knowledge to some or all of the individuals in the group. For example, in Hutchins's examples we can identify a particular central individual who receives and acts on the information supplied by the other individuals (and objects) in the system. The response to the very last point is that while in some systems it may be effective to have a single, central individual in such a role, that is certainly not required, and many distributed cognitive systems lack such an individual—air traffic control is an important example. In large-scale local science, while the Principal Investigator or Programme Director may have an overview of the functioning of the project, she will not necessarily be a cognitive central node in the system; conversely, as Knorr Cetina describes the HEP experiments, those with responsibility for scientific outcomes of sub-projects and their communication to other parts of the experiment find themselves in the middle of the management structure. Such projects may produce papers with dozens of authors, where the content of the paper cannot be said to be fully known (in an individual way) by any of them (papers with hundreds of authors are increasingly common).[12]

More generally, group knowledge does not reduce to the knowledge of any individuals in the group. Indeed there can be scientific knowledge without any individual knowing. Consider this example:

Dr N. is working in mainstream science, but in a field that currently attracts only a little interest. He makes a discovery, writes it up and sends his paper to the *Journal of X-ology*, which publishes the paper after the normal peer-review process. A few years later, at time *t*, Dr N. has died. All the referees of the paper for the journal and its editor have also died or forgotten all about the paper. The same is true of the small handful of people who read the paper when it appeared. A few years later yet, Professor O. is engaged in research that needs to draw on results in Dr N.'s field. She carries out a search in the indexes and comes across Dr N.'s discovery in the *Journal of X-ology*. She cites Dr N.'s work in her own widely-read research and because of its importance to the new field, Dr N.'s paper is now read and cited by many more scientists.

I claim (Bird 2010) that Dr N.'s contribution to knowledge did not cease with his death. Rather his discovery is a contribution to what is known in wider science in virtue of its publication and remains known thanks to the accessibility of that publication. From the perspective of wider science what is important is not whether some individual knows or not but rather whether they can use that knowledge in their own work if so required, and that is what publication ensures. Contrast that with a parallel case where a reclusive scientist does not publish his work—that work cannot be a contribution to wider science because it is inaccessible.

This example illustrates one aspect of distributed cognition—the importance of non-human forms of representation. For the system to know something, what is in peoples' heads is not important; what is important is the availability of the information known for the various social purposes the system may have. And that information may be made available through non-human means. (Libraries and the web do genuinely contain knowledge.) Another common feature of distributed cognition is the division of cognitive labour, illustrated by the following example (Bird 2010):

Dr X., a physicist, and Dr Y., a mathematician, collaborate on a project to demonstrate the truth of the conjecture that q. Their project can be broken down into three parts. Part one is a problem in physics, the problem of showing that p, which will be the work of Dr X. alone. Part two is a problem in pure mathematics, that of proving that if p then q, for which Dr Y. takes sole responsibility. Part three is an application of modus ponens to the results of

---

[12] Usually those listed are not all 'authors' in the normal sense—they are participants in the project; even so many papers are collaboratively written with different authors contributing different sections according to their expertise.

parts one and two. They arrange for an assistant to publish a paper if and only if the assistant receives from X the demonstration that p is true and from Y the proof of $p \to q$ (the brief final part with the application of modus ponens has been pre-written). We can imagine that X and Y have no other communication with each other or with the assistant and so do not know at the time of publication that q has been proven.

These examples show two things. First, that what the social epistemic subject knows does not depend on what the individuals know. Pettit (2003: 191) and Tuomela (2004: 112) subscribe to a supervenience claim, that the knowledge (and other intentional states) of a group supervene on the relevant mental states of the individuals.[13] The supervenience claim is false for states of social knowing brought about by distributed cognition. Note that the falsity of the supervenience claim does not show that there are mysterious group-level entities that act independently of other things. Rather, it indicates that the true supervenience basis for facts about a social epistemic subject extends beyond the mental sates of individuals: the supervenience basis includes non-human entities as well as human ones and also facts about the relationships between individuals (which need not themselves supervene on individual states). Secondly, and as a consequence of the preceding point, we cannot reduce states of social knowing to states of individuals; so positing such states cannot be regarded as *merely* inflationary, inflating ontology without bringing explanatory benefit.

2.3.3. Subjectless knowing?

In the two preceding subsections I have argued first that we have reason to believe that there are social entities and then that we can sometimes attribute epistemic states to them. This approach assumes that if there is to be knowing at all, there must be a subject who is the knower, whether individual or social. Some philosophers of science are reluctant to ascribe a subject to this social knowing; they will agree with the claim that there is social knowing, but deny that we have to find an entity to which we can ascribe this state. Popper (1979: 109) famously held that 'knowledge in the objective sense is knowledge without a knower: it is knowledge without a knowing subject'. Giere comments on Knorr Cetina's suggestion that in a large scale experiment, it is the experiment that knows (Knorr Cetina 1999). Giere (2002a) prefers the idea that the knowledge produced by the experiment does not belong to any epistemic subject. The forgoing arguments suggest that we

---

[13] Gilbert (2000) also says, 'According to the conception of collective belief I put forward, collective beliefs are a matter of how it is with the individual members of the group in question'; as she goes on to emphasize, the 'how it is' is not just a matter of the corresponding beliefs of the individuals. Other features of individuals are relevant according to her view, for example, as has been noted above, commitments by the individuals.

do not need to avoid identifying a knowing subject. On this view Knorr Cetina is right, when we take 'the experiment' to be the total system of the team working on the experiment and its analysis, plus the equipment and infrastructure that enables them to reach their results. We might prefer the terms 'project' or 'program'. It does not sound at all odd to assign epistemic properties to such entities, saying, for example, 'the Manhattan project discovered how to harness the power of nuclear fission'.

A further reason for rejecting the subjectless knower view is that it is difficult to reconcile with the best argument that there is social knowing at all. The best argument is the functionalist one articulated above. That argument requires, in outline, that we regard social states as having functions and where the functions can be regarded as cognitive, the states are epistemic. But states of *what*? One cannot identify a state as having a function without there being a reasonably determinate thing that has that function. One cannot identify functions independently of the things they are functions of. Hence our best argument for social knowing requires that there is a social entity that does the knowing.

2.4. When is There a Social Epistemic Subject, and of What is it Composed?

We have established that there are grounds for holding that there are social subjects with epistemic states. The arguments given allow us to answer the following questions:

1. When is it that a social epistemic subject exists?
2. Of what is the social epistemic subject composed?

A social subject exists when there is sufficient social glue (cohesion, solidarity) to join the components together. I have argued that the glue need not be joint commitment. Division of labour is another source of solidarity. Put less abstractly, the fact that certain people have mutually interacting jobs or roles may be sufficient to bind them together in the relevant way, as for example it is on a naval ship. That division of labour, those different job-roles, determine the distinct individual functions that contribute to the various functions possessed by the social whole thus bound together. If the latter include cognitive functions, then the social whole is an epistemic social subject. (While it may be vague when there is enough of the right kind of cohesion and distinctness that a social entity exists, that is no objection to the claims being made. It is often vague when a physical object has enough cohesion to be regarded as an entity, e.g. a cloud, melting iceberg, etc.)

In what does this social subject consist? At least the individuals performing the functions contributing to the function of the whole. That much is clear. The lesson of distributed cognition and the anti-supervenience arguments is that we must include relevant non-human entities also. Describing the function of the navigation on the *Palau* makes no sense without including the crew's navigational equipment and indeed the ship herself. While that answer gives us the correct supervenience basis for the epistemic state, it does not mean that these are the only components of the social epistemic subject. Jane knows that Edinburgh is the capital of Scotland but John does not; Jane's hand is not part of the supervenience basis for this knowledge. Still, that hand is part of the knowing subject (Jane) whereas John's hand is not. That is because Jane is not just an epistemic subject; we identify her as having cognitive functions as part and parcel of identifying other functional states. If she knows which direction is North, she may demonstrate this by pointing with her hand. Turning now to the *Palau*, the whole of interest extends beyond just the navigation team. For the cognitive function of knowing the bearing of Hampton Roads is related to the locomotive function of steering the vessel into Hampton Roads. And there will be crew members performing that function who have no role in the cognitive function. Given the connections between the various functions, those functions must be attributed to an entity comprising the whole crew (and the ship).

What are the consequences of this approach for wider science? Let us start with not-so-wide science, the science in the North Korean nuclear weapons programme. That scientific programme is functioning as part of the North Korean state, with a view to enabling that state to fulfil its goals. However, the social entity in question goes beyond just the officials of the state; it will include the citizens of North Korea also, since they are functionally connected to the weapons programme in a number of ways: their labour (even if coerced) pays for the programme; they have other obligations to the state and military (e.g. military service); they live within the boundaries of the country that the weapons programme aims to protect. So those citizens have a functional relationship to the knowledge generated by the weapons programme that the citizens of other nations do not. This explains why it is appropriate to say 'North Korea knows how to build a nuclear weapon, but Burma does not' (or 'the North Koreans know how to build a nuclear weapon, but the Burmese do not').

Now we can think about wider science, as practiced in universities and publicly-funded research institutes across the world. Scientific collaboration, the division of cognitive labour, and the dissemination of results are international and typically accessible to anyone who has sufficient background knowledge to understand them. Yet others will be indirect consumers of the knowledge, for example, through the technology it creates. Consequently, membership of the social group of wider science may be considered to be very extensive, potentially encompassing much of the world's population. Such a conclusion is neither trivial nor absurd. For if we are all part of a global village, participating, willingly or otherwise, in a highly internationalized economy, it is not absurd to think of others, even if geographically remote from us, as part of some of same social entities.[14] Science in particular has been international from an early date, with scientists in different European countries as well as America communicating with one another regularly from the seventeenth century forward.

2.5. Conclusion

This paper has contributed arguments in support of three claims: (i) that there are social entities; (ii) that such entities can have epistemic states; (iii) that wider science is one such entity.

The claim (i) that there are social groups is controversial. It is perhaps natural for those wishing to defend this view to take a conservative approach. The group's existence is closely tied to the intentions of its members; their commitment to the group provides it with the unity that makes it a genuine entity. The commitment model adds detail in order to gives its groups epistemic/cognitive states as required by (ii). Doxastic states are provided by certain commitments to propositions. Epistemic states, such as knowledge, will come about as a result of the mechanism the group uses to reach its shared conclusion.

However, in order to answer (i), we can see that there are other ways of binding people together into a social unity, forms of Durkheimian organic solidarity, where differences between members, such as those based on division of labour, can connect people via relations of dependence. An account of group epistemic states arises naturally from a model of group unity based on organic solidarity; for example, if organic solidarity arises from division of cognitive labour, then it will be natural to see the group as having cognitive states. Systems exhibiting distributed cognition exemplify such groups. It will be necessary to regard the group as having a cognitive goal, but doing so does not require that the goal has been intentionally chosen or that the system has been explicitly designed (as in many examples of distributed cognition); evolved entities can have goals and functions, and some groups' cognitive goals may be seen in this light.

---

[14] This point has an ethical dimension. For example, even if we in the West are under an obligation to help relieve poverty wherever it exists, that obligation seems all the stronger when the poor in question are those making the cheap goods we buy.

Finally, claim (iii) requires that we show that wider science can be understood as a social entity with group epistemic states. Above I argued, as have Giere (2002b) and Brown (2009), that wider science is a distributed cognitive system. When added to the arguments for (i) and (ii) this makes it a plausible conjecture that wider science is indeed an entity with epistemic states—states of 'scientific knowledge' in the impersonal sense. To add confirming evidence to the plausibility of the conjecture will require detailed work regarding the structures of science showing how they do have the coordination towards a cognitive goal that one would expect of a distributed cognitive system, even though the system is an evolved rather than designed one. And it will also need to be argued that the ties that bind not only scientists but also the downstream consumers of science are sufficient for genuine unity. These, it strikes me, are promising lines of enquiry.

References

Bird, A. 2007. "What is scientific progress?" *Noûs* **41**: 64–89.
Bird, A. 2010. "Social knowing." *Philosophical Perspectives* **24**: 23–56.
Brown, M. 2009. Science as socially distributed cognition: Bridging philosophy and sociology of science. In K. Francois, B. Löwe, T. Müller, and B. V. Kerkhove (eds.), *Foundations of the Formal Sciences VII*. London: College Publications.
Clark, A. 1997. *Being There: Putting brain, body, and world together again*. Cambridge MA: MIT Press.
Durkheim, E. 1893. *De la division du travail social*. Paris: Alcan. Translated as *The Division of Labor in Society*, by W. D. Halls, New York: The Free Press, 1984.
Giere, R. N. 2002a. "Distributed cognition in epistemic cultures." *Philosophy of Science* **69**: 637–44.
Giere, R. N. 2002b. Scientific cognition as distributed cognition. In P. Carruthers, S. Stich, and M. Siegal (eds.), *The Cognitive Basis of Science*, pp. 285–99. Cambridge: Cambridge University Press.
Gilbert, M. 1987. "Modelling collective belief." *Synthese* **73**: 185–204.
Gilbert, M. 1989. *On Social Facts*. London: Routledge.
Gilbert, M. 2000. *Sociality and Responsibility: New essays in plural subject theory*. Lanham, MD: Rowman and Littlefield.
Gilbert, M. 2004. "Collective epistemology." *Episteme* **1**: 95–107.
Hardwig, J. 1991. "The role of trust in knowledge." *Journal of Philosophy* **88**: 693–708.
Hutchins, E. 1995a. *Cognition in the Wild*. Cambridge MA: MIT Press.
Hutchins, E. 1995b. "How a cockpit remembers its speeds." *Cognitive Science* **19**: 265–88.
Kanai, R. and M. Banissy 2010. "Are two heads better than one? It depends." *Scientific American*. August 2012. URL: http://www.scientificamerican.com/article.cfm?id=are-two-heads-betterthan accessed 25 Sept 2012.
Kitcher, P. 1993. *The Advancement of Science*. New York: Oxford University Press.
Knorr Cetina, K. 1999. *Epistemic Cultures: How the sciences make knowledge*. Cambridge MA: Harvard University Press.

Kuhn, T. S. 1962. *The Structure of Scientific Revolutions*. Chicago, IL: University of Chicago Press.

Magnus, P. D. 2007. "Distributed cognition and the task of science." *Social Studies of Science* 37: 297–310.

Merton, R. K. 1973. The normative structure of science. In N. W. Storer (Ed.), *The Sociology of Science*, pp. 267–73. Chicago, IL: University of Chicago Press.

Pettit, P. 2003. Groups with minds of their own. In F. F. Schmitt (Ed.), *Socializing metaphysics*, pp. 167–93. Lanham, MD: Rowman and Littlefield.

Popper, K. 1979. *Objective Knowledge* (Revised ed.). Oxford: Clarendon Press.

Schmitt, F. 1994. The justification of group beliefs. In F. F. Schmitt (Ed.), *Socializing Epistemology: The Social Dimensions of Knowledge*, pp. 257–87. Lanham, MD: Rowman and Littlefield.

Tuomela, R. 1992. "Group beliefs." *Synthese* 91: 285–318.

Tuomela, R. 2004. "Group knowledge analyzed." *Episteme* 1: 109–27.

3

A Deflationary Account of Group Testimony

Jennifer Lackey

The topic of this paper is group testimony as a *source of knowledge* and the questions that will be the focus of my discussion are these: when we acquire knowledge from the testimony of a group, who is the source? Is it an individual or set of individuals or is it somehow the group itself? Both negative and positive answers have been given to these questions. According to a *reductionist* account, a group's testimony that *p* is epistemologically reducible to the testimony of some individuals. The standard reductionist theory is the *summative* view, according to which a group testifying that *p* can be understood in the minimal sense that all or some members of the group would testify that *p* were the relevant opportunity to arise. The distinction between summative and non-summative accounts is due to Anthony Quinton (1975/1976), though he focuses on such accounts of groups *simpliciter* rather than of group testimony. He writes:

> We do, of course, speak freely of the mental properties and acts of a group in the way we do of individual people. Groups are said to have beliefs, emotions, and attitudes and to take decisions and make promises. But these ways of speaking are plainly metaphorical. To ascribe mental predicates to a group is always an indirect way of ascribing such predicates to its members. With such mental states as beliefs and attitudes, the ascriptions are of what I have called a summative kind. To say that the industrial working class is determined to resist anti-trade union laws is to say that all or most industrial workers are so minded. (Quinton 1975/1976, p. 17)[1]

---

[1] Compare Quinton on summative accounts of groups with Margaret Gilbert on summative views of group beliefs: "What is it for *us* to believe that such-and-such, according to our everyday understanding? It is common to answer this question with some form of 'summative' account. For *us* to believe that *p* is for all or most of us to believe that *p*. Or perhaps a 'common knowledge' condition may be added: for *us* to believe that *p* is for all or most of us to believe that *p*, while this is common knowledge among us. Whatever the precise account given, the core of it is a number of individuals who personally believe that *p*" (Gilbert 1994, p. 235). See also Goldman (2009).

Applying Quinton's remarks[2] to the topic at hand, we can say that there is nothing epistemologically distinctive about group testimony when understood in a summative way—one's general epistemology of testimony can simply be applied to the individual members whose testimony constitutes that of the group.[3]

Summative accounts of group judgments also result from various aggregation procedures for combining individual judgments held by the members of a group into collective ones. "Aggregation procedures are mechanisms a multimember group can use to combine ('aggregate') the individual beliefs or judgments held by the group members into collective beliefs or judgments endorsed by the group as a whole" (List 2005, p. 25).[4] If these group judgments can then be communicated or otherwise conveyed, these accounts can naturally be construed as reductionist and summative views of group testimony. For instance, a dictatorial procedure, "whereby the collective judgments are always those of some antecedently fixed group member (the 'dictator')" (List 2005, p. 28) reduces the judgment of the group to the judgment of a single member—the dictator. A majority procedure, "whereby a group judges a given proposition to be true whenever a majority of group members judges it to be true," reduces the judgment of the group to a majority of its individual members (List 2005, p. 27). A supermajority procedure, whereby a group judges a given proposition to be true whenever a supermajority of group members judges it to be true, reduces the judgment of the group to a supermajority of its individual members. And a unanimity procedure, "whereby the group makes a judgment on a proposition if and only if the group members unanimously endorse that judgment," (List 2005, p. 30) reduces the judgment of the group to all of its members when there is unanimous agreement. Though there are obvious differences between the reductive bases on such views, they are all both reductionist and summative: the judgments of the group are reducible to the judgments of all or some of the members that comprise it.

---

[2] There are two different views of group testimony suggested in this passage from Quinton. On the one hand, there is the *eliminativist* view, according to which it is literally false that groups testify to things and hence attributions of testimony to group are simply metaphorical. On the other hand, there is the *reductionist* view, according to which it is literally true that groups testify to things, but such claims are made true by individual members of the group testifying to things. The summative account, as I am understanding it in this paper, is reductionist, not eliminativist.

[3] According to Deborah Tollefsen, the summative view of testimony can be understood as follows: "...when a group offers testimony it is really understood as the testimony of all or some of the members—what they would testify to if given the opportunity. Another way to understand this summative approach would be to say that a group's testimony *p* expresses the views of all or some of the members of the group" (2007, p. 300). For reasons that will become apparent later in this paper, I do not think that these two characterizations of the summative account of group testimony are equivalent.

[4] For more on the theory of judgment aggregation, see List and Pettit (2002, 2004), Dietrich (2005), List (2005), and Pauly and van Hees (2006).

In contrast, a *non-reductionist* account of group testimony maintains that the testimony of a group is irreducible to that of all or some of its member.[5] In particular, such a view holds that in some very important sense, the group itself is the source of the knowledge, where the epistemological status of the testimony in question is over and above, or otherwise distinct from, the testimony of any of its individual members. According to a *non-summative* view in particular, a group testifying that p cannot be understood in the sense that all or some members of the group would testify that p were the relevant opportunity to arise. So, a more precise version of the question at issue in this paper can be expressed as follows: is there an epistemologically significant sense in which groups are a source of testimonial knowledge?

In this paper, I shall defend a negative answer to this question. I shall begin by considering the most compelling arguments offered on behalf of a non-reductionist, non-summative account of group testimony. Although I argue that such arguments fail, at least one of the considerations here succeeds in undermining summativism. Those working in collective epistemology have failed to notice, however, that a rejection of a summative account of group testimony does not necessitate embracing a non-reductionist or "inflationary" view of this phenomenon. I then develop a *deflationary account of group testimony* according to which a group's testimony *is* reducible to that of one or more individuals, though not necessarily ones who are members of the group in question. Thus my view is unlike any existing account of group testimony in the literature since it is both reductionist and non-summative in nature.

3.1. A Non-Reductionist View of Group Testimony—Some Considerations

There are several reasons why a non-reductionist or non-summative view of group testimony is deemed epistemologically necessary. The first, and by far the most commonly cited consideration, is what we may call *Lack of Belief*: not a single member of the group in question may believe that p, yet hearers can nonetheless acquire knowledge that p on the basis of the group's testimony that p. Philip Pettit's arguments on behalf of collective judgments and intentions can be adapted along these lines. For instance, he discusses a case involving the employees of a company deciding whether to forgo a pay-raise in order to spend the

---

[5] The use of reductionism and non-reductionism in this context should not be confused with reductionism and non-reductionism as it applies to views of the justification of individual testimonial beliefs. For a discussion of the latter, see Coady (1992), Fricker (1994 and 1995), and Lackey (2008).

saved money on implementing a set of workplace safety measures. The employees are supposed to make their decision on the basis of considering three separable issues: "first, how serious the danger is; second, how effective the safety measures that a pay-sacrifice would buy is likely to be; and third, whether the pay-sacrifice is bearable for members individually. If an employee thinks that the danger is sufficiently serious, the safety measure sufficiently effective, and the pay-sacrifice sufficiently bearable, he or she will vote for the sacrifice; otherwise he or she will vote against" (Pettit 2003, p. 171). Imagine now that the company's three employees vote in the following way:

Serious danger?	Effective measure?	Bearable loss?	Pay sacrifice?
A. Yes	No	Yes	No
B. No	Yes	Yes	No
C. Yes	Yes	No	No

If the group judgment is determined by how the members vote on the premises, then the group conclusion is to accept the pay sacrifice since there are more "Yes"s than "No"s in each of the premise columns. In such a case, "the group will form a judgment on the question of the pay-sacrifice that is directly in conflict with the unanimous vote of its members. It will form a judgment that is in the starkest possible discontinuity with the corresponding judgments of its members" (Pettit 2003, p. 183). Because of cases such as this, combined with the plausible claim that considerations about judgments can be naturally extended to intentions, Pettit concludes that groups are intentional subjects that are distinct from, and exist "over and beyond," their individual members. He writes: "These discontinuities between collective judgments and intentions, on the one hand, and the judgments and intentions of members, on the other, make vivid the sense in which a social integrate is an intentional subject that is distinct from its members" (Pettit 2003, p. 184). If we assume that a group can report or otherwise convey its judgments and intentions, a non-summative account of group testimony seems to follow naturally from Pettit's conclusion.

A similar argument is put forth by Frederick Schmitt, who rejects summative accounts of group belief on the following grounds:

Suppose the Library Committee and the Budget Committee must each judge whether last year's library budget is adequate for this year. The Budget Committee judges so, while the Library Committee judges not. Yet their members are the same (and let us suppose, to make matters simple, judge alike). It follows that one of the two committees believes a proposition p that no member believes. These points are enough to cast doubt on a summative account of group belief.... (Schmitt 1994, p. 261)

Here, Schmitt maintains that because a group may believe that p without a single of its members believing that p, the plausibility of a summative account of group belief is seriously undermined.[6] Once again, since a group can certainly communicate its beliefs through, for instance, published documents, verbal reports via spokespeople, and so on, it seems to follow that a non-summative or otherwise inflationary account of group testimony should be embraced.

Deborah Tollefsen argues directly for a non-summative or non-reductionist account of group testimony by asking us to consider a report issued in 2002 by the UN Population Commission, entitled *Charting the Progress of Populations*, that provides information on twelve socio-economic indicators relevant to populations. According to Tollefsen, "[t]his report is the testimony of the UN Population Commission," where this cannot be reduced to the testimony of all or some of its forty-seven members. She writes:

> No one member is the source of the report as a piece of testimony since no one individual member had all of the views or information expressed in the document. Indeed, we can imagine that the status of birth rates in, say, South America was a subject that no member had a view on until they read the report compiled by their committee. We can also imagine that, despite the committee's report, each member remains skeptical. They do not believe the contents of the report, yet it remains the report of the committee because of the organizational context in which it was written. (Tollefsen 2007, p. 301).

Given that the information contained in the report about the status of birth rates in South America is the testimony of the UN Population Commission and yet there may not be a single member of the commission who believes it, it seems to follow that group testimony understood in a non-summative fashion has to be countenanced. Otherwise put, how could the testimony found in the report be reduced to that of all or some of the members of the UN Population Commission if no single individual member even believes its content?

The second reason for countenancing group testimony, which we may call *Lack of Information*, is also suggested by the above considerations: not a single member of the group may be privy to all of the information conveyed by the testimony that p, yet hearers can nonetheless acquire knowledge that p on the basis of the group's testimony that p. This is not an uncommon phenomenon: a group works together on a project, each member being assigned to one aspect of it, and one person—who may not even be a member of the group—compiles all of the relevant information into a single report that is issued. In such a case, no member of the group has access to the information being conveyed, so there is only the group itself, where this is understood in a non-summative fashion, to plausibly serve as the epistemic source of the knowledge acquired by hearers.

---

[6] For additional inflationary accounts of group belief, see Gilbert (1989 and 1994) and Tuomela (1992).

The third, and closely related, piece of evidence on behalf of group testimony is what we may call *Lack of Reliability*: not a single member of the group may be reliable regarding the testimony that p, yet hearers can nonetheless acquire knowledge that p on the basis of the group's testimony that p. This follows from the previous point: if there isn't a single member of a given group who is privy to the content of the report being testified to, then surely no such member is a reliable epistemic source regarding the information thereby conveyed. As Tollefsen says, "Each individual member may be a reliable source with respect to the information they contributed but no one individual is a reliable source with respect to the whole report because no one individual contributed all of the information" (Tollefsen 2007, p. 305). For this reason, the group itself has to be recognized as the relevant epistemic source.

Finally, there is what we may call the *Group Citation* consideration in support of an inflationary view of group testimony: we routinely cite groups as the source of the knowledge that we possess. I may say, "I found out from the American Kennel Club that the Labrador retriever is the most popular purebred dog in the United States," or "I learned from the Catholic Church that the Pope is taken to be infallible with respect to his official declarations." In such cases, I cite groups as the source of my knowledge, and these descriptions intuitively seem accurate since there is not an individual who obviously shoulders the epistemic burden of the information possessed. Similarly, there are instances of testimony that appear to represent the view of a collective rather than an individual entity. Christian List provides the following examples of this sort of group testimony: "an expert panel or research group that publishes a joint report on some scientific matter, the monetary policy committee of a central bank that makes an economic forecast, or a court that publicly announces its factual judgments relevant to some case" (List 2005, p. 26). In all of these cases, the testimony in question conveys the position of the groups in question, regardless of the views of the individual members themselves. Thus, it seems to follow that a non-reductionist or inflationary view of testimony should be espoused.

We have seen that there are various considerations that purport to establish the need for a non-reductionist or non-summative view of group testimony. In the next two sections, I will take a very close look at Lack of Belief and a variation of it. There are two central reasons for the extended focus on this specific consideration. First, Lack of Belief is the most commonly cited argument in favor of an inflationary account of group testimony, and thus it appears to be what proponents of such an account find most compelling. Second, and more importantly, responses to the other considerations will come with far greater ease and clarity after I argue against Lack of Belief and develop my own deflationary view of group testimony.

Given this, I will return to Lack of Information, Lack of Reliability, and Group Citation at a later stage in this paper.

3.2. Lack of Belief

To begin, recall that Lack of Belief concludes that a non-reductionist view of group testimony must be countenanced because there may not be a single member of the group who holds the relevant belief. More precisely:

Argument 1

(1) A group, G, can provide testimony that p, even in cases where no single member of G believes that p.

(2) Therefore, G itself is the source of the testimony that p.

It should be immediately obvious that in order for (2) to follow from (1), a further premise needs to be added; namely:

(Speaker Belief) A speaker, S, can testify that p only if S believes that p.[7]

For if it is the lack of belief that p on the part of the individual members of G that requires that G itself to be the source of the testimony that p, this must be because belief that p is thought to be necessary for testifying that p. But surely (Speaker Belief) is an implausible premise. When, for instance, a person commits perjury by lying under oath, it is never concluded that she failed to provide testimony; instead, it is said that she offered testimony that is false or unreliable, but testimony nonetheless. This is further supported by the fact that there is not a single view of testimony in the existing literature that endorses (Speaker Belief). For instance, Elizabeth Fricker characterizes testimony as "tellings generally" with "no restrictions either on subject matter, or on the speaker's epistemic relation to it" (Fricker 1995, pp. 396-7). Similarly, Robert Audi claims that we must understand testimony as "...people's telling us things" (Audi 1997, p. 406). Even those views of testimony that are more restrictive than Fricker's and Audi's do not require belief. For instance, Catherine Elgin characterizes testimony as "...utterances and inscriptions that purport to convey information and transmit warrant for the information they convey" (Elgin 2002, p. 292). C.A.J. Coady argues that S testifies by making

---

[7] Strictly speaking, there is yet another premise that needs to be added to Argument 1, which can be formulated as follows:
 (Group Belief) G itself can believe that p, even if no single member of G shares that belief.
 Since (Group Belief) will not figure prominently in this paper, I will leave its role in Argument 1 implicit in the text.

some statement that *p* if and only if: (i) S's stating that *p* is evidence that *p* and is offered as evidence that *p*; (ii) S has the relevant competence, authority, or credentials to state truly that *p*; and (iii) S's statement that *p* is relevant to some disputed or unresolved question (which may or may not be whether *p*) and is directed to those who are in need of evidence on the matter. (Coady 1992, p. 42) And according to my view of testimony, "S testifies that *p* by making an act of communication *a* if and only if (in part) in virtue of *a*'s communicable content, (1) S reasonably intends to convey the information that *p* or [8] (2) *a* is reasonably taken as conveying the information that *p*" (Lackey 2008, p. 30).[9] Though there are obvious and important differences among these competing accounts of testimony, it is telling that not a single one requires belief that *p* in order to testify that *p*. This provides compelling evidence against granting (Speaker Belief), thereby undermining the Lack of Belief consideration on behalf of group testimony.

Despite this, there is a related argument supporting group testimony that is significantly more promising. It can be formulated in the following way:

Argument 2

(3) A hearer, H, can come to know that *p* on the basis of the testimony that *p* provided by a group, G, yet it may be the case that no single member of G believes, and hence no single member of G knows, that *p*.

(4) Therefore, G's testimony that *p* is the source of H's knowledge.

In order for (4) to follow from (3) in Argument 2, an additional premise is needed, which can be expressed as follows:

(Speaker Knowledge) A hearer, H, can come to know that *p* on the basis of a speaker, S's, testimony that *p* only if S knows that *p*.[10]

---

[8] This, of course, is not an exclusive 'or'; both (1) and (2) could be satisfied simultaneously.

[9] There are views of testimony in the literature other than those cited in the text. For instance, Peter Graham maintains that S testifies by making some statement that *p* if and only if: (i) S's stating that *p* is offered as evidence that *p*; (ii) S intends that his audience believe that he has the relevant competence, authority, or credentials to state truly that *p*; and (iii) S's statement that *p* is believed by S to be relevant to some question that he believes is disputed or unresolved (which may or may not be whether *p*) and is directed at those whom he believes to be in need of evidence on the matter. (Graham 1997, p. 227) And James Ross offers a definition of testimony that bears some similarities to Graham's account. According to Ross, testimony is "... any verbalized reporting of a purported state of affairs where the reporter intends that the hearer (reader, viewer, etc.) will take it on his report that the state of affairs is *as* reported" (Ross 1975, p. 3).

[10] Argument 2 also depends on:
(Group Knowledge) G itself can know that *p*, even if no single member of G knows that *p*.
However, for the purposes of this paper, I will simply grant this principle.

According to Argument 2, hearers can acquire testimonial knowledge from groups, even when no single member of the group possesses the knowledge in question (due to lack of belief). Since speaker-knowledge is a necessary condition for the acquisition of testimonial knowledge, someone must shoulder the epistemic burden in such a case. Assuming that groups can possess knowledge, the group itself is a natural candidate for occupying this role. Hence, groups can be the source of testimonial knowledge.

Unlike Argument 1, which depends on the highly implausible (Speaker Belief), Argument 2 relies on (Speaker Knowledge), which is very widely accepted in the literature in the epistemology of testimony. For instance, Robert Audi writes: "*I* cannot (testimonially) give you knowledge that *p* without knowing that *p*.... Testimonially based knowledge is received by transmission and so depends on the attester's knowing that *p*" (Audi 1997, p. 410). In a similar spirit, Tyler Burge says: "If the recipient depends on interlocution for knowledge, the recipient's knowledge depends on the source's having knowledge as well. For if the source does not believe the proposition, or if the proposition is not true, or if the source is not justified, the recipient cannot know the proposition" (Burge 1993, p. 486). And Steven Reynolds claims that "... if you tell me that *p*, I can thereby come to know that *p* only if you already know it" (Reynolds 2002, p. 142). These quotations are characteristic of (Speaker Knowledge) and it is this view of testimonial knowledge that dominates the current epistemological literature.[11]

Support for (Speaker Knowledge) derives from a purported analogy between testimony and memory. While memory is thought to be capable of only *preserving* epistemic properties from one time to another—and cannot therefore *generate* new epistemic properties—testimony is said to be capable of only *transmitting* epistemic properties from one person to another. So, for instance, just as I cannot know that *p* on the basis of memory unless I non-memorially knew that *p* at an earlier time, the thought underlying this picture of testimonial knowledge is that a hearer cannot know that *p* on the basis of testimony unless the speaker from whom it was acquired herself knows that *p*. Thus, if testimonial knowledge is acquired only via transmission, then there always needs to be a *knowledgeable source* to shoulder the epistemic burden in question. If no single member of a group believes, and hence no single member knows, that *p* and yet knowledge that *p* is acquired via testimony, then the group itself has to be the knowledgeable source.

---

[11] Proponents of various versions of this thesis, some of which focus on epistemic justification or warrant, include Welbourne (1979, 1981, 1986, and 1994), Hardwig (1985 and 1991), Ross (1986), Burge (1993 and 1997), Plantinga (1993), Dummett (1994), McDowell (1994), Williamson (2000), Audi (1997, 1998, and 2006), Owens (2000 and 2006), Reynolds (2002), Adler (2006), Faulkner (2006), and Schmitt (2006).

In addition to the wide acceptance and intuitive plausibility of (Speaker Knowledge), motivating a non-reductionist view of group testimony via this principle has several advantages. First, it can explain the intuition underlying Lack of Belief: lack of belief on the part of the members of a group is relevant to group testimony because it entails a lack of knowledge on their part, which in turn rules out the possibility of hearers acquiring knowledge via their testimony. Hence, the epistemic source in question must be testimony provided by the group itself. (Speaker Knowledge) also provides a compelling explanation of the relevance of both Lack of Information and Lack of Reliability to the view of group testimony at issue here. Acquiring testimonial knowledge requires a knowledgeable source. Being such a knowledgeable source relative to p requires that one have the information that p and that one be reliable with respect to its conveyance. Since no one individual of a given group needs to satisfy these desiderata in order for testimonial knowledge to be acquired via its testimony, the group itself must be the source of the testimonial knowledge.

Despite this, I will argue in what follows that (Speaker Knowledge) is false, and hence that this principle cannot provide support for the view that group testimony is an irreducible epistemic source.

3.3. Arguments against (Speaker Knowledge)

To begin, there are two general types of counterexamples against the thesis that speaker-knowledge is a necessary condition for testimonial knowledge. The first type involves speakers who fail to believe, and hence fail to know, a proposition to which they are testifying, but nevertheless reliably convey the information in question through their testimony. So, for instance, consider the following:

CREATIONIST TEACHER: Stella is a devoutly Christian fourth-grade teacher, and her religious beliefs are grounded in a deep faith that she has had since she was a very young child. Part of this faith includes a belief in the truth of creationism and, accordingly, a belief in the falsity of evolutionary theory. Despite this, she fully recognizes that there is an overwhelming amount of scientific evidence against both of these beliefs. Indeed, she readily admits that she is not basing her own commitment to creationism on evidence at all but, rather, on the personal faith that she has in an all-powerful Creator. Because of this, Stella does not think that religion is something that she should impose on those around her, and this is especially true with respect to her fourth-grade students. Instead, she regards her duty as a teacher to include presenting material that is best supported by the available evidence, which clearly includes the truth of evolutionary theory. As a result, after consulting reliable sources in the library and developing reliable lecture notes, Stella asserts to her students, "Modern day *Homo sapiens* evolved from *Homo erectus*," while presenting her biology lesson today. Though Stella herself neither believes nor knows this proposition, she never shares her own personal faith-based views with her students, and so they form the corresponding true belief solely on the basis of her reliable testimony.

Now, given Stella's commitment to creationism, she does not know that modern day *Homo sapiens* evolved from *Homo erectus* because she does not believe this proposition. i.e., she fails the belief condition of knowledge. But because she reliably conveys this information to her fourth-grade students, and does not provide them with any evidence to the contrary, they acquire the knowledge in question on the basis of her testimony. Moreover, we can flesh out CREATIONIST TEACHER in various ways so that the students clearly satisfy the justification or warrant condition of knowledge, no matter what view of these concepts is at issue. For instance, we can suppose that the children have grown up in environments in which they have not acquired any reasons to favor evolutionary theory over creationism or vice versa. We can also assume that the students have excellent positive reasons for accepting the testimony of Stella, e.g., her reports typically covary with their perceptual experiences, the reports of their parents and classmates, and so on. Thus, according to both broadly externalist and internalist accounts of justification or warrant, the children clearly acquire the knowledge in question on the basis of Stella's testimony.

What CREATIONIST TEACHER reveals is that an *unreliable believer* may nonetheless be a *reliable testifier*, and so may reliably convey knowledge to a hearer despite the fact that she fails to possess it herself.[12] For although Stella ignores the relevant evidence with respect to her doxastic states concerning evolutionary theory—thereby leading her to lack the belief that modern day *Homo sapiens* evolved from *Homo erectus*—she bases her testimony regarding this topic firmly on such evidence. This enables Stella to impart knowledge to her students that she fails to possess herself, thereby showing that (Speaker Knowledge) is false.[13]

The second type of counterexample against (Speaker Knowledge) involves speakers who have an undefeated defeater for believing a proposition to which they are testifying, but nevertheless reliably convey such a proposition through their testimony without transmitting the defeater in question to their hearers. There are two central kinds of defeaters that are typically taken to be incompatible with testimonial knowledge. First, there are what we might call *psychological*

---

[12] It should be noted that CREATIONIST TEACHER undermines views that are even weaker than (Speaker Knowledge). For instance, John Hardwig argues in his (1991) that a speaker must *believe* that *p* in order for her testimony to give a hearer a good reason to believe that *p*. But obviously Stella's testimony can give her students a good reason to believe that *Homo sapiens* evolved from *Homo erectus*, despite the fact that she does not believe this proposition herself. Hence, even Hardwig's much weaker thesis is falsified by CREATIONIST TEACHER.

[13] This type of argument can be found in my (2006 and 2008).

defeaters. A psychological defeater is a doubt or belief that is had by S, and indicates that S's belief that *p* is either false or unreliably formed or sustained. Defeaters in this sense function by virtue of being *had* by S, regardless of their truth-value or epistemic status.[14] Second, there are what we might call *normative defeaters*. A normative defeater is a doubt or belief that S ought to have, and indicates that S's belief that *p* is either false or unreliably formed or sustained. Defeaters in this sense function by virtue of being doubts or beliefs that S *should have* (whether or not S does have them) given the presence of certain available evidence.[15] The underlying thought here is that certain kinds of doubts and beliefs contribute epistemically unacceptable *irrationality* to doxastic systems and, accordingly, justification can be defeated or undermined by their presence.

Moreover, a defeater may itself be either defeated or undefeated. Suppose, for instance, that Harold believes that there is a bobcat in his backyard because he saw it there this morning, but Rosemary tells him, and he thereby comes to believe, that the animal is instead a lynx. Now, the justification that Harold had for believing that there is a bobcat in his backyard has been defeated by the belief that he acquires on the basis of Rosemary's testimony. But since psychological defeaters can themselves be beliefs, they, too, are candidates for defeat. For instance, suppose that Harold consults a North American wildlife book and discovers that the white tip of the animal's tail confirms that it was indeed a bobcat, thereby providing him with a *defeater-defeater* for his original belief that there is a bobcat in his backyard. And, as should be suspected, defeater-defeaters can also be defeated by further doubts and beliefs, which, in turn, can be defeated by further doubts and beliefs, and so on. Similar considerations involving reasons, rather than doubts and beliefs, apply in the case of normative defeaters. When one has a defeater for one's belief that *p* that is not itself defeated, one has what is called an *undefeated defeater* for one's belief that *p*. It is the presence of undefeated defeaters, not merely of defeaters, that is incompatible with testimonial justification.

With these thoughts in mind, consider the following:[16]

---

[14] For various views of what I call psychological defeaters see, for example, BonJour (1980 and 1985), Nozick (1981), Pollock (1986), Goldman (1986), Plantinga (1993), Lackey (1999, 2006, and 2008), Bergmann (1997 and 2004), and Reed (2006).

[15] For discussions involving what I call normative defeaters, approached in a number of different ways, see BonJour (1980 and 1985), Goldman (1986), Fricker (1987 and 1994), Chisholm (1989), Burge (1993 and 1997), McDowell (1994), Audi (1997 and 1998), Williams (1999), Lackey (1999, 2006c, and 2008), BonJour and Sosa (2003), Hawthorne (2004), and Reed (2006). What all of these discussions have in common is simply the idea that evidence can defeat knowledge even when the subject does not form any corresponding doubts or beliefs from the evidence in question.

[16] This case is adapted from Goldman (1986, pp. 53–4), though I am using it for a very different purpose.

PERSISTENT BELIEVER: Millicent in fact possesses her normal visual powers, but she has cogent reasons to believe that these powers are temporarily deranged. She is the subject of a neurosurgeon's experiments, and the surgeon falsely tells her that there are implantations causing malfunction in her visual cortex. While she is persuaded that her present visual appearances are an entirely unreliable guide to reality, she continues to place credence in her visual appearances. She ignores her well-supported belief in the incapacitation of her visual faculty; she persists in believing, on the basis of her visual experiences, that a chair is before her, that the neurosurgeon is smiling, and so on. These beliefs are all, in fact, true and they are formed by the usual, quite reliable, perceptual processes. As Millicent is walking out of the neurosurgeon's office, she is the only person to see a badger in Big Bear Field. On the basis of this visual experience, she forms the corresponding true belief that there was a badger in this field, and then later reports this fact to her friend Bradley without communicating the neurosurgeon's testimony to him. Bradley, who has ample reason to trust Millicent from their past interaction as friends, forms the corresponding true belief solely on the basis of her testimony.

The first point to notice about PERSISTENT BELIEVER is that *Millicent does not know that there was a badger in Big Bear Field* because *she is not justified or warranted in holding this belief*. In particular, the fact that she believes the neurosurgeon that her visual powers are an entirely unreliable guide to reality, without holding any other relevant beliefs, provides her with an undefeated defeater for her visual beliefs. As Goldman says, "...are [Millicent's visual beliefs] specimens of knowledge? Intuitively, no. The reason is that Millicent is not justified in holding these beliefs; they contravene her best evidence" (Goldman 1986, p. 54).

The second point to notice about this case is that *Bradley does know that there was a badger in Big Bear Field on the basis of Millicent's testimony*. For not only does Bradley have excellent positive reasons for accepting Millicent's testimony, he also possesses no relevant undefeated defeaters. Specifically, since he does not know anything about the neurosurgeon's testimony, he does not believe, nor does he have reason to believe, that Millicent's visual powers are an unreliable guide to reality. Given this, Bradley comes to know that there was a badger in Big Bear Field on the basis of Millicent's testimony, even though her believing the neurosurgeon's report undermines her knowing this. In this way, Millicent fails the justification or warrant condition of knowledge because she *has* an undefeated defeater for believing that there was a badger in Big Bear Field, Bradley satisfies the justification or warrant condition of knowledge because he does *not* have such a defeater, and thus it is possible for a hearer to acquire knowledge on the basis of a speaker's testimony even when the speaker does not possess the knowledge in question herself.

What PERSISTENT BELIEVER reveals is that defeaters do not simply "come along for the ride" when a speaker offers testimony to a hearer. For though the neurosurgeon's testimony defeats the epistemic status of Millicent's perceptual belief about the badger in the field, Bradley has no reason for doubting either Millicent's perceptual or testimonial practices. Because of this, even though it is irrational for Millicent to trust her visual experiences in the face of the neurosurgeon's testimony, such irrationality is not transferred to Bradley via her testimony. This enables her to impart knowledge to him that she fails to possess herself, thereby once again showing that (Speaker Knowledge) is false.[17]

We have seen, then, that (Speaker Knowledge) is false and thus that this principle cannot provide support for the view that group testimony is an irreducible source of knowledge. Given that Argument 2 was the most promising line of defense on behalf of a non-reductionist view of group testimony, serious doubt has been cast on the conclusion that there is an epistemologically important sense in which groups are a basis of testimonial knowledge.

3.4. Speaker Reliability, the Statement View, and a Deflationary Account of Group Testimony

One of the central conclusions that the arguments from the previous sections support is the replacement of (Speaker Knowledge) with a thesis that focuses on the *statements* of speakers rather than on their states of believing or knowing. For instance, CREATIONIST TEACHER and PERSISTENT BELIEVER both reveal that when unreliable believers are nonetheless reliable testifiers, speakers can impart knowledge to hearers that they fail to possess themselves. This motivates replacing (Speaker Knowledge) with the following (Speaker Reliability) principle:

(Speaker Reliability) A hearer, H, can come to know that p on the basis of a speaker, S's, testimony that p only if S's statement that p is reliable or otherwise truth-conducive.

The requisite reliability of the statement in question can, in turn, be fleshed out in any number of ways. For instance, it may be necessary that the speaker's statement be sensitive, safe, properly or virtuously formed, and so on.[18] The central point of (Speaker Reliability), in contrast to (Speaker Knowledge), is that the speaker's states of believing and knowing are epistemically relevant only insofar as they bear on her capacity to be a competent testifier.[19]

---

[17] This sort of argument can be found in my (1999).
[18] See Nozick (1981), Sosa (1996, 1999, 2000, and 2002), Williamson (2000), and Pritchard (2005), Plantinga (1993), and Sosa (1991), respectively.
[19] Of course, often times, it is precisely *because* a speaker is insincere or an incompetent believer that she is an incompetent or unreliable testifier. For instance, if I frequently lie or form inaccurate beliefs, more often than not this will prevent you from acquiring knowledge on the basis of my testimony. But the reason why you are so prevented is that my insincerity or incompetence has made my testimony unreliable. Moreover, a *hearer's beliefs* about a speaker's sincerity and competence can have

Now, as with (Speaker Knowledge), (Speaker Reliability) expresses only a necessary condition for testimonial knowledge. A complete epistemology of testimony will, then, require further conditions. At a minimum, we can propose what I have elsewhere called the *Statement View of Testimony* (SVT):

SVT: For every speaker, S, and hearer, H, H knows that *p* on the basis of S's testimony only if (1) S's statement is reliable or otherwise truth-conducive, (2) H understands that *p* and comes to truly believe that *p* on the basis of the content of S's statement, and (3) H has no undefeated defeaters for believing that *p*.[20]

Condition (1) is simply the Speaker Reliability principle. (2) is required so as to ensure that the knowledge in question is testimonial. If, for instance, I come to know that you have a soprano voice by hearing you say, in a soprano voice, that you do, then my resulting knowledge is testimonial only if it is based on the content of your report rather than on features about your testimony, such as the way in which it was expressed.[21] And (3) is included to prevent testimonial knowledge from being compatible with the subject's possessing explicit counterevidence to the contrary, which is a condition nearly universally accepted in the epistemological literature.[22] Further conditions may be needed for a complete view of testimonial knowledge. But regardless of what is added to the SVT, such a view handles with ease how knowledge is acquired in cases such as CREATIONIST TEACHER and PERSISTENT BELIEVER. Moreover, the SVT can capture the intuitions underlying (Speaker Knowledge)—a speaker's statement that *p* can be reliably connected with the truth via a speaker sincerely reporting her knowledge that *p*. But as should be clear, this is only *one* of the ways in which such reliability can be secured.

We are now in a position to see how the SVT motivates and supports a broadly reductionist account of group testimony's epistemological significance. Let us begin by considering one of the paradigmatic instances of group testimony discussed earlier: the UN Population Commission, which is comprised of forty-seven individual members, issues a report entitled *Charting the Progress of Populations*. Now suppose that a person—call her Sam—who is not a member of the UN Population Commission, interprets and compiles all of the data contributed by the members of this group into the published report and serves as the group's spokesperson. Suppose further that one of the statements in this report is, "the

---

epistemic significance. For instance, if I believe that you are a compulsive liar or an unreliable epistemic source, then even if you are neither of these, the mere fact that I believe that you are can provide me with a defeater for accepting your testimony. Hence, my beliefs about your sincerity and competence can prevent me from acquiring knowledge on the basis of your testimony.

[20] For a defense of the SVT, see my (2008).
[21] This sort of case can be found in Audi (1997).
[22] See the references in notes 14 and 15.

birth rate of Latinos in the US is on the rise," of which not a single member of the UN Population Commission is aware. We have seen that the standard picture in the epistemology of testimony, according to which (Speaker Knowledge) is true and hence knowledge is acquired through testimony only via transmission, leads naturally to a non-reductionist account of group testimony. Since H can know that p on the basis of S's testimony that p only if S knows that p, the group itself must be the source of testimonial knowledge that p in cases where there is no single member of the group who believes that p. On my Statement View of Testimony, however, neither knowledge that p nor even belief that p is necessary for a hearer to acquire knowledge that p on the basis of a speaker's testimony. So the mere absence of belief and knowledge on the part of the members of a given group who testifies that p does not, by itself, necessitate positing someone who does believe or know that p. This is the negative conclusion of applying the SVT to the issue of group testimony. According to the positive aspect of my Statement View of Testimony, the acquisition of testimonial knowledge is largely determined by the reliability of the proffered statement. I propose that group testimony be treated epistemologically just like any instance of individual testimony and, in particular, that the epistemology of group testimony be subsumed under the SVT.

To flesh this out in more detail, let us consider the statement issued by the UN Population Commission that the birth rate of Latinos in the US is on the rise. The statement itself is conveyed by Sam, the spokesperson for the group. So, on my view, whether this statement is reliable will depend upon facts about Sam as a testifier of this information. For instance, one way of understanding this reliability constraint is via Nozick's notion of *sensitivity*, i.e., Sam would not state that p if p were false.[23] Alternatively, reliability can be fleshed out in terms of the *safety* requirement endorsed by Pritchard, Sosa, and Williamson, i.e., Sam would not state that p without it being so that p.[24] Or it may be the case that general facts about Sam's history as a testimony-producing source or as a virtuous testifier determine whether her statement about the birth rate of Latinos in the US is reliable.[25] But regardless of how the details of reliability are worked out, the central point I wish to emphasize here is that *Sam* is the one issuing the statement in question, and hence whether hearers acquire knowledge on the basis of her testimony will depend on whether *she* is a reliable testifier of this information.[26] Thus, on my view of group testimony, the epistemic status of the testimony of the UN Population

---

[23] See Nozick (1981).
[24] See Pritchard (2005), Sosa (1996, 1999, 2000, and 2002), and Williamson (2000).
[25] See, for instance, Goldman (1976 and 1979) and Sosa (1991).
[26] There are interesting questions about the metaphysics of being a spokesperson for a group, but they lie outside the scope of this paper.

Commission on the birth rate of Latinos in the US reduces to the epistemic status of Sam's statement about this fact. In this sense, then, my view of group testimony is *reductionist*. It is, however, perhaps even better described as *deflationary* since there is no special epistemology of group testimony at all—it is simply subsumed by my general Statement View of Testimony.

One feature of my deflationary account of group testimony that should be emphasized is its *non-summative* nature. Recall that on a summative view, one's general epistemology of testimony can simply be applied to all or some of the individual members whose testimony constitutes that of the group. As far as I know, summative views are the only reductionist accounts of group testimony in the literature. On my view, however, the epistemic status of the testimony of a group can reduce to the epistemic status of an individual *who is not even a member of the group in question*. This is the case with Sam who, *ex hypothesi*, is not a member of the UN Population Commission but nonetheless issues a statement on its behalf about the birth rate of Latinos in the US. In such a case, my view holds that we treat Sam's report, which conveys the testimony of the group, just like any other instance of testimony; hence, whether a hearer can come to know this fact on the basis of her report depends largely on the reliability of her statement. Given this, my deflationary view is broadly reductionist, though non-summative: the epistemic status of a group's testimony is reducible to that of one or more individuals, though not necessarily ones who are members of the group in question. Specifically, the conditions expressed in the SVT apply to the testifier of the group's statement, regardless of whether this spokesperson is a member of the group. My deflationary account is the only view of group testimony in the literature that is both reductionist and non-summative.[27]

We can now return to the considerations on behalf of a non-reductionist or non-summative account of group testimony with which this paper began. We have already seen how my deflationary view handles Lack of Belief—since the SVT makes clear that a speaker need not believe that p in order for a hearer to acquire knowledge that p on the basis of her testimony, there is no reason to think that lack of belief on the part of members of a group precludes hearers from knowing

---

[27] It may be asked how my view accounts for a case where all of the members of a group assert that p in unison. By way of answering this question, the first point to notice is that much will depend on how the details of the case are described. If the individuals in question are all entirely and appropriately independent of one another, then this may turn out to be a group of individuals offering many different statements, each of which will be assessed for its own reliability. Once dependence among the beliefs of the group's members is introduced, various complications arise that lie beyond the scope of this paper to address. For a detailed discussion of some of these issues, see my (2013). It should be noted, however, that no matter how my view accounts for the various "unison" cases, none supports a non-reductionist view of group testimony.

that *p* on the basis of their testimony. Thus, lack of belief on the part of group members does not motivate a non-reductionist account of group testimony. With respect to the Lack of Information consideration, my account shows that the testifier of a group's report need not have access to all of the information relevant to the testimony in question in order to reliably state that *p*. This is true not only in cases of group testimony, but with respect to individual testimony as well. Stella in CREATIONIST TEACHER need not be privy to all of the information relevant to evolutionary theory in order to reliably impart the knowledge that *Homo sapiens* evolved from *Homo erectus*. Similarly, a spokesperson on behalf of a group may be such that she would not state that *p* if *p* were false and would not state that *p* without it being so that *p* without being privy to all of the information relevant to the question whether *p*. Thus, a non-reductionist view of group testimony does not follow from the Lack of Information consideration offered on its behalf. Finally, let us consider the Lack of Reliability reason, which is best expressed by the following quotation from Tollefsen: "Each individual member [of a group] may be a reliable source with respect to the information they contributed but no one individual is a reliable source with respect to the whole report because no one individual contributed all of the information" (Tollefsen 2007, p. 305). My deflationary view of testimony explains this sort of phenomenon in different ways, depending on how the details are fleshed out. If the testimony being envisaged is one in which each member of the group indeed literally wrote down a part of a single document, I would regard this as less a case of group testimony and more a case of a single report that contains multiple instances of individual testimony. Each statement in the report may have differing degrees of reliability, which determines whether hearers can acquire knowledge via each instance of testimony. If the testimony involves only some members of a group working up a document together that is then publicly conveyed, their individual reliability with respect to conveying the relevant information will establish whether testimonial knowledge is possessed by the recipients in question. And if the group testimony is issued by a spokesperson, her reliability as a testifier matters for the acquisition of testimonial knowledge. Any way it is characterized, however, the Lack of Reliability consideration does not necessitate a non-reductionist view of group testimony.

A question that may be asked at this point is how precisely my view of group testimony accommodates the case offered by Pettit at the start of the paper in which the employees of a company are deciding whether to forgo a pay-raise in order to spend the saved money on implementing a set of workplace safety measures. It may be recalled that Pettit claims that if the group judgment is determined by how the members vote on the premises, then the group will form a judgment on the question of the pay-sacrifice that is directly in conflict with the unanimous vote of its members. Because of this, he concludes that groups are intentional subjects that are distinct from, and exist "over and beyond," their individual members. Now, as the case is presented, it is not clear what my view would say about it since the situation itself is under described. For instance, it is not specified how the information is publicly conveyed on behalf of the group, who transmits the collective judgment, whether the spokesperson is reliable or not, and so on. Once these details are filled in, the application of my view to such a case will be fairly straightforward.

Even more importantly, however, the considerations underlying Pettit's argument may be turned on their head to provide a general argument against inflationary accounts of group judgments. To see this, recall that there are many different aggregation procedures that may be used to generate a group judgment in any given case. Now, notice that Pettit produces the conflict between the collective and the individual judgments in his example by assuming a premise-based aggregation procedure. But another viable procedure for aggregating the judgments in such a case is a conclusion-based one and this method altogether eliminates the conflict between the group and its individual members. Moreover, as was noted earlier, there are other aggregation procedures—such as dictatorial, majority voting, supermajority voting, and unanimity ones—some of which generate the same collective judgment as the premise-based procedure, some the same as the conclusion-based one, and some an incomplete collective judgment. What is of interest for our purposes here, however, is that there is not a fact of the matter about which aggregation procedure should be used—each has its virtues and its vices. Fabrizio Cariani begins his overview of the literature on judgment aggregation with this point:

Judgment Aggregation studies how collective judgments arise from the aggregation of individual opinions. Its motivating observation is that prima facie plausible rules for aggregating judgments do not (and cannot) have all the features we take to be desirable. Judgment Aggregation, then, aims to classify the various aggregation rules by means of the properties they do satisfy and to select those that are, in some sense, best. (Cariani 2011, p. 22)[28]

Given that competing aggregation procedures can result in radically different group judgments despite holding fixed the individuals and their respective

---

[28] Similarly, List and Pettit (2002) defend the following Impossibility Theorem:
There exists no aggregation procedure generating complete and consistent collective judgments that satisfies the following three conditions simultaneously:
Universal domain. The procedure accepts as admissible input any logically possible combinations of complete and consistent individual judgments on the propositions.
Anonymity. The judgments of all individuals have equal weight in determining collective judgments.
Systematicity. The collective judgment on each proposition depends only on the individual judgments on the proposition, and the same pattern of dependence holds for all propositions.

judgments, combined with the point that there is not always a fact of the matter about which procedure to use, there also does not seem to be a fact of the matter about what a given group's judgment is in such cases. This conclusion provides a further reason to reject an inflationary account of group judgment and testimony.

The final consideration on behalf of a non-reductionist account of group testimony that needs to be addressed is Group Citation. As mentioned earlier, it seems clear that we often cite groups as the source of our knowledge—for instance, I say that I learned from the American Academy of Pediatrics that the MMR vaccination is not linked to autism. On my deflationary account of group testimony, however, the source of this knowledge may in fact be a spokesperson for the group who is not even a member of the American Academy of Pediatrics. Thus, my view has the peculiar consequence that the way in which we ordinarily cite the sources of our knowledge can deviate significantly from what our sources of knowledge actually are.

There are two responses that I should like to offer here to this consideration. First, there is also frequently an asymmetry between the way in which we cite the sources of our knowledge and what our sources of knowledge actually are in the case of individual testimony. For instance, it is not at all uncommon for us to report having learned from the President that there will be a tax cut, when in fact the source of our information is *The New York Times* reporting the President's new policies. Or for us to cite having learned from Sylvia Plath's diary that she was depressed, when in fact our epistemic source is a biographer of Plath writing about the contents of her diary. So, to the extent that there is this deviation between our cited epistemic sources and our actual sources of knowledge, it is not unique to my deflationary view of group testimony.

Second, while on my view it is true that, strictly speaking, the testifier of the group's statement is the source of the resulting testimonial knowledge, it does not follow from this that there isn't a broader sense in which the group itself is also the source. In the case of Sam—the spokesperson for the UN Population Commission—while her testimony that the birth rate of Latinos in the US is on the rise is the source of my corresponding knowledge, many features about the members of the commission will be relevant to whether she is a reliable source of information on this topic. For instance, how competent the members are in acquiring the relevant data, how accurate they are in compiling it, how trustworthy they are in communicating their findings, and so on, will all partly determine Sam's reliability as a testifier. In this sense, then, the recipients of Sam's testimony do learn from the UN Population Commission, despite the fact that Sam is the testimonial source of their knowledge. Hence, the deviation between our cited epistemic sources and our actual sources of knowledge on my view may not be quite as stark as it seemed.

3.5. Objections and Replies

There are several objections that may be immediately raised against my deflationary account of group testimony. The first is that my view is implausibly individualistic. How could it possibly be the case that features of the members of the group itself do not figure into the epistemology of their group testimony? Surely, for instance, in the case of the UN Population Commission, it matters whether its members were epistemically responsible in their collection of the relevant data or reliable in their documentation of it. Yet such features are noticeably absent from my deflationary account of group testimony.

To respond to this objection, consider again my SVT as it is applied to individual reports. On this account, what is necessary for the acquisition of testimonial knowledge is that the speaker's statement be reliable or otherwise truth-conducive. This can be secured in a number of different ways. One way that this can happen is via knowledge of the speaker: S may know that p, sincerely report that p to H, and H may acquire testimonial knowledge on this basis. But as CREATIONIST TEACHER and PERSISTENT BELIEVER made clear, this is merely *one* of the ways in which a speaker's statement can be rendered reliable. Another way is when S fails to believe and hence fails to know that p, but nonetheless reliably states that p. This can happen, as it does with Stella in CREATIONIST TEACHER, when a speaker grounds her doxastic states in faith-oriented reasons, but bases her reports on cogent scientific evidence. A further way that the reliability of the proffered statement can be secured is when S fails to justifiedly believe that p because S possesses an undefeated defeater for this belief, but nonetheless reliably conveys the information that p via her testimony without thereby transmitting her defeater. This is the scenario found in PERSISTENT BELIEVER. The point that I wish to emphasize here, however, is that while the reliability of the speaker's statement is the central focus of my SVT, numerous factors will contribute to whether and how this condition obtains. That (Speaker Reliability) can be secured via various different routes is not unique to this condition—(Speaker Knowledge) can obtain through a speaker seeing that p, remembering that p, introspecting that p, receiving testimony that p, reasoning to the conclusion that p, and so on. With respect to both conditions, the primary level of explanation is either the reliability or the knowledge of the speaker. But in understanding whether and how these conditions obtain, countless other features will be relevant.

The same is true of my deflationary account of group testimony. While the primary level of explanation concerns the reliability of the statement proffered on behalf of the group, this can obtain in a number of ways. All of the members of the group may believe that p and one such member may reliably convey this information on behalf of the group. Or some members of the group may know that p and choose an outside spokesperson, who also knows that p, to publicly convey their reliable report. Or not a single member of the group may believe that p and may choose an outside spokesperson to reliably offer their statement. Thus, in understanding whether and how the (Speaker Reliability) condition has been satisfied in cases of group testimony, many features of the members of the group will be relevant, such as how honest they are, how reliable they are in acquiring the information in question, how responsibly they convey it to their spokesperson, and so on. So the epistemic status of the members of the group are not absent from my account; they are simply subsumed by the central requirement of the SVT—that the statement in question be reliable or otherwise truth-conducive.

Moreover, multiple layers of testimony may, and frequently do, contribute to whether a given statement is reliable. Consider the case of individual testimony first—when Stella reports that *Homo sapiens* evolved from *Homo erectus*, the reliability of her testimony may depend in part on a textbook from which she learned this fact which, in turn, may rely upon the testimony of the biologist from whom the author acquired this knowledge which, in turn, may be grounded in the writings of numerous scientists who made original contributions to the theory of evolution which, in turn, may ultimately be traced back to the work of Darwin himself. Thus even individual testimony is often deeply social. Obviously the same is true in the case of group testimony: one instance of group testimony may be indebted to the epistemic contributions of countless testifiers. For instance, the reliability of a speaker reporting on behalf of the American Academy of Pediatrics that there is not a causal link between the MMR and autism will depend on the testimony of the immunologists who researched this issue which, in turn, may rely upon the reports of the technicians and assistants who assisted with the interpretation of the data which, in turn, may depend on the testimony of the parents whose children were diagnosed with autism, and so on. Given the deeply social nature of nearly all testimony, worries about my deflationary account of group testimony being problematically individualistic seem misguided.

The second strategy for resisting my deflationary account of group testimony is to deny that the statements issued by a spokesperson like Sam are properly regarded as testimony. In particular, it may be argued that a spokesperson functions as a parrot of the thoughts of the group and, since parrots do not offer testimony, neither does the spokesperson. If the spokesperson is not testifying, and yet the resulting knowledge is testimonial in nature, then we need to look elsewhere for the epistemic source. And, of course, the group that the spokesperson is representing is the most natural candidate for occupying this role.

By way of response to this objection, the first point to notice is that Sam's statement that the birth rate of Latinos in the US is on the rise satisfies every existing theory of the nature of testimony offered in the literature. Obviously, her report is plausibly regarded as a "telling," and so it fulfills the broad characterizations of testimony offered by Fricker and Audi. Sam's statement is also an utterance that purports to convey information and transmit warrant for the information that it conveys, thereby qualifying as testimony on Elgin's view. Moreover, she is a competent speaker who offers a statement that is evidence in an objective sense, and we can certainly imagine that it is relevant to some disputed or unresolved question and is directed to those who are in need of evidence on the matter. Thus, there is no obstacle to Sam's report qualifying as testimony on Coady's view as well. And finally, Sam reasonably intends to convey information in virtue of the communicable content of her assertion, and hence her statement is testimony on my view, too. According to every view of testimony mentioned earlier in this paper, then, Sam satisfies the requisite conditions for testifying, and there are no other theories in the literature where the results would be different.

Moreover, Sam is unlike a parrot in various crucial respects. When Sam states that the birth rate of Latinos in the US is on the rise, she is offering an act of communication, which requires that she have the *intention to express communicable content*. To clarify this notion, consider a case in which, unbeknownst to me, Chloe has headphones on and is bopping her head to the beat of the music. I walk into the room, ask her if there is any cake left, and, seeing her bop her head, think that she has intended to communicate to me that there is cake left in the kitchen. This sort of case may be an example of *ostensible testimony*, but it should not qualify as genuine testimony in any sense of the word. The reason for this is that Chloe's head-bopping is not an act of communication *since she did not intend to express communicable content*. This is true of a parrot's offering a string of sounds as well. When a parrot merely repeats what it hears, it does not have the intention to express communicable content. In this way, the parrot *mimics* an act of communication, but does not *make* one. So, there is no reason to compare Sam's statement about the birth rate of Latinos in the US to the sounds produced by a parrot. Hence, I see no compelling reason to deny that a spokesperson is offering testimony.

The third objection that may be raised against my deflationary account of group testimony can be motivated by considering the following: suppose that while Sam is serving as a spokesperson for the UN Population Commission, she is extremely reliable when offering the statement that the birth rate of Latinos in the US is on the rise. In particular, when she testifies to this proposition on behalf of the group, she grounds her statement in the competently acquired data and results of the Commission. Suppose further, however, that while Sam is testifying on her own about this matter, she is highly unreliable. Specifically, when she speaks for herself about the birth rate of Latinos in the US, she bases her assertion in limited, anecdotal evidence that she has acquired from living in a neighborhood with a disproportionately large Latino population. Given that Sam's reliability with respect to the statement in question differs significantly when testifying on behalf of the group and when speaking for herself, there is reason to think that there are two different statements here. And this, it may be argued, supports an inflationary account of group testimony since the natural explanation of this multiplicity of statements is that one of them is the group's and one of them is Sam's.

Notice, however, that the phenomenon highlighted in the above objection is not at all unique to cases involving the testimony of groups; it is found equally in instances of individual testimony. Stella in CREATIONIST TEACHER, for instance, is extremely reliable when she reports that *Homo sapiens* evolved from *Homo erectus* to her students in the classroom but not when she testifies about this matter in the coffee shop with her fellow creationist friends. We do not conclude from this common phenomenon that there are two different statements, the teacher's and Stella's, where the former is understood as over and above the latter in any substantive sense. Even more importantly, this same phenomenon is found in cases not involving testimony at all. For example, a young child may have a highly reliable mathematical intuition about an addition fact when she is guided by her teacher but not when she is doing her homework alone. Again, we do not take this to show that the child's intuition in the former scenario should be given an inflationary account that renders it importantly distinct from that in the latter. Or a subject may have an extremely reliable perceptual experience of a sparrow in a tree when wearing her prescription eyeglasses but not without them. Once again, we do not conclude that there are two perceptions, one that is over and above the other in some metaphysically robust sense. Given that this phenomenon is widespread across all of the epistemic sources, and yet there is no reason to suppose that these considerations support inflationary accounts in these domains, there is no reason to draw such a conclusion in the case of group testimony.

A fourth objection to my deflationary account of group testimony arises from considering cases in which conclusions are automatically generated via various ways of aggregating the views of a group of individuals. For example, James Surowiecki discusses a case in *The Wisdom of Crowds* in which the mean of the estimates of the weight of a fat ox offered by a diverse group of 787 people visiting the West of England Fat Stock and Poultry Exhibition in 1906 was far more accurate than that proposed by individual experts, such as butchers and farmers (the mean was 1,197 pounds and the ox weighed 1,198 pounds). Similarly, the Iowa Electronic Markets offer predictions of political elections by allowing traders to buy and sell contracts through the use of a free market model, and the results turn out to again be far more accurate than those of traditional polling.[29] Now, if such automatically generated estimations and predictions can be understood as representing the testimony of the groups in question, then an argument can be made on behalf of an inflationary account of group intention. For testifying to a proposition seems to require at least the intention to express communicable content—as noted earlier, this is what distinguishes bopping one's head to the beat of the music from responding affirmatively to a question with a nod. But there is no individual in these cases of automatically generated conclusions to shoulder this intentional burden. Thus it must be the group, where this is understood as over and above any of the relevant individuals, that possesses the intention to express the communicable content in question. Otherwise put, given that intentional activity is necessary to testify and assuming that automatically generated conclusions are instances of group testimony, then at least an inflationary account of group intention seems to follow. But once we countenance a non-reductionist or non-summative account of group intention, it is no longer clear why we should resist a similar view with respect to group testimony.

By way of response to this objection, notice first that there is no reason at all to regard the published aggregation of the views of just any collection of individuals as constituting group testimony in an interesting sense. If I conduct a survey of the political views of randomly chosen people walking on Michigan Avenue in Chicago on Wednesday at 11:18 a.m., aggregate their judgments, and then convey the results, the conclusion does not amount to group testimony in any substantive sense. This can be supported by considering a couple of different criteria that have been proposed for the metaphysical requirements necessary for a collection of individuals to appropriately qualify as a group in the relevant sense. For instance, Christian List suggests that in order to be a group in this sense, a collection of individuals must be an agent which, in turn, requires the satisfaction of certain constraints of rationality. He writes:

...to be an agent, a group must exhibit patterns of behaviour vis-à-vis the outside world that robustly satisfy certain rationality conditions. Many groups fail to exhibit such rational integration in their behaviour. For example, a group of people who happen to be at London's Leicester Square at the same time lacks the required level of integration. On the other hand,

---

[29] These sorts of cases are also discussed in Tollefsen (2007).

a well organized committee or organization with clearly established decision making procedures might well qualify as sufficiently integrated. (List 2005, p. 26)[30]

And according to Deborah Tollefsen:

What is required for an assertion to count as the group's testimony is some form of sanction that allows an assertion to be that of the group, and such an assertion must occur within the proper normative context. That is, the group must be authorized to offer this assertion or assertions as testimony by the community or proper authority. The social mechanisms for the transforming of assertions into a piece of group testimony will vary depending on the social context. The role of spokesperson, for instance, is one mechanism for sanctioning assertions as those of the group. (Tollefsen 2007, p. 302)

Now surely a random group of people, either at the West of England Fat Stock and Poultry Exhibition estimating the weight of a fat ox or of traders buying and selling contracts via the Iowa Electronic Markets, do not exhibit rational integration in their behavior, nor do they typically sanction that a given assertion represents them as a group. Indeed, such cases are best described as simply a collection of instances of individual testimony that have been gathered together or aggregated in various ways. Thus, there is reason to doubt that either example in the above objection involves group testimony at all.

But what if it were simply stipulated that the collection of individuals at the West of England Fat Stock and Poultry Exhibition or trading in the Iowa Electronic Markets satisfied whatever criteria are necessary for membership in a given group? Even if it could be rendered plausible that such individuals are *groups* in the relevant sense, it doesn't follow that an automatically generated conclusion based on their views is their *testimony*. For if the conclusion in question is indeed automatically generated and does not involve any intention to express communicable content, then the information may represent the view of a group. But there is no reason to conclude from this that testimony is being offered. Of course, the epistemological significance of this verdict may be only marginal, since my account of group testimony can easily subsume or explain it. In particular, if the automatically generated conclusion is reliably produced, then it has the potential to amount to knowledge in those who consume it, regardless of whether it is testimony or not. The point I wish to emphasize here, however, is that without the intention to express communicable content, which clearly seems absent in cases of such automatically generated conclusions, there are good grounds for denying that testimony is involved in the first place.

---

[30] See also Pettit (2003) and List and Pettit (2005).

The final objection that may be raised to my view is that the interesting epistemological work about groups is simply being pushed to the question of the reliability of the statement in question. In particular, since many features of the group in question are relevant to determining whether a particular statement is in fact reliable—such as how competent the members are, how trustworthy they are with respect to one another, and so on—there will be substantive issues about groups that arise at this level. And, it may be thought, my view offers little by way of settling these issues.

In response to this objection, notice that facts about the reliability of groups are being handled in the same way as they would be in the case of individual testimony, when there is a chain of testifiers. This shows that we do not need *new* conceptual resources for understanding the phenomenon of group testimony. Granted, in any particular case, there might be a very complicated story about how this works, but this does not mean that we haven't made substantial progress in recognizing this general point. Compare reductionism in the philosophy of mind—the view that mental properties reduce to physical properties. To show, in general, that this project can succeed is a substantive philosophical conclusion. Of course, there is still plenty of work to be done to flesh out how each particular property reduces, but this does not mean that all of the explanatory work has been pushed to the project of identifying the specific physical bases of mental phenomena. Establishing that the mental can in fact be reduced to the physical—and that there is no need for further, categorically different conceptual resources in accounting for the mental—is surely an important result in its own right. The same holds in the case of group testimony. Showing that the testimony of groups can be reduced to that of individuals—and that there is no need for additional conceptual machinery in explaining group testimony—is clearly a significant philosophical conclusion in its own right.

3.6. Conclusion

In this paper, I have defended a deflationary account of group testimony, according to which the epistemic status of the testimony of groups can simply be subsumed by my Statement View of (individual) Testimony. There are at least two significant benefits to adopting a deflationary account of this sort. First, there is no mystery to the phenomenon of group testimony. To the extent that we understand the epistemology of individual testimony, we thereby also understand the epistemology of group testimony. Second, a non-reductionist account of group testimony will face several difficult explanatory burdens. For example, if the group itself—as distinct from any of its members or a spokesperson—is the source of the testimony in question, then the group must be offering an *act* of communication. It must *intend* to be conveying communicable content. But how, exactly, can a group either act or have intentions, especially where we understand these as being over and above the acts and intentions of its members? Perhaps defensible accounts can be given of these things.[31] But it is an advantage of my deflationary account that it does not depend on the successful completion of these sorts of projects.[32]

References

Adler, Jonathan E. (2002) *Belief's Own Ethics*. Cambridge, MA: The MIT Press.
Audi, Robert. (1997) "The Place of Testimony in the Fabric of Knowledge and Justification." *American Philosophical Quarterly 34*: 405–22.
———. (1998) *Epistemology: A Contemporary Introduction to the Theory of Knowledge*. London: Routledge.
———. (2006) "Testimony, Credulity, and Veracity," in Jennifer Lackey and Ernest Sosa (eds.), *The Epistemology of Testimony*. Oxford: Oxford University Press: 25–49.
Bergmann, Michael. (1997) "Internalism, Externalism and the No-Defeater Condition." *Synthese 110*: 399–417.
———. (2004) "Epistemic Circularity: Malignant and Benign." *Philosophy and Phenomenological Research 69*: 709–27.
BonJour, Laurence. (1980) "Externalist Theories of Epistemic Justification." *Midwest Studies in Philosophy 5*: 53–73.
———. (1985) *The Structure of Empirical Knowledge*. Cambridge, MA: Harvard University Press.
BonJour, Laurence and Ernest Sosa. (2003) *Epistemic Justification: Internalism vs. Externalism, Foundations vs. Virtues*. Oxford: Blackwell Publishing.
Burge, Tyler. (1993) "Content Preservation." *The Philosophical Review 102*: 457–88.
———. (1997) "Interlocution, Perception, and Memory." *Philosophical Studies 86*: 21–47.
Cariani, Fabrizio. (2011) "Judgment Aggregation." *Philosophy Compass 6*: 22–32.
Chisholm, Roderick M. (1989) *Theory of Knowledge*, 3rd ed. Englewood Cliffs, N.J.: Prentice-Hall.
Coady, C.A.J. (1992) *Testimony: A Philosophical Study*. Oxford: Clarendon Press.
———. (1994) "Testimony, Observation and 'Autonomous Knowledge,'" in Bimal Krishna Matilal and Arindam Chakrabarti (eds.), *Knowing from Words*. Dordrecht: Kluwer Academic Publishers: 225–50.
Dietrich, Franz. (2005) "Judgment Aggregation: (Im)possibility Theorems." *Journal of Economic Theory 126*: 286–98.

---

[31] For an attempt to do just this, see Gilbert (1989).
[32] I am grateful to Louise Antony, Fabrizio Cariani, Sandy Goldberg, Alvin Goldman, Hilary Kornblith, Ernie Sosa, Tim Sundell, John Turri, audience members at Amherst College, Pontifícia Universidade Católica do Rio Grande do Sul, the University of Waterloo, the University of Edinburgh, the Workshop on the Epistemology of Groups at Northwestern University, the 34th International Wittgenstein Symposium in Kirchberg, Austria, the University of Buenos Aires, and, especially, Baron Reed for helpful comments on earlier drafts of this paper.

Dummett, Michael. (1994) "Testimony and Memory," in Bimal Krishna Matilal and Arindam Chakrabarti (eds.), *Knowing from Words*. Dordrecht: Kluwer Academic Publishers: 251–72.

Elgin, Catherine Z. (2002) "Take It from Me: The Epistemological Status of Testimony." *Philosophy and Phenomenological Research 65*: 291–308.

Faulkner, Paul. (2000) "The Social Character of Testimonial Knowledge." *The Journal of Philosophy 97*: 581–601.

Fricker, Elizabeth. (1987) "The Epistemology of Testimony." *Proceedings of the* Aristotelian Society 61: 57–83.

———. (1994) "Against Gullibility," in Bimal Krishna Matilal and Arindam Chakrabarti (eds.), *Knowing from Words*. Dordrecht: Kluwer Academic Publishers: 125–61.

———. (1995) "Telling and Trusting: Reductionism and Anti-Reductionism in the Epistemology of Testimony." *Mind 104*: 393–411.

Gilbert, Margaret. (1989) *On Social Facts*. London: Routledge.

———. (1994) "Remarks on Collective Belief," in Frederick F. Schmitt (ed.), *Socializing Epistemology: The Social Dimensions of Knowledge*. Lanham, MD: Rowman & Littlefield Publishers: 235–56.

Goldman, Alvin I. (1976). "Discrimination and Perceptual Knowledge." *Journal of Philosophy 73*: 771–91.

———. (1979). "What Is Justified Belief?" in George Pappas (ed.), *Justification and Knowledge*. Dordrecht: Reidel: 1–23.

———. (2009). "Social Epistemology." *The Stanford Encyclopedia of Philosophy*, Edward N. Zalta (ed.), URL = <http://plato.stanford.edu/archives/fall2009/entries/epistemology-social/>.

———. (1986) *Epistemology and Cognition*. Cambridge, MA: Harvard University Press.

Graham, Peter J. (1997) "What is Testimony?" *The Philosophical Quarterly 47*: 227–32.

Hardwig, John. (1985) "Epistemic Dependence." *The Journal of Philosophy 82*: 335–49.

———. (1991) "The Role of Trust in Knowledge." *The Journal of Philosophy 88*: 693–708.

Hawthorne, John. (2004) *Knowledge and Lotteries*. Oxford: Oxford University Press.

Lackey, Jennifer. (1999) "Testimonial Knowledge and Transmission." *The Philosophical Quarterly 49*: 471–90.

———. (2006) "Learning from Words." *Philosophy and Phenomenological Research 73*: 77–101.

———. (2008) *Learning from Words*. Oxford: Oxford University Press.

———. (2013) "Disagreement and Belief Dependence: Why Numbers Matter," in David Christensen and Jennifer Lackey (eds.), *The Epistemology of Disagreement: New Essays* (Oxford: Oxford University Press): 243–68.

List, Christian. (2005) "Group Knowledge and Group Rationality: A Judgment Aggregation Perspective." *Episteme 2*: 25–38.

List, Christian and Phillip Pettit. (2002) "Aggregating Sets of Judgments: An Impossibility Result." *Economics and Philosophy 18*: 89–110.

———. (2004) "Aggregating Sets of Judgments: Two Impossibility Results Compared." *Synthese 140*: 207–35.

———. (2005) "On the Many as One." *Philosophy and Public Affairs 33*: 377–90.

McDowell, John. (1994) "Knowledge by Hearsay," in Bimal Krishna Matilal and Arindam Chakrabarti (eds.), *Knowing from Words*. Dordrecht: Kluwer Academic Publishers: 195–224.

Nozick, Robert. (1981) *Philosophical Explanations*. Cambridge, MA: The Belknap Press.
Owens, David. (2000) *Reason without Freedom: The Problem of Epistemic Normativity*. London: Routledge.
Pauly, Marc and Martin, van Hees. (2006) "Logical Constraints on Judgement Aggregation." *Journal of Philosophical Logic 35*: 569–85.
Pettit, Philip. (2003) "Groups with Minds of Their Own," in Frederick Schmitt (ed.), *Socializing Metaphysics*. New York: Rowman and Littlefield: 167–93.
Plantinga, Alvin. (1993) *Warrant and Proper Function*. Oxford: Oxford University Press.
Pollock, John. (1986) *Contemporary Theories of Knowledge*. Totowa, N.J.: Rowman and Littlefield.
Pritchard, Duncan. (2005) *Epistemic Luck*. Oxford: Oxford University Press.
Quinton, Anthony. (1975/1976) "Social Objects." *Proceedings of the Aristotelian Society 75*: 1–27.
Reed, Baron. (2006) "Epistemic Circularity Squared? Skepticism about Common Sense." *Philosophy and Phenomenological Research 73*: 186–97.
Reynolds, Steven L. (2002) "Testimony, Knowledge, and Epistemic Goals." *Philosophical Studies 110*: 139–61.
Ross, Angus. (1986) "Why Do We Believe What We Are Told?" *Ratio 28*: 69–88.
Ross, James. (1975) "Testimonial Evidence" in Keith Lehrer (ed.), *Analysis and Metaphysics: Essays in Honor of R.M. Chisholm*. Dordrecht: Reidel.
Schmitt, Frederick F. (1994) "The Justification of Group Beliefs," in Frederick F. Schmitt (ed.), *Socializing Epistemology: The Social Dimensions of Knowledge*. Lanham, MD: Rowman & Littlefield: 257–87.
——. (2006) "Testimonial Justification and Transindividual Reasons," in Jennifer Lackey and Ernest Sosa (eds.), *The Epistemology of Testimony*. Oxford: Oxford University Press: 193–224.
Sosa, Ernest. (1991) *Knowledge in Perspective: Selected Essays in Epistemology*. Cambridge: Cambridge University Press.
——. (1996) "Postscript to 'Proper Functionalism and Virtue Epistemology,'" in John L. Kvanvig (ed.), *Warrant in Contemporary Epistemology*. Lanham, MD: Rowman & Littlefield: 271–81.
——. (1999) "How Must Knowledge Be Modally Related to What Is Known?" *Philosophical Topics 26*: 373–84.
——. (2000) "Contextualism and Skepticism." *Philosophical Issues 34*: 94–107.
——. (2002) "Tracking, Competence, and Knowledge," in Paul Moser (ed.), *The Oxford Handbook of Epistemology*. Oxford: Oxford University Press: 264–87.
Surowiecki, James. (2005) *The Wisdom of Crowds*. New York: Anchor Books, A Division of Random House.
Tuomela, Raimo (1992) "Group Beliefs." *Synthese 91*: 285–318.
Tollefsen, Deborah. (2007) "Group Testimony." *Social Epistemology 21*: 299–311.
Welbourne, Michael. (1979) "The Transmission of Knowledge." *The Philosophical Quarterly 29*: 1–9.
——. (1981) "The Community of Knowledge." *The Philosophical Quarterly 31*: 302–14.
——. (1986) *The Community of Knowledge*. Aberdeen: Aberdeen University Press.

———. (1994) "Testimony, Knowledge and Belief," in Bimal Krishna Matilal and Arindam Chakrabarti (eds.), *Knowing from Words*. Dordrecht: Kluwer Academic Publishers: 297–313.

Williams, Michael. (1999) *Groundless Belief: An Essay on the Possibility of Epistemology*, 2nd. edn. Princeton: Princeton University Press.

Williamson, Timothy. (2000) *Knowledge and its Limits*. Oxford: Oxford University Press.

PART II

General Epistemic Concepts in the Collective Domain

4

How to Tell if a Group Is an Agent

Philip Pettit

Introduction

I take a human group to be a collection of individual human beings whose identity as a group over time, or over counterfactual possibilities, need not require sameness of membership. The typical group can remain the same group even as its membership changes, with some members leaving or dying, others joining or being born into the group. As we envisage the possibility of changes in the membership of such a group, even ones that are never going to materialize, we think of them as changes in one and the same, continuing entity.[1]

This conception of a group distinguishes it from a set or collection, where a change of members necessarily entails a change of set. But it still encompasses a generous range of social bodies, since it says nothing about the basis on which we individuate a group over time or possibility. It allows us to take almost any property, whether of origin or ethnicity, belief or commitment, career or hobby, even height or weight, to fix the identity of a group. The Irish, the Catholics, the lawyers, the stamp collectors and the obese can constitute groups. Thus while groups may vary in how important their individuating property is, and in how far it is socially significant for members or non-members, the information that a collection constitutes a group is no big news.

Among groups in this common, downbeat sense, however, some stand out from the crowd. These are groups that perform as agents, incorporating in a way that enables them to mimic the performance of individual human beings. They make judgments, form commitments, plan initiatives, and, relying

---

[1] As Chad McIntosh has reminded me, a group might be defined so that it is required to have certain individuals as members. Hence the cautious phrasing about the difference between collections and groups.

on members who act in their name, undertake actions in any of a range of domains. Examples are the partnerships and companies that operate in commercial space, the associations and movements that characterize civil society, and the churches and states that shape the lives of people throughout the world. Such entities certainly involve collections of individuals in coordinated relationships, and they certainly count as groups since they are individuated by their common acquiescence in what is done in their name. But their capacity to act, and more generally to perform as agents, marks them out. They are a class apart.

This claim is not uncontentious, however, since there are many instances where we ascribe agent-like features to groups without any real suggestion that they count as agents proper. Thus we say that the bond market is unsettled by the indecisiveness of the Eurozone leadership, or that the X-generation has lost its affection for video games, or that the sun-worshippers on a beach acted courageously in helping to save a swimmer in difficulty. Yet most of us will agree that the bond market is just a network of bond traders, each with his or her own goals; that the X-generation is just the collection of people born between about 1965 and 1980, allegedly characterized by certain shared traits; and that if those on the beach acted courageously, that just means that they each played a part in a coordinating plan, not that they formed a distinct agent. In none of these cases is there a serious candidate for the role of a group agent.

If I am to support my belief in group agents, then, I have to be able to give an account of how we can tell bona fide group agents apart from mere pretenders like these. That is what I try to do in this paper, building on work done jointly with Christian List (2011). I begin with a discussion of agency in general, distinguishing between non-personal and personal agency, and argue that we have a special way of detecting personal agency: by the direct experience or indirect evidence of interpersonal engagement. And then I try to show that under plausible epistemic scenarios such experience or evidence is necessary for the ascription of agency to a group.

The paper is in four main sections. In the first I provide a general account of agency, concentrating on simple cases. In the second I argue for the distinctions advertised between different modes of agency and of agency-detection. And in the third I use this material to argue that in our ordinary practice only direct or indirect evidence of interpersonal engagement provides a warrant for ascribing agency to groups. This means that the only group agents that we generally recognize are agents of a personal kind and in the final section, connecting with the work done with Christian List (2011), I argue that such group agents count as real, non-fictional agents.

4.1. The Conception of Agency

A system is an agent insofar as it is organized to instantiate a set of goals and a set of representations and to pursue those goals in accordance with those representations. This notion of an agent is best introduced with a simple example. Imagine that you return home one evening to find that your whiz-kid sister has set up a knee-high robot in the kitchen, which she invites you to observe. You see that it has bug-like eyes that appear to scan the room, wheels on which it can move about, and arms suited to lifting and adjusting objects up to its own size. Your sister drops a can on the floor and, to your surprise, the robot moves towards it, lifts it in an awkward embrace, then takes it to a trash bin in the corner and deposits it there. Amazed, you check for reliability by dropping an orange on the ground and, once again, the robot makes its way to the orange, lays hold of it with its arms, and takes it to be deposited in the bin. You double-check on its capacity by moving the robot, the trash bin and the orange to another room and, as before, you find that the robot performs up to par. You carry on with similar checks and it turns out that with only a few exceptions the robot performs quite reliably to this pattern.

There is a clear sense in which this system gives evidence of being a goal-seeking, representation-guided system and makes a claim to count as an agent: it more or less reliably acts to realize a certain goal or purpose according to more or less reliable representations. The goal is that things on the floor are put in the bin; this counts as a goal insofar as it is a condition whose non-fulfillment prompts rectifying action on the robot's part. The representations are states in the agent that provide information about the environment; these count as representations insofar as they come and go with the presence and absence of the conditions on which they provide information. The robot is so organized that, depending on whether or not its representations indicate that there is an object on the floor, it will act or not act; and depending on where the representations locate the object relative to robot and bin, they will guide its movements and other adjustments.

Or at least the robot is so organized that it will perform to this standard when independently plausible conditions of functioning are satisfied: when the lights are on, it is not misled by pictures of objects, its batteries are not run down, and so on. Assuming such conditions are met, the robot functions quite reliably in representing the environment and in acting for its goal in accordance with those representations. It is constituted so that in the absence of factors that plausibly impede its functioning, it reliably moves any objects on the floor to the bin area, operating on the basis of its reliable representational faculties. It displays that behavior in actual circumstances and in a range of variations on the actual circumstances where the goal remains relevant and attainable and its functioning—its forming and acting on its representations—is not impeded. The robot is marked out as an agent by the evidence of this robust, if conditioned pattern of behavior.²

Is such evidence sufficient in itself to ensure that the system counts as an agent? Not strictly, since the system may not be organized, as I put it earlier, so as to behave in the purpose-driven, representation-guided mode described; it may do so under purely external rigging. It may turn out to be following instructions, for example, from a spatially distant controller like a marionette (Peacocke 1983). Or it may be conforming to a look-up tree, implanted by a temporally distant controller who foresaw every situation the system might confront and pre-programmed its response (Block 1981). But if the system is enduringly organized within itself so that it displays the required pattern of behavior, then there can be no room for doubt about its agential status (Jackson and Pettit 1990a; Jackson 1992).

The robust pattern of behavior displayed by the toy system of our example is about as simple as it is possible to imagine. But we can see that a similar story can hold as we go to more and more complex patterns, and more and more complex agents. The purposes pursued by agents may be multiple, and variously ordered. The representations formed by agents may extend into a number of sensory modalities, they may assume the form of memories as well as current representations, they may become abstract or propositional as well as concrete or perceptual, and they may include representations of how things might be as well as of how things actually are. And those representations, as well as the purposes they serve, may be endorsed in degrees, as well as in the on-off manner envisaged so far. The variations and developments possible are legion and are evident across the spectrum from simple to complex robots, from simple to complex non-human animals, and from non-human animals to our own kind. Still, despite complexities of these kinds, the category of agency retains its common form across those variations. Each of the systems imagined, no matter how complex, is organized so as to reliably promote certain goals or purposes under the guidance of reliable representations, when there are no factors present that impede its functioning (List and Pettit 2011, Ch 1).

This discussion of the nature of agency and the evidence for agency leaves one question unanswered. How robust does the conditioned pattern of behavior that is characteristic of agency have to be? Absent factors that impede its functioning,

---

² We cannot invoke impeding factors, it should be noticed, in a free or undisciplined manner. There has to be reason to posit a contingent factor that gets in the way of the operation of the system. Suppose that the robot performed the part described but only on a random basis. In that case we would have little reason for recognizing it as an agent, unless there were evidence that a particular perturber was randomly getting in the way.

what range of variations ought to make no difference to the performance of an agent?

An extreme line on this question might be that no such variation ought to make any difference to the reliability of the agent in responding to evidence and executing its actions. But this is likely to be unrealistic with naturalistic, essentially limited subjects and I shall only assume that there is some threshold in variations, perhaps sensitive to context, such that it is enough for agency that a system proves to be evidentially and executively reliable beyond that threshold.

I do not have anything to say on where that threshold might lie but, wherever it lies, there are two fronts, internal and situational, on which any system must display the required degree of evidential and executive reliability (Pettit 2009). I defend two claims, bearing on these two forms of robustness. First, if the agent does not achieve internal robustness, there will be no reason to trace its behavior to states like representations and purposes as distinct from the many possible neural or electronic realizers of those states. And, second, if it does not achieve situational robustness, then the states to which we trace it, even if they are multiply realizable, will not be fit to count as representations and purposes.

The first claim is that the purposive and representational states or attitudes that are taken to prompt the agent's behavior must do so over a range of possible variations in how they are realized within the system. For example, the kitchen robot does not have to be given evidence of an object on the floor that strikes its bug-like eyes from just one particular angle, making one particular retinal impression and triggering one particular computational process. It responds appropriately no matter what the angle of vision and no matter what the retinal impression and computational process that realizes its representation of the object. In the absence of robustness over variations in the internal, physical realizers of representations and indeed purposes, there would be no reason to posit representations and purposes at the origin of the behavior; there would be no reason to posit anything other than the physical realizers themselves. The claim of purposive and representational attitudes to causal relevance consists in their programming for behavioral responses: that is, in their leading to the responses over variations in how they are realized at lower levels (Jackson and Pettit 1990b; List and Menzies 2009). Absent internal robustness, there would be no grounds for taking them to have any such causal relevance to the behavior produced.

The second claim is that an agent must display a purposive-representational pattern of behavior over situational as well as internal variations. Assume that impeding factors are absent. In order for a state to count as a representation that p it must form in response to evidence that p and unform in response to evidence that not p. And in order for a state to count as a purposive state of seeking to X, it must prompt different behaviors under different representations as to the opportunities and means of X-ing. This means that the representational attitude must form and unform in response to evidence, even when there are other variations in situation, and that the purposive attitude must prompt suitable initiatives over parallel variations; otherwise they would not count respectively as representational and purposive. Absent impeding factors, then, to take a system to act for a certain purpose according to a certain representation is necessarily to assume that it would do so over suitable situational variations: that is, variations in which the representation continues to be supported and the purpose continues to be capable of implementation.[3]

4.2. Two Modes of Agency and Agency-Detection

4.2.1. Personal and non-personal agency

While the considerations in the last section introduce the basic conception of agency with which I shall be working here, they ignore the fact that there are two modes of agency that stand in deep contrast with one another. On the one side there is what I shall describe as the non-personal agency exhibited by the toy robot—and, I suspect, all other robots and all non-human animals. And on the other there is the personal agency that we human beings generally display. Non-personal agency, as should be clear already, comes in many varieties and appears at many distinct levels of sophistication; there is a deep gulf between even the family pooch and the kitchen-cleaning robot. But variegated as it is, non-personal agency still contrasts in the deepest possible fashion with our own personal form of agency.

In order to bring out the distinctive character of personal agency let me rehearse in a set of dot-points certain things that you—and human beings in general—can more or less clearly do but which no animal or robot can approximate (Pettit 1993; McGeer and Pettit 2002). These points are inevitably telegraphic, given restrictions of space, but I hope that they are intuitively clear and plausible.

- Like robots and other animals, you can form purposes and representations, beliefs and desires, relying on your non-intentional, usually unconscious processing—for short, your sub-personal processing—to guide the formation of those attitudes under the flow of incoming evidence, perceptual and otherwise. But you can also do much more.

---

[3] The requirement of situational robustness is close to John Searle's (1983) requirement that an agent satisfy "the background" condition of having sufficient skills to be able to adjust appropriately under situational variation.

- You can assent to, dissent from, or suspend judgment on sentences or propositions that express attitudes you hold or might hold; and you can do this in light of considering the evidence for and against those propositions. A proposition expresses a certain attitude when acting as if the proposition were true—acting as if things were as it says they are—amounts to acting according to that attitude. In this sense 'p' expresses the belief that p; ' "q" is attractive' expresses the desire that q (as well as the belief that "q" is attractive); and 'I will do X' expresses the intention to X (as well as the belief that you will do it).
- In passing judgment in this way on a proposition, you reveal—or perhaps make it the case for the first time—that you hold the corresponding attitude. Exercising judgment over propositions is a way of forming or revealing attitudes that is distinct from the spontaneous, sub-personal way of forming attitudes associated with basic agency and the behavioral mode of revealing the attitudes that you form in that way.
- Many of your attitudes will be spontaneously formed, of course, and perhaps never become associated with judgment. But on pain of not being an interpretable agent—even an interpretable agent for yourself—there had better be a general coherence between the attitudes that form spontaneously within you and the attitudes formed or confirmed via the exercise of judgment. In particular, the attitudes you hold spontaneously ought to expand or contract or alter in response to the judgments you make. Were they to come regularly apart, then you would have two inconsistent profiles as an agent.
- While coherence is likely to be generally assured by your subpersonal make-up, judgment may come apart from attitude in particular cases. You may make your judgment without sufficient attention to the evidence and your spontaneously formed attitudes, being better attuned to evidence, may not vary as a result of the judgment. Or you may make your judgment thoughtfully, as when you come to reject the gambler's fallacy, but your spontaneously formed attitudes may not fall in line: you may forget yourself at the casino table (McGeer and Pettit 2002). But you can guard against this occasional incoherence between assent and attitude by taking measures to ensure greater care in making judgments and greater caution in acting on related beliefs.
- Assuming coherence between judgment and attitude, the fact that you assent to 'p' or dissent from 'p' will indicate that you hold the attitude that 'p' or 'not-p' expresses: the act of assent or dissent will induce or perhaps reveal that attitude within you, ensuring the presence of a disposition to manifest associated patterns of behavior. And, assuming coherence, the fact that you suspend judgment on whether or not p will indicate that you hold neither attitude: you have an open mind.

- All of this being so, you are able to prompt the formation of attitudes in any area, or at least reveal their presence—that is, bring them to consciousness—by resort to judgment: by seeing whether or not the available evidence leads you to give assent to relevant propositions. You can intentionally make up your mind, as we say, passing judgment on whether the weather is improving or Pythagoras's theorem is sound; on whether it would be fun to go to town or whether to take a break.

It should be clear that the capacities at which I gesture here mean that you and human beings in general are very different from other sorts of agents. The regular agent is at the mercy of the beliefs and desires and intentions that happen to form within it—and at the mercy of how sensitive they are to evidence—acting under the ebb and flow of their influence. But as a human being you are able to have a sort of intentional control over whether or not you form certain beliefs and desires in a given area, over how well the attitudes you form are faithful to available evidence and over whether they satisfy related conditions: whether they are consistent with one another, and whether they are closed under entailment.

What desires are likely to guide you in the exercise of such intentional control? You will want to form beliefs and other attitudes in any domain where you are required or otherwise motivated to act; this will be necessary for shaping what you do. And as a prerequisite of satisfactory agency you will want to form beliefs and other attitudes that are faithful to the evidence, consistent with one another and even to some extent closed. Any failure in such regards is liable to limit your capacity to perform as an agent, your ability to act effectively for whatever purposes you happen to embrace.

The control you can exercise on these lines is essentially epistemic, allowing you to determine the matters on which you form beliefs and other attitudes and to promote the broadly evidential quality of the attitudes you form. But there is also another sort of control, evaluative rather than epistemic in character, which your expressive and judgmental capacities as a human being ought also to make possible. This is control over what purposes you embrace rather than control over how you pursue those purposes.[4]

On the picture sketched you are able with any desire you have—say, the desire that p—to register and assent to the proposition that 'p' is an attractive prospect;

---

[4] It may be more appropriate to speak of checking rather than controlling in the epistemic and indeed the evaluative context. In a given case your belief as to whether the evidence argues that p may be incorrect and your spontaneously formed belief that p correct rather than the other way around. But the capacity to form the evidential belief puts a check on spontaneous belief-formation, making it more likely that you will end up satisfying epistemic ideals (Pettit 2007).

you can judge and believe that that is so at the same time as you are attracted to the prospect. But suppose, plausibly, that experience gives you a basis for judging that while the p-prospect is attractive here and now, it is not reliably or robustly attractive. Like the gratification of a passing impulse, it is a prospect that you will wish you hadn't sought as you look at what you chose from the perspective of a later self or a perspective that you share with other people. If you can now predict and privilege your standpoint as an intertemporally enduring, interpersonally engaged self, forming beliefs about what is robustly attractive, it will be rational to take a critical attitude towards your current desire. And human experience suggests that by taking a critical attitude—by forming the belief, under epistemic control, that the prospect is not attractive in a suitably robust way—you can exercise a distinct evaluative control over your desires and purposes; the beliefs you form may provide you with the means of disabling offensive desires or prompting more satisfactory alternatives (Smith 1994).

Assuming that you have control over how far the attitudes you form on the basis of available evidence are epistemically and perhaps evaluatively satisfactory, you will meet standard conditions for being fit to be held responsible—fit to be praised or blamed—for the formation of relevant attitudes and for the deeds they lead you to enact (Pettit and Smith 1996). Faced with the issue of whether or to form a belief that p, it will be intuitively up to you whether you are attentive to the evidence; you will have a capacity to promote such attention, even if you fail to exercise it. And faced with the issue of whether to form a desire that q or that not-q, it will equally be up to you whether you form a desire that accords with your beliefs about the robust attractiveness—the desirability—of the prospects; again you will have the required capacity, even if you fail to exercise it. In each case, then, you will be fit to be held responsible for performing well or badly by epistemic and evaluative standards in the attitudes you embrace or fail to embrace.

In ordinary parlance, this is to say that you will be personally responsible for the attitudes you form—or fail to form—as distinct from just being causally responsible for them. Even the simple robot or animal is causally responsible for the attitudes it forms, since it is the sub-personal processing of the system that produces those attitudes, updating in response to the evidence it confronts. But you will be personally responsible for relevant attitudes insofar as you can be called to book for them: you can be exposed to praise or blame for what you do or do not believe or desire or intend—and for how you consequently act or fail to act—whether on an epistemic or evaluative basis. It is this dimension of personal responsibility that leads me to describe the sort of agency that you and other human beings display as a personal form of agency, distinguishing it from the non-personal agency of simpler systems like robots and other animals.[5]

4.2.2. Two ways of detecting agency

In determining whether a simple system like our robot is an agent we rely on induction from the evidence of how it interacts with what we may describe as an impersonal environment: how it performs in the limited range of cases that we explore as we put different objects at different places on the floor, or as we observe its reactions to differences introduced by other hands. It will give evidence of being an agent just insofar as it is disposed to act after a certain pattern in an indefinite range of possible scenarios, of which the limited range explored is a subset. The limited range offers an inductive basis for ascribing the wider disposition. The existence of the disposition, realized in its internal organization, offers the best explanation for why it behaves as it does in the cases actually investigated.

We know from long-established psychological studies that we human beings have a powerful tendency to look for agency, being prompted to ascribe it even in cases where the systems involved—for example, the geometrical shapes in a simple, cartoon movie (Heider and Simmel 1944)—are manifestly incapable of agency. We are hair-triggered to move from the most slender behavioral evidence to the postulation of the robust capacities that agency requires. It's as if we are pre-programmed to be animists. We worry about overlooking any agents that may inhabit our world and, for the sake of avoiding that possibility, we routinely run the risk of taking many non-agential systems to be agents proper.

But despite this readiness to leap to ascriptions of agency, we don't primarily rely on induction from interaction with an impersonal environment when we ascribe agency to other human beings. As human beings we are personal agents. And as personal agents we have a special basis for recognizing the agency of other personal agents, at least to the extent that we share expressive resources. What we mainly rely on in ascribing agency to other human beings is induction from their interpersonal interaction with other persons, whether we engage directly in that

---

[5] Under the argument presented, of course, the domain of personal responsibility will be restricted to attitudes that are capable of being expressed in our common language. But that is not a particularly problematic constraint. If you are fit to be held responsible for forming or acting on attitudes engaging matters for which you and we have resources of expression—say, matters to do with the nature of the liquid in the glass before you, the position of that cup, and the desirability of drinking from it—then it will not matter that we have no words in which to express other presupposed attitudes: say, the sub-personal representation of the precise size of the glass, and its orientation from your body, that presumably plays a role in guiding your arm and the grasping motion of your fingers. We can hold you responsible for drinking the gin, even though we don't hold you responsible for the precise way in which you grasp and raise the glass.

interaction ourselves or have indirect evidence of the interaction in their relations with others.

In order to see how we can gain access to your agency, recognizing the presence of suitable attitudes, I add some dot-points to the list already constructed. These register ways in which we, as engaged interlocutors, can come to determine the agential presence and operation of attitudes of belief, desire, intention, and the like. They reflect capacities that are more or less clearly within the capacity of any normal human being and within your capacity in particular.

- Assuming that you can make up your mind on certain propositions, determining your own attitudes, you can know your mind on those matters other than by reviewing yourself introspectively. You can test yourself on your response to an arbitrary proposition and depending on how you judge, you can know whether or not you believe the proposition—and in relevant cases hold or do not hold a corresponding desire or intention.
- On those matters where you make up and know your mind, you can speak for yourself by making up your mind and displaying that knowledge publicly in assertion. If you assert that 'p' then, assuming sincerity, that will manifestly communicate that you have knowingly made up your mind that p and that you believe that p; it will amount to avowing the belief, as we say.
- Communicating by avowal that you believe that p—or have any other attitude—contrasts with communicating your belief by reporting that you believe that p: it seems to you, as you might put it, that you believe that p. With a report you can excuse a later failure to act as if p in either of two ways: by explaining that the introspective evidence on your belief misled you; or by explaining that you changed your mind, say by discovering new perceptual or other evidence against 'p'.
- In avowing a belief that p, communicating that you have made up your mind, you will communicate at the same time that you cannot excuse a later failure to act as if p by the claim that the introspective evidence on your believing that p was inadequate or misleading; that would be inconsistent with your having made up your mind which, in traditional terminology, gives you a maker's rather than a reporter's knowledge of your attitude. The change-of-mind excuse will remain available but not the misleading-evidence excuse.
- With any belief and desire or intention on which you can make up your mind, you have a choice between avowing and reporting it.[6] The fact that

---

[6] If you choose to report that you have a certain attitude—say, that you believe that p—then you cannot help but avow a distinct attitude: your belief that you believe that p. Although you can avoid avowal with any particular attitude, then, you cannot avoid avowing some attitudes.

you manifestly and voluntarily avow it rules out excusing a failure to display the attitude by appeal to misleading evidence on your attitudes, as a reporter might excuse such a failure; it amounts to a commitment not to try to escape that cost, should it be incurred.

- Since the avowal of an attitude is more costly than reporting the attitude— reporting it as you might report the attitudes of another—it is also more credible than a mere report; and being more credible it is likely to be more appealing: it will have a better chance of shaping the expectations of your audience and coordinating with them to your mutual benefit.
- You can make your ascriptions of future actions more credible and more appealing in a parallel way, by strengthening an avowal into a promise. Like the avowal, the promise rules out the excuse of having been misled about your attitudes when you fail to act according to an attitude previously avowed. But it also rules out the excuse of having changed your mind since making the avowal. Promise that you'll meet me at the theater and you cannot claim in later excuse either that you got your intention wrong or that a better opportunity presented itself and you dropped the intention.[7]

What these points emphasize is that if you are a personal agent, then there are very exacting expectations to which we, your interlocutors, will hold you. We will expect you in suitable areas to be able to speak with authority to what you believe and desire and intend; to be willing to make commitments to us— avowals or promises—and not just to report on yourself as you might report on another; to prove capable of living up to those commitments in the general run, displaying the beliefs and desires, the intentions and actions, to which your words testify; and, where you occasionally fail to live up to those words, to be able to recognize the failures and to be willing to make excuses or apologies that suggest a determination to improve. Being a personal agent, you will be expected to prove yourself a conversable agent too: someone we find it possible to reach in the realm of words and to engage to our mutual benefit.

The fact that we tie your agential status to such a rich array of expectations means that if you are not an agent—or at least not an agent for whom your words speak—then that will show up very quickly. And the fact that those expectations are very exacting means that as you begin to meet the expectations, it will quickly

---

[7] The fact of having avowed a belief does not give you a new reason for believing it; should the evidence change, you can excusably change your belief. But the fact of having promised to do something does give you a new reason for desiring and acting accordingly: it puts your reputation at stake and constrains any changes of mind.

become plausible that you are an agent.[8] Induction plays a central role in the exercise of establishing that you are a personal, conversable agent but the exercise is very different from the inductive procedure that we have to follow with the robot in our earlier example. To put the difference in a slogan, it involves induction from interpersonal interaction rather than induction from impersonal interaction.

We see that you are a personal agent in virtue of probing your attitudes, eliciting avowals and promises, and finding that you do not let us down: that is, in virtue of vindicating your status in interaction with us. Or we see that you are a personal agent by learning of the pattern of interpersonal interaction that you enjoy with third parties. We rely just on induction from evidence of impersonal interaction in the case of a non-personal agent like the robot, whether this be a form of interaction we sponsor in experiment or register as mere observers: whether in that sense it be direct or indirect. But in the case of personal agents like you and any other human being we can also rely on induction from evidence of interpersonal interaction, whether this be interaction in which we directly engage or interaction with third parties that we learn about indirectly.

4.3. Recognizing Group Agents

The discussion so far suggests that if groups are agents, then they may be non-personal agents like robots and animals or personal agents like you and me. And it suggests that whether they count as agents of one or the other kind will correlate with the sort of evidence we find appropriate for establishing their agency. I argue for two theses in this section, one positive, the other negative. First, that we can certainly establish the agency of some groups by finding them conversable in the manner of personal agents: that is, by interacting with them interpersonally or having evidence of such interaction with others. And second, that we cannot plausibly establish the agency of any group just on the basis of evidence, direct or indirect, of an impersonal form of interaction. The upshot is that the only groups we can plausibly expect to count as agents are groups that succeed in attaining conversability.

---

[8] Notice, as registered in (List and Pettit 2011, Ch 1), that this extra evidence may serve in the case of a conversable agent to override the evidence of behavioral failure that might lead us to doubt the agency of an impersonal system. If you fail to behave according to the attitudes of which we have independent evidence but admit the failure, perhaps even apologizing for it, then that will provide an assurance that you are an agent that would be hard to attain in the case of a non-personal agent.

4.3.1. Ascribing group agency on the basis of interpersonal interaction

Most of the groups that make a persuasive claim to count as agents speak for themselves in the manner of individual human beings, having individuals or bodies that serve as corporate spokespersons. In claiming to speak for the group—that is, for all the members—on any issue, such spokespersons lay claim to an authority, based on the individual acquiescence of members to live up to the words they utter on the group's behalf. Thus the agential status of the group will be manifest in the fact that the declarations that the spokespersons make are ones that other members honor, acting as the words require of them, now in this situation, now in that. As we deal with the group through its spokespersons, we find that it vindicates its status as an agent by how it interacts with us. And we find no difficulty in this, since the authority claimed and manifested by spokespersons testifies to explicit or implicit commitments on the part of members—presumably capable of confirmation in individual interaction with them—to abide by the utterances of suitable representatives.

The spokespersons for any group may be individuals or assemblies of individuals and while no group need have the same spokesperson on every issue, different spokespersons must speak with a single voice, ensuring by whatever means that the avowals and promises they make on behalf of the group form a coherent whole. The group's accepted mode of organization and decision-making will usually ensure this coherence among spokespersons, as it will ensure that members know how they are required to behave by the utterances of such authorities (French 1984; List and Pettit 2011). A group agent may fail on occasion to live up to those utterances, of course, as an individual may fail too. But the mode of organization ought at least to make it capable in such a case of proving responsive to complaints about the breakdown, enabling it to recognize when an excuse is available, or an apology due, and to act accordingly.

What sorts of declarations do spokespersons make on behalf of a group agent? They avow the beliefs of the group, as when the church outlines its tenets of faith, the political party presents its analysis of the economy, or the corporation explains why its profits fell in a recent quarter. They avow equally the wishes and values and intentions of the group as when the church expounds what it stands for, the party embraces certain principles or policies, and the corporation endorses a strategic statement and a statement of medium-term tactics. And they promise future action in one or another domain, as when the church promises greater openness about priestly abuse, the party commits itself to one or another initiative in government, and the corporation enters contracts with its suppliers and customers.

Is it excessive to take the declarations of spokespersons to be avowals and promises? Absolutely not, for the declarations are taken in common usage to rule out excuses of misleading evidence or change of mind in the way that is characteristic of avowals and promises. Suppose a group fails to live up to a belief or value ascribed by an authorized spokesperson. It will not do for that spokesperson to excuse what was said on the grounds of having mistaken the evidence about what the group held. The spokesperson's only recourse will be to resign from the role assigned by the group or, maintaining that role, to try to offer another excuse for the failure or to make an apology on the group's behalf. Or suppose a group fails to live up to a promise that the spokesperson made on its behalf. In this case the spokesperson can invoke neither the misleading-evidence excuse nor the change-of-mind excuse. Again the alternatives will be as stark as before: resign, excuse on other grounds, or make an apology.

Let us assume that a group designates unique spokespersons in different domains, then, and that it robustly lives up to the words of its spokespersons. And let us assume, as this implies, that the voice supported by the different spokespersons is reasonably coherent, offering a self-consistent, if developing story of the group's attitudes. Or let us assume at least that, when the voice fails to be coherent, the spokespersons respect the demand to speak with one voice, making amendments that restore coherence. If such conditions are fulfilled, then there can be little doubt about the grounds for treating the group as an agent. The words of the spokespersons project a robust pattern of goal-seeking, representation-guided action and the group is systematically organized to live up to those words and keep faith with the projected pattern.

More specifically, the words of the spokespersons project that robust pattern—that pattern of evidentially and executively reliable performance—on the two fronts, internal and situational. On the internal front, they give us evidence that the members of the group will perform appropriately, living up to what the group demands of them, across a raft of variations in their personal attitudes: any variations, at any rate, that are consistent with their remaining committed to the group. And on the situational front, they indicate that the members of the group will perform appropriately as circumstances change, giving rise to a change in what attitudes are supported or what action would be appropriate for enacting the group's attitudes.

We have grounds at least as solid as in the robot case for treating such a collectivity as an agent. Moreover, indeed, we have grounds that entitle us to treat it as a personal agent that can be held responsible for its attitudes, given the capacity it must have to take account of epistemic or evaluative critiques of the attitudes it embraces. The spokespersons that speak for the group, whether these be individuals or assemblies, will presumably be as capable of responding to such challenges when they act for the group as they are when they act for themselves. They may refuse on occasion to answer a particular challenge but the pressures of credibility on any group that claims to support coherent attitudes, and to invite relationships with individuals and with other groups, will argue for not making a habit of such refusal. Within its domain of operation, it must purport and prove itself to be a conversable subject: an entity capable of being reached and engaged in speech.

The conditions identified in these observations are satisfied over and over in the social world. Our societies teem with commercial, ecclesiastical, associational and political groups, each with its own mode of organization, its own way of generating a single, self-representative voice and its own way of guaranteeing fidelity in action to the words uttered in its name. As the law of incorporation has grown over the last century or so, these entities have become ever more powerful, gaining a capacity to act in different areas, to change their area of action as they will, to adopt and amend the goals that they pursue there, and to do all of this on the basis of resources that are strictly corporate, with the liability of members for group bankruptcy being severely limited.

4.3.2. *Ascribing group agency from evidence of impersonal interaction*

Evidence of interpersonal interaction, direct or indirect, would clearly be sufficient for thinking of certain groups as agents: specifically, as conversable agents. But is evidence of interpersonal interaction necessary for establishing the status of a group as an agent? Or might the evidence of impersonal interaction alone suffice to establish a group's claim to agency, and presumably to agency of a non-personal kind? Might we be reasonably led to cast a group as an agent just by finding that it displays an agential pattern of interaction of broadly the kind illustrated by the robot? In particular, might we be reasonably led to do this without making assumptions that can only be confirmed by recourse to evidence of interpersonal interaction? I argue that the answer is, no.[9]

Every group, in the nature of the case, is made up of individual human beings, each with a mind of their own. Thus whatever goal-seeking patterns are postulated at the group level, they have to emanate from individual actions: the actions whereby some or all of the members do their bit, whatever that is, in sustaining the group-level patterns. And whatever representations are supposed to guide

---

[9] Questions naturally arise about what to say of groups where the evidence from interpersonal interaction is mixed—for example, where would-be spokespersons are in conflict—but the evidence of impersonal interaction is strong: for example, it suggests that some of the spokespersons are reliable, others not. I do not address such questions here but stick for simplicity to the purer cases.

the group in its fidelity to those patterns, they have to be formed on the basis of representations formed in some or all of its members: the members, after all, are the group's eyes and ears. If we are to treat a group as an agent, then there has to be good ground for expecting that it will robustly display any goal-seeking, representation-guided patterns we postulate. And that means that there has to be good ground for expecting that it will do this over possible variations in how, independently of the group, members individually see things and are individually disposed to act. It has to be evidentially and executively reliable, as we put it earlier, over certain variations on the internal front: that is, in the individuals who make it up.

The dependence of the behavior of a group on the intentional profiles of its members generates a dilemma for anyone who thinks that observing the impersonal interaction of a group might be enough on its own to provide adequate evidence of group agency. Suppose that we come across a group such that its interaction with an impersonal environment—and such impersonal interaction only—suggests that there is a purpose or set of purposes that it is pursuing in light of representations it forms about the opportunities and means of action at its disposal. Either the behavior of members of the group will be intelligible just in light of their individual profiles—their group-independent beliefs and desires. Or the behavior of the group will not be intelligible on that basis. And in neither case are we likely to think that the interaction of the group with its impersonal environment provides sufficient evidence for casting it as an agent.

If the behavior of the group is intelligible in light of the group-independent, individual profiles of members, then there will no reason to postulate a group agent, since the pattern displayed by the group as a whole will not be robust over relevant sorts of internal variation within the group: that is, variations in the group-independent profiles of the members. Take the example of a market in some domain of commodities, which advances the purpose of establishing the relative prices at which those goods can be successfully cleared, in light of information about—and, we might think, a representation of—the level of aggregate demand. This apparently purposive-representational pattern ought not to lead us to think of the market as an agent. The pattern is only as robust as the group-independent desires of members to trade with one another at maximal returns to themselves.[10]

Let us turn now to the second possibility, that the pattern displayed in a group's interaction with an impersonal environment—a pattern like that illustrated in

---

[10] And even if that were not thought to be an objection, canons of parsimony would argue against invoking group agency to explain a pattern that is already explicable by the group-independent profiles of the group's members.

the market—is not intelligible in light of the group-independent, individual profiles of its members. Might the evidence of such a pattern suffice on its own to establish the agency of the group? I do not think so. We would hardly find that pattern compelling unless we had some explanation as to why members should support it, given that they may be disposed by their group-independent attitudes to act in an unsupportive manner. And the only explanation that would have any plausibility in such a scenario would require confirmation, direct or indirect, by reference to interpersonal interaction. This explanation is that the members are committed to live up to avowals and promises made in their name: that in that sense their behavior is determined by group-dependent, not group-independent, attitudes.

Imagine that you are hovering in a helicopter and watching the rush hour traffic clog the main highway out of town. And suppose you notice that the line of traffic is systematically blocking an ambulance from crossing that highway. All the crossings give priority to the highway and you see the ambulance being blocked, now at this crossing, now at another, now at a third. You might think of the traffic as a group agent that aims at frustrating the ambulance; after all, the evidence of its impersonal interaction with the ambulance suggests that that's what it is doing. But could you sensibly reach that conclusion just on the basis of such evidence? I think not.

The problem is that, whatever the group-level evidence, you are bound to assume that individual drivers each have group-independent attitudes of their own; you are hardly going to take them to be automatons or zombies. And under that assumption it would be a miracle—a cosmic accident—if the attitudes robustly fell in line with the requirements of the alleged group goal. The only basis on which you could reasonably conclude that the traffic had an agential character, with the frustration of the ambulance as a goal, is the belief that the individual drivers are committed, as under a rule of authorized spokespersons, to the service of that group-level goal. You might not be clear about how they could be guided by a spokesperson and might even be forced to postulate channels of hidden electronic communication. But any such postulate, no matter how unlikely, would be more reasonable than taking them to constitute an agent, without reliance on the possibility of confirmation by direct or indirect evidence of interpersonal interaction.[11]

---

[11] You might drop the belief in the agential status of the individuals, as certain radical ontologies would do. But this would be a resort of radical despair. For a critique of the option see Chapter 3 of my book *The Common Mind* (Pettit 1993).

4.3.3. The bottom line

The considerations in this section suggest that under plausible epistemic scenarios, the only evidence that we can take as determinative of the presence of a group agent is evidence of interpersonal interaction. That means that the only sort of group we are ever likely to recognize as an agent is a conversable body. Such a group will have spokespersons that maintain a single voice and a mode of organization that gives credibility to their words, prompting other members to keep faith with those words when they act in the name of the group. It will count as a personal rather than a non-personal agent.

This line ought not to be surprising in view of the history of the concept of group agency. The concept emerged in medieval Europe, where guilds and orders and other novel entities flourished, and it quickly gained a wide currency. It applied to any group of people who united together in such a way that collectively they appeared in law, and figured in the courts, in the manner of an individual subject. The paradigm example was the group that could own property and enter contracts, sue others and be sued in turn, and operate legally in the manner of an individual agent. What struck the legal theorists of the time was that in an entity like a guild or parish or town certain individuals or assemblies were authorized to speak for the corporate body, avowing the judgments or purposes of that body on the basis of the authority vested in them, and incurring commitments for the body in promising to take one or another action. Such spokespersons were expected to maintain a coherence of voice, not holding by inconsistent claims or plans. And ordinary members of the body were required under the rules of incorporation to keep faith with the words given in their name, living up to the avowals and promises that their spokespersons made.

Congenially with the view developed here, the authorities or spokespersons in this image were generally cast as playing a representative role, and groups were held to perform as agents just to the extent that the members rallied behind the words of their representatives. Thus in 1354, Albericus de Rosciate could say that a collegial agent, although it is constituted out of many members, is one by virtue of representation: *collegium, licet constituatur ex pluribus, est tamen unum per repraesentationem* (Eschmann 1944, 33, fn 145). The theme dominates the work of legal theorists of the time like Bartolus of Sasseferrato and his pupil, Baldus de Ubaldis, who make much of the way a suitably represented group, in particular the represented people of a city, could figure as a corporate agent or person (Woolf 1913; Canning 1983). Arguing that the *populus liber*, the free people of a city republic, is a corporate person, Baldus explains that this is because the council—the representative, rotating council—represents the mind of that people: *concilium repraesentat mentem populi* (Canning 1987, 198).

This conversability criterion makes clear why churches and political parties and commercial firms are certainly group agents. But, to go back to earlier examples, the model makes equally clear why there is no temptation to ascribe group agency to the bond market, or the X-generation, or even the group of people who coordinate their efforts to save a swimmer.

There is no purpose pursued as such by the bond-market or the X-generation, no pressure on them to agree on representations to guide the pursuit of that purpose, and so no basis for expecting them to perform robustly as agents in their own right. But what of the beach group? The members in this sort of group do have a shared purpose, and do agree on the means of furthering it, and there may seem to be a better case for treating it as an agent.

On reflection, however, it should be clear that this sort of group will not constitute a group agent either. There is no reason to expect such a group to display the internal or situational robustness that we associate with agency. We might be able to predict on the basis of the individual character of the members that faced with a similar crisis in the mountains, they would almost certainly respond in some equally altruistic way. But there would be nothing about the group as such—nothing about its authorization of spokespersons or the mode of its organization—that would support such extrapolation across changes of situation, let alone changes in its internal make-up.[12]

4.4. The Reality of Group Agents

Despite the fact that the argument provided appears to support the reality of conversable group agents—and only indeed of group agents of that kind—a common approach suggests that still such agents should count only as fictions. They may perform as if they were agents but really they are not. They are merely the projections of the individual agents who make them up; they are the fronts or avatars behind which the members, who are the only real agents, operate for their own purposes.

---

[12] In the beach case there is certainly a joint action on the part of the participants, sponsored by a joint intention that they form. This might materialize insofar as it is manifest to each that they all want to save the swimmer, that they can do so only together, that the salient way of doing so is to link arms and form a chain into the water, and that if anyone starts the chain then others will join up. Joint intention is certainly required for the formation of a group agent, as that is described here; it is implicit in the acquiescence of members in the identification of spokespersons and in the authorization of their words. But necessary as joint intention may be for the formation of a group agent, it is not sufficient on its own to ensure the presence of such an agent (Pettit and Schweikard 2006; List and Pettit 2011) There is a large literature on what occurs when people form and act on a joint intention; see for example (Tuomela 1995; Bratman 1999; Gilbert 2001). The account that fits best with my comments here is probably Bratman's.

This sort of fiction theory goes back to Thomas Hobbes (1994, Ch 16), in particular to his discussion of how a group of individuals can authorize a spokesperson to speak for them, thereby constituting a conversable body, capable of making and living up to commitments (Skinner 2010). Hobbes, a seventeenth-century philosopher, stands out among his predecessors for insisting that the spokesperson that speaks for a group has to be capable of performing as a pre-existing agent or agency. His idea is that a corporate agent will form just insofar as such a pre-existing agent or agency takes on the role of spokesperson for members of the group. 'A multitude of men are made one person, when they are by one man, or one person, represented'. But their spokesperson or representative may be a committee, not just an individual, provided that the committee forms its judgments by majority vote, making suitable accommodation for ties: 'if the representative consist of many men, the voice of the greater number must be considered as the voice of them all'.

Hobbes assumes that the spokesperson for any group agent exists prior to the formation of that entity as an independent individual or committee and provides unity for the group agent insofar as its words can be treated as the words of the group, not 'truly', but 'by fiction'.[13] Thus in order to deflate the representation whereby group agents form—he often describes this as personation—he insists that it involves nothing more than the representation whereby an individual may speak for a wholly inanimate object, as in asserting its rights. 'There are few things that are incapable of being represented by fiction. Inanimate things, as a church, a hospital, a bridge, may be personated by a rector, master, or overseer'.

Does the account given here support the sort of fiction theory that Hobbes espouses and that continues to be espoused in contemporary circles, particularly among economists and economically minded lawyers (Grantham 1998)? No, it does not. It is possible in principle for a group agent to form around a single, dictatorial spokesperson, as Hobbes envisages, but this would be a degenerate case of group agency; it might be as well cast as an example of an individual agent with a multitude of helpers. And, even more importantly, it is not possible for a group agent to form around a single, majoritarian committee, whether this be an elite committee or a committee of the whole.

Hobbes assumes, as many assumed before and since, that a committee can function like an individual agent, mechanically generating its judgments and purposes

---

[13] This fiction theory is important to Hobbes, since it undermines the idea that the commonwealth—for him, the supreme group agent—might be formed on the basis of a mixed, republican constitution that requires different spokespersons to agree in determining the voice of the state. He thought that such a constitution would create civil war, rejecting it on the grounds that it would create 'not one independent commonwealth, but three independent factions' (Hobbes 1994, Ch 29, s 6).

from the bottom up via majority voting. That is why he thinks that a committee can serve like a dictator to speak for a group and establish it as a conversable agent, capable of entering and keeping commitments. But it turns out that he is quite mistaken about that, as the discursive dilemma makes clear (Pettit 2001, Ch 5; List 2006). A majoritarian committee cannot reliably function like an independent agent, in the way Hobbes envisages, because majority voting among individually consistent members can generate inconsistency in the group judgments on various connected issues.

Suppose that you, Bloggs and I want to form a group agent and that we must decide on the attitudes of the group on three propositions, 'p', 'q', and 'p&q'. You and Bloggs may vote for 'p', I against, and Bloggs and I for 'q', you against. How then will we cast our votes on 'p&q'? You and I will vote against and only Bloggs vote for. Thus our majority voting pattern will lead us as a group into embracing, incoherently, the package: p, q, not-p&q. We will then face a discursive dilemma. Let that package stand and we must reject the aspiration to collective rationality. Alter the package so as to ensure collective rationality and we must reject the aspiration to individual responsiveness.

This simple observation shows that the majoritarian committee cannot be recruited to the role of a spokesperson, allowing the group for which it speaks to count as an agent. In order for the three of us to establish a group agent we have to follow a procedure that targets the requirements for such an agent to exist, ensuring in particular that it is reliably consistent and coherent. Thus we might follow a straw-vote procedure under which every attitude supported by a majority vote is checked for consistency with other attitudes adopted; if it is consistent, we endorse it; and if it is not consistent, as in the case illustrated, we make a decision on which member of the conflicting subset to reject, whether that be the new candidate or something accepted in the past. This might lead us as a group to endorse the claims 'p, q, p&q', as it might have led us to endorse 'not-p, q, not-p&q', 'p, not-q, not-p&-q'. In any such event it will enable us to preserve collective rationality, and to allow us to form a group agent, but require us to sacrifice individual, majoritarian responsiveness; there will be at least one proposition we endorse as a group that a majority of members individually reject.

The group agent that we might form in this way, via the straw-vote procedure, is not an agent that we, an independently existing agency, go through the motions of representing, giving it a fictional existence. No, it is a group agent that comes into existence by dint of our individual efforts, in particular our efforts to ensure that the conditions for the existence of the group agent are met. As individual, bottom-up voting proceeds, we gather feedback on the emerging pattern of judgments and purposes that this would generate for the group and, when necessary, we act top-down to ensure that that pattern is fit for agency: we suspend the effect of a vote and revise the overall results of voting, past and present, so as to ensure our coherence as a group agent. Before the appearance of that group agent, we exist as individuals, of course, being required to bring the group into existence. But before its appearance there is no other agent or agency—nothing like the dictatorial spokesperson—such that by contrast with that entity the group agent created is merely a fiction.

The discursive dilemma shows that one particular pattern of bottom-up responsiveness to member votes— that which majority voting would ensure—is ruled out by the requirement of collective rationality and so that a majority committee could not play the agential, representative role that the fiction theory of group agents requires. But could a group agent be represented in any other bottom-up way—say, under another other voting system—by a single committee or indeed by a network of committees with complementary tasks? No, it could not. The recent impossibility theorems on judgment-aggregation generalize the lesson illustrated by the discursive dilemma and support that negative line (List and Pettit 2002; List and Polak 2010). They show, roughly, that when individuals construct a group agent—a reliably rational entity—the exercise will be effective only if the judgments and purposes they assign to the group are not constrained to be a reflection, majoritarian or otherwise, of the corresponding attitudes of the members. And that means, as in the straw-vote case, that the individuals have to construct a group agent *de novo*: they have to construct an agent such that there is no pre-existing agency—no pre-existing spokesperson—in comparison with which it might look like a fiction.

And so to the denouement. It may be, as we saw earlier, that the only plausible basis for ascribing agency to groups is evidence of interpersonal interaction, and that only groups whose members organize to make them conversable have a claim to constitute agents. But still, so our concluding observations suggest, such a group agent is not just a fiction or pretense: a dummy agent that reflects only the voices of a ventriloquist master, in the way in which the dicatatorial agent would reflect the voice of the dictator. Any group agent will be the same collection as the set of its members at or over time, since it does not have any existence apart from them. But it will not be the same agent.[14] Indeed, prior to the formation of the group entity,

---

[14] A further consideration in support of this view is that a given collection of individuals might constitute one group agent, with its own commitments, in one context, and a different group agent, with different commitments, in another. The town council might have just the same members, for example, as the hospital board. To hold that either group was the same agent as its members would be to imply, absurdly, that the town council is the same agent as the hospital board.

the collection of individuals who construct it will not be an agent of any kind; as Hobbes would say, it will be merely a multitude.[15]

References

Block, N. (1981). "Psychologism and Behaviorism." *Philosophical Review* 90: 5–43.

Bratman, M. (1999). *Faces of Intention: Selected Essays on Intention and Agency*. Cambridge, Cambridge University Press.

Canning, J. (1987). *The Political Thought of Baldus de Ubaldis*. Cambridge, Cambridge University Press.

Canning, J. P. (1983). "Ideas of the State in Thirteenth and Fourteenth Century Commentators on the Roman Law." *Transactions of the Royal Historical Society* 33: 1–27.

Eschmann, T. (1944). "Studies on the Notion of Society in St Thomas Aquinas: St Thomas and the Decretal of Innocent IV Romana Ecclesia, Ceterum." *Medieval Studies*: 1–42.

French, P. A. (1984). *Collective and Corporate Responsibility*. New York, Columbia University Press.

Gilbert, M. (2001). "Collective Preferences, Obligations, and Rational Choice." *Economics and Philosophy* (17): 109–20.

Grantham, R. (1998). "The Doctrinal Basis of the Rights of Company Shareholders." *Cambridge Law Journal* 57: 554–88.

Heider, F. and M. Simmel (1944). "An experimental study of apparent behavior." *American Journal of Psychology* 13: 243–59.

Hobbes, T. (1994). *Leviathan*. ed E.Curley. Indianapolis, Hackett.

Jackson, F. (1992). Block's Challenge. *Ontology, Causality, and Mind: Essays on the Philosophy of David Armstrong*. K. Campbell, J. Bacon and L. Rhinehart. Cambridge, Cambridge University Press.

Jackson, F. and P. Pettit (1990a). "In Defence of Folk Psychology." *Philosophical Studies* 57: 7–30; reprinted in F.Jackson, P.Pettit and M.Smith, 2004, Mind, Morality and Explanation, Oxford, Oxford University Press.

Jackson, F. and P. Pettit (1990b). "Program Explanation: A General Perspective." *Analysis* 50: 107–17; reprinted in F. Jackson, P. Pettit, and M. Smith, 2004, Mind, Morality and Explanation, Oxford, Oxford University Press.

List, C. (2006). "The Discursive Dilemma and Public Reason." *Ethics* 116: 362–402.

List, C. and P. Menzies (2009). "Non-reductive physicalism and the limits of the exclusion principle." *Journal of Philosophy* 106: 475–502.

List, C. and P. Pettit (2002). "Aggregating Sets of Judgments: An Impossibility Result." *Economics and Philosophy* 18: 89–110.

---

[15] My thanks for the many helpful comments I received at a number of events where a version of this paper was presented: at an American Philosophical Association meeting in Chicago and at workshops in the University of Vienna, University College, Dublin and the University of Copenhagen. The paper draws heavily on my joint work with Christian List, of course, and I am deeply indebted to him. I am grateful to Rachael Briggs and Jennifer Lackey, who provided very helpful comments on earlier drafts.

List, C. and P. Pettit (2011). *Group Agency: The Possibility, Design and Status of Corporate Agents*. Oxford, Oxford University Press.

List, C. and B. Polak (2010). "Symposium on Judgment Aggregation." *Journal of Economic Theory* 145 (2).

McGeer, V. and P. Pettit (2002). "The Self-regulating Mind." *Language and Communication* 22: 281–99.

Peacocke, C. (1983). *Sense and Content*. Oxford, Oxford University Press.

Pettit, P. (1993). *The Common Mind: An Essay on Psychology, Society and Politics*, paperback edition 1996. New York, Oxford University Press.

Pettit, P. (2001). *A Theory of Freedom: From the Psychology to the Politics of Agency*. Cambridge and New York, Polity and Oxford University Press.

Pettit, P. (2007). "Rationality, Reasoning and Group Agency." *Dialectica* 61: 495–519.

Pettit, P. (2009). The Reality of Group Agents. *Philosophy of the Social Sciences: Philosophical Theory and Scientific Practice*. C. Mantzavinos. Cambridge, Cambridge University Press: 67–91.

Pettit, P. and D. Schweikard (2006). "Joint Action and Group Agency." *Philosophy of the Social Sciences* 36: 18–39.

Pettit, P. and M. Smith (1996). "Freedom in Belief and Desire." *Journal of Philosophy* 93: 429–49; reprinted in F. Jackson, P. Pettit, and M. Smith, 2004, Mind, Morality and Explanation, Oxford, Oxford University Press.

Searle, J. R. (1983). *Intentionality*. Cambridge, Cambridge University Press.

Skinner, Q. (2010). A Genealogy of the Modern State. London.

Smith, M. (1994). *The Moral Problem*. Oxford, Blackwell.

Tuomela, R. (1995). *The Importance of Us*. Stanford, CA, Stanford University Press.

Woolf, C. N. S. (1913). *Bartolus of Sassoferrato*. Cambridge, Cambridge University Press.

5

The Stoic Epistemic Virtues of Groups

Sarah Wright

How do epistemic virtues, ordinarily applied to individual cognizers, apply to groups acting for epistemic purposes? In this paper I will focus specifically on the Stoic approach to the virtues (moral and epistemic) and demonstrate why those virtues are well-poised to be smoothly extended to cover groups as well. I start by explaining a distinction from the ancient Stoics between the *telos* of our lives and the *skopos* of our actions. I examine the ways that aiming at these two types of goals interacts in the individualistic moral and epistemic virtues, and then extend this model to cover group epistemic virtues. Our individual epistemic *skopoi* are obtaining true beliefs for ourselves or others, and I will argue that a natural extension of the *skopos* of the individual to the *skopos* of the group allows for a focus either on the beliefs of its members or the beliefs of the group as a whole. I then consider an objection to this approach which argues that groups cannot have beliefs, so they cannot aim at true belief for the group. Looking in detail at the Stoic account of the agency in our beliefs and actions, I show that the Stoic approach clearly allows groups to have beliefs. After addressing this potential problem with the *skopos* of group epistemic virtue, I turn to a potential objection to the idea that groups can have a determinate *telos*. Since the purpose of a group is often freely chosen, stated explicitly, and can be wildly variable between different groups, it may appear that there is no fixed *telos* of groups to which we can appeal. I argue that, insofar as groups can engage in actions and belief they should be held to the standard of acting and believing well. While this standard is loose enough to permit groups to have many different purposes, those groups will all have a shared *telos* on the basis of which they may be evaluated.

5.1. Stoic Virtue Theory

Before applying a virtue theory to groups, it is important to understand the model of the virtues that is being proposed. Within Ancient Greek virtue theories, the best way to do this is to focus on the *telos* of human life proposed by the theory. Eudaemonist theories are unified in agreeing that there is a single *telos* for human life and that reaching this *telos* is the only way to achieve eudaemonia. Despite this superficial agreement, the differences between theories come in the way that they spell out what *eudaemonia* and the human *telos* are.[1] The Stoics are noted in this regard for having a very clear (and perhaps austere) approach on which virtue is both necessary and sufficient for *eudaemonea*. Their commitment to the "sufficiency thesis" leads them to the seemingly paradoxical statement that the virtuous person is happy even when being tortured on the rack. Of course the virtuous person reasonably wants to avoid being tortured, but the Stoic claim here is that being tortured does not undermine the fact that the virtuous person has reached the human *telos* and as a result counts as having a good human life.

This claim on the part of the Stoics gives them reason to make a clear distinction between the *telos* of a human life and the *skopos* (or target) of particular actions. Introducing the idea of a *skopos* allows us to recognize that there are things outside of virtue at which we reasonably aim. Health, success, material goods, and (at the extreme) avoiding torture are all things at which a virtuous and reasonable person may aim, as a *skopos*. But, on the Stoic picture they are not required for having a good human life.

The Stoics call virtue the "skill of living."[2] They demonstrate their commitment to the "sufficiency thesis" by choosing the skills associated with the stochastic crafts as those on which they model the skill of living. As Brad Inwood explains:

"Stochastic crafts are those, like rhetoric and medicine, in which the achievement of the stated aim of the craft can and must be distinguished from the question whether the craft is being practiced perfectly."[3]

Stochastic crafts help us to understand the *telos/skopos* distinction. They are those crafts in which one may achieve the *telos* (of that craft) even when one is unable to reach the particular *skopoi* which are the reasonable and characteristic aims of the craft.

---

[1] Julia Annas argues for this interpretation in her (1993).
[2] Julia Annas also argues that virtues should not be seen as opposed to skills but rather as a type of skill in her (1995).
[3] Inwood 1986, 549.

Looking to an ancient example we can consider the stochastic craft of medicine. Consider a doctor, Anna, working with a patient to restore a full range of motion in his shoulder after a rotator cuff injury. Her target or *skopos* in treating this patent is the restoration of a full range of motion. Anna is skilled in facilitating patient recovery from injuries; this implies that Anna has reached her *telos* of the craft of medicine (at least within her specialization). Anna uses her medical skill in choosing the best course of treatment to address the injury. However, despite her best efforts, she may not be able to help her patient. The patient's injuries may be too severe; there may be too much scar tissue for any amount of rehabilitation to work. The patient may fail to perform the prescribed stretches and exercises needed for a full recovery. Or the patient may simply stop coming to his appointments. In any of these cases, Anna will fail to reach the goal of her treatment; she will miss her *skopos*. But that failure neither reflects on nor undermines the fact that Anna is a skilled doctor or the fact that she is currently practicing the craft of medicine well. These facts depend on Anna's performance, not on the outcomes of the procedures that she prescribes. Skillfully practicing the craft of medicine is the true *telos* of a doctor (*qua* doctor).

The Stoics choose stochastic crafts like medicine as their model for virtue in part because they are concerned that the virtues, and our reaching our *telos*, should depend only on what is up to us. Our overall *telos* should not depend on anything that is outside our control. We ought to act in ways we think will accomplish good ends, but we should also recognize that we may not be able to bring about those results.[4] For example, a courageous firefighter, Dan, arriving on the scene at of a burning house, may quickly identify that there is a person in the building and rush into the house in order to pull the victim from the flames. Dan's courage, an addition to his knowledge of firefighting, leads him to take as a *skopos* the rescue of the person in the building. His courage is exercised and demonstrated in the way that he makes this choice. Despite Dan's brave choice, his attempts at rescue may fail. The fire may compromise the roof causing it to fall in. The victim may have already died from smoke inhalation. Or the victim may refuse to be rescued, running further into the burning house. In each of these cases Dan will fail to reach the goal of his rescue; he will miss his *skopos*, for reaching his *skopos* is not something over which he has control. But this failure does not undermine the fact that Dan is a courageous firefighter, or the fact that he was acting from the virtue of courage in his rescue attempts. Those facts depend on Dan's actions, and are not marred by a negative outcome. Dan, if he possesses all the virtues in addition to courage, will still attain the *telos* of a human life.

---

[4] "The difference between the fulfillment of the *telos* and the attainment of the *skopos* is between what lies in our power (the inner decision) and what lies outside (external goods)." A. A. Long (1967, 82)

This same distinction applies equally well when considering what we might label the "epistemic virtues." Unlike Aristotle, the Stoics do not make a clear distinction between these two types of virtues; instead they tend to focus on the character of the "sage" who is virtuous in all regards. But just as we might consider courage abstracted from the other virtues, we might also think of epistemic virtues similarly abstracted. The epistemic virtue of carefulness may motivate Elizabeth, when taking a class on the poetry of John Donne, to investigate which other poets Donne read. Thus, in the course of her studies, she takes as a *skopos* the target of believing the true answer to her question.[5] She may ask her professor about influences on Donne, after researching and discovering that her professor is a well-respected author of a biography of Donne. This research and choice of *skopos* demonstrate Elizabeth's epistemic virtue of carefulness. Despite all her care, however, she may come to have a false belief about the issue at hand. Perhaps the best historians have come to the wrong conclusion about which poets influenced Donne. Perhaps she mishears the answer her professor gives her. Or perhaps her professor lies to her, giving an incorrect list of influences that best fit his own pet theory. In any of these cases, Elizabeth will fail to reach the goal of her inquiry; she will form a relevant belief, but the belief will be false. She will miss her *skopos* of true belief, for reaching this *skopos* is not something over which she has control. But this failure does not undermine the fact that Elizabeth is careful, or the fact that she was acting from that virtue in her research. Those facts depend on Elizabeth's actions, and are not undermined by a negative outcome. Elizabeth's epistemic *telos* is believing well (as part of her overall *telos* of living well). She may still attain that *telos* despite her failure to reach the truth in a particular instance.

Thus we can see that Stoic virtues, both moral and epistemic, take the same form and that these virtues, unlike those proposed by other ancient virtue theories, involve both a *telos* and a *skopos*. The addition of the *skopos* allows a more pure or rarified approach to the *telos*, one on which virtue is sufficient for reaching that *telos*, despite failures to reach the *skopos*.

5.2. Extending Stoic Epistemic Virtues to Groups

Having highlighted what is distinctive about Stoic virtue theory, and noting that goals and targets play an essential role in the Stoic approach, we may now consider how that theory might be extended to cover groups as the agents of virtues.

---

[5] This is in contrast with Sherman and White's interpretation on which true belief is the epistemic *telos*. But their interpretation leads to problems with the Stoic view applied to epistemic virtues. See Annas (2003) for an argument that true belief is the *skopos*.

Focusing only on epistemic virtues, we can ask whether the *telos* and *skopos* of individual epistemic virtues can be extended to cover groups as well. The *skopos* of individual cognitive acts is true belief. In inquiry and subsequent belief, the target is to have a belief only if it is true. This *skopos* can clearly extend to groups. Even before considering whether groups may themselves have beliefs, we should note that groups may often have as a *skopos* true belief on the part of their members. A bowling club, in aiming to have all their players at the right bowling alley on the right evening and time, aims to produce in its members true beliefs about the location and time of the next match. Such a goal might apply to all group members; there might be other cases where the *skopos* is true belief on the part of a single member. It is best for the club as a whole for the treasurer of the bowling club to have many true beliefs about the finances of the club; this then is a reasonable *skopos* for the club as a whole to have. These examples illustrate that even groups with non-epistemic purposes will have many epistemic *skopoi* for individuals in the course of their operations. This will be even truer for groups with an explicitly epistemic purpose. The task force charged with discovering the cause of the BP oil spill has an explicitly epistemic goal. Its *skopoi* will include true beliefs on the part of its own members and on the part of the larger public. All of these examples, in aiming for true belief, not for the group, but for individuals in or out of the group, might be classified as instances of other-regarding epistemic virtues.[6] Such virtues may be exemplified by individuals as well; they are clearly the sorts of virtues that we most want from our educators.

In addition to other-regarding epistemic virtues, we might also look to extend self-regarding epistemic virtues to groups. These self-regarding epistemic virtues would take as their *skopoi* true belief on the part of the group, not just on the part of some of its members. Such a proposal requires that it is possible to have group beliefs distinct from individual belief. As noted by many authors, our ordinary ways of talking about groups recognize this as a live possibility.[7] We often ascribe beliefs to groups, and do so in a natural way that is not obviously metaphorical. This presents prima facie reason to believe that groups may have beliefs. If so, then the truth of the group belief would be an appropriate *skopos* for a group.

The *telos* of the cognitive life of an individual is the more general and long-standing disposition to believe well, that is, to believe in accordance with the epistemic virtues as part of the overall goal of living well. If a group is capable of believing and it extends through time, then it should also be capable of possessing

---

[6] A category for which Jason Kawall has argued in his (2002).
[7] For examples of group belief attributions see Margaret Gilbert (2002 and 2004) and Deborah Tollefsen (2003). For group knowledge attributions see Jennifer Lackey (2012), and List and Pettit (2011).

the disposition to believe well. This disposition in the individual cannot be retained or supported by the emotions within the Stoic view, for, as is well known, the Stoics hold that the virtuous person will avoid any emotions. Even if the motivational structure of a group is radically different than that of the individual, this difference should not stand in the way of the instantiation of this individual disposition to believe well in a larger group. Since on the Stoic picture virtue is necessary and sufficient for reaching the *telos*, and group that is disposed to believe well, thus reaching the epistemic *telos*, must also possess the epistemic virtues. Thus the Stoic model of the epistemic virtues is well-designed to be smoothly extended to apply to groups.

Of course there are potential problem that might be raised in light of this extension. I will categorize those objections into those that address the *skopoi* of groups and those that address the *telos* of groups and will address each type separately.

5.3. Objections Concerning the Group *Skopoi*

As stated above, the *skopoi* of groups on a stoic virtue epistemic model would be true beliefs, often true beliefs for the group itself, not just for its members. The target would be unreachable if groups were unable to form beliefs. K. Brad Wray has argued that groups cannot have beliefs, only acceptances. He argues this on the basis of a distinction be makes between belief and acceptance:

The foregoing analyses suggest that belief and acceptance differ in the following respects:
1. you can accept things you do not believe, whereas you cannot believe what you do not accept;
2. acceptance often results from a consideration of one's goals, and thus results from adopting a policy to pursue a particular goal;
3. belief results in a feeling, in particular, a feeling that something is true;
4. and, acceptance can be voluntary, whereas belief is not.[8]

While Wray points out all four of these features as relevant differences between acceptance and belief, his emphasis in his argument that groups cannot believe but only accept is on the second of these features. Wray's argument has been extensively addressed in responses by Gilbert and Tollefsen, who have focused on the application to groups of the second and fourth features most extensively.[9]

---

[8] Wray 2001, 325.
[9] In Gilbert's (2002) and Tollefsen's (2003)

To this debate, I would only like to add a note about the types of examples already in play in this debate. Wray's second reason to think that groups do not form beliefs, only acceptances, is that "acceptance often results from consideration of one's goals," while he claims that "[p]roper beliefs are not...tailored to our goals."[10] Wray illustrates this point by considering examples of group belief presented by Gilbert, showing why he takes them to be more properly characterized as examples of group acceptance. One salient example is that of parents deciding what curfew to give their child.[11] Though they each have a different idea of what an ideal curfew would be, they compromise to find a shared curfew they can enforce. The enforceability of the curfew is the practical goal that drives their compromise and subsequent acceptance of a shared view on curfews.

While this example does demonstrate that practical concerns can be the relevant goal driving the search for a shared view, it does not demonstrate that practical interests are always the goal sought when a group comes to a shared view. For example, we might consider Gilbert's example of a group of scientists who come to the group belief that "their subfield is moving in a fruitful direction."[12] In such a case, while practical concerns are served in the coordination of action by the group, a goal that is also relevant is that the group only hold this view if it is true; it is neither epistemologically nor practically desirable (in the long run) for the group to pursue a subfield if it is not fruitful. Thus the epistemic goals of a group can determine the claims that they accept, as well as their practical goals. But accepting a proposition in light of purely epistemic goals does not seem to disqualify it from the status of belief.

This point about the epistemic goals of groups can be made without reference to any of the specific features of the Stoic account of epistemic virtues and of the structure of belief. However once we introduce the Stoic notions of *telos* and *skopos* we can illustrate this point even more clearly. Notice that on all ancient virtue theories the actions and beliefs of an individual are thought to have a single shared goal—the *telos* of human life. On the Stoic virtue theory each action and belief also has its own *skopos*. Each action will aim at bringing about a state in the world, while each belief will aim at being true. Since these are *skopoi*, they are differently related to evaluation than other types of goals might be; as shown above, failure to reach one's *skopos* does not reflect negatively on the act or the actor. But this subtlety of relation does not undermine the fact that the *skopos* is a goal. Thus, contra

---

[10] Wray 2001, 325.
[11] Example from Gilbert 1994, explained in Wray 2001.
[12] Example from Gilbert 1994, explained in Wray 2001.

Wray, proper beliefs are tailored to our epistemic goals. Being tailored to a goal does not disqualify a cognitive state from being a belief.

In addition to noting the particular points within Wray's objections, we should also notice that the Stoics will come to the following general conclusion: Any group that is organized in such a way that it can take group action is in a position to have group beliefs.[13] While this conclusion might seem at first controversial, it follows directly from the overall Stoic picture of agency on which our beliefs and actions are both equally the result of our own choices and both equally reflect our characters. Thus an exploration of the Stoic model of agency is needed to reach this general conclusion about group belief.

5.4. Stoic Epistemic Agency and a Response to Wray

A natural place to begin is by exploring the agency the Stoics find in perceptual belief. According to the Stoics, an instance of perception produces in us an impression. The term impression comes from the impression that a seal makes in wax.[14] A clear perceptual impression captures all the (relevant) details of the object perceived, just as a clear wax impression captures all the (relevant) details of the seal.[15] However, the wax metaphor might be misleading in that the contents of the perceptual impressions are not unconceptualized physical shapes; rather the content of the impression is already conceptualized and perceptual impressions take the form of a *lekton* (a sayable), having the form of a complete sentence.[16] This conceptual content allows the impression to be a single step in the cognitive process. One does not perceive then conceptualize; conception is part of perception. Thus rather than having the impression of a set of shapes and colors which I must then classify and understand as an object, I have the perceptual impression of a cup of

---

[13] Note that this formulation focuses on actions taken as a group, not actions in which members of a group participate independently. Even if the actions of A, B, and C taken together result in an outcome, it will not count as a group action unless the actions of the individuals are part of a plan or course of action chosen by the group.

[14] "For, just as the seals on rings always stamp all their markings precisely on the wax, so those who have cognition of objects should notice all their peculiarities." Sextus Empiricus, *Against the professors* 7.247–52 (SVF 2.65). Also see Annas (1992) for a more complete explanation.

[15] The Stoics were engaged in an internal debate about whether all details or only the relevant details were included in the (cognitive) impression. But this distinction only makes a difference when we move from the general structure of perception to our epistemic evaluation of that perception. The insistence that all details of the thing perceived are contained in the impression is forced on the Stoics through their debates with the Academics and their joint search for certainty.

[16] "They [the Stoics] say that a 'sayable' is what subsists in accordance with a rational impression, and a rational impression is one in which the content of the impression can be exhibited in language." Sextus Empiricus, *Against the* professors 8.70 (SVF 2.187). See also Annas 1992, 76ff.

coffee sitting on the table to my right. As a result, the contents of my impressions will be limited by both my conceptual and perceptual resources. Some impressions will be more expert than others.[17] Julia Annas gives the example of perceiving a silver birch; if I do not have the concept of a silver birch I may not have such an impression. Rather I might only have the impression of a birch. However, conceptual resources are not sufficient to provide more detailed impressions; I must also have the perceptual resources to apply those concepts. A bird-watching expert who has forgotten her glasses will be unable to identify the species of a bird by sight; she may only have the impression that a bird is on the tree before her. Over time or through the use of perceptual aids we may improve our capacities to form more detailed impressions; we can make our impression more expert. But our control over the detail and precision of our impressions, while present, is limited.

What we do control completely is our assent to impressions. The birdwatcher lacking her glasses may be tempted to identify a bird as a ruby throated warbler. That is, she may have the (perhaps indistinct) perceptual impression that the bird before her is a ruby-throated warbler. However, noting that she currently has limited eyesight, and that she is identifying the bird primarily by its distinctive markings, the epistemically virtuous bird watcher will not assent to that impression; instead she will withhold belief on the issue.[18] Refusing to assent to the impression in compromised circumstances marks off the epistemically virtuous; the capacity to assent marks off humans from other animals:

"A rational animal, however, in addition to its impressionistic nature, has reason which passes judgment on impressions, rejecting some of these and accepting others, in order that the animal may be guided accordingly."[19]

This judgment is not something that follows our beliefs, checking on some of them after they have been established as beliefs; the judgment is what turns impressions into beliefs. It is also the one thing that is thought to be entirely under our control:

"Fittingly enough, the one thing which the gods have placed in our power is the one of supreme importance, the correct use of impressions. The other things they have not placed in our power."[20]

Since assent is the one thing that is in our power, it must be the ultimate source for all our agency, including our epistemic agency. As with impressions, this should not be thought of as two steps, but as a single step. My assenting to the impression

---

[17] Julia Annas 1992, 82ff.
[18] "Suspension of judgment is the wise man's response to every case where his impressions fail to discriminate objects with the requisite clarity and distinctness." Long and Sedley (1987), 252.
[19] Origen, *On principles* 3.1.2–3 (SVF 2.988) in Long and Sedley (1987).
[20] Epictetus, *Discourses* 1.1.7–12.

does not lead to my believing; my assenting to an impression constitutes my believing the content of that impression.

Not all impressions to which I may assent are perceptual impressions. In addition there are non-perceptual impressions and impulsive impressions. Remaining in the realm of belief, we should address non-perceptual impressions first. Since beliefs on the Stoic account are just assents to impressions, there is a need for a category of non-perceptual impressions to allow belief about absent objects and abstract objects such as numbers. These impressions will not come from outside through our perceptual capacities, but will be generated internally as we imagine or consider possibilities. Thus, I might wonder if it is raining in New Orleans today. In so doing I am considering the non-perceptual impression that it is raining in New Orleans. I have the capacity to assent to this impression, but lacking any evidence about the weather in Louisiana, the epistemically virtuous move here would be to refrain from assenting to this impression.

Assenting to either perceptual or non-perceptual impressions constitutes belief. But assenting to a third kind of impression, the impulsive impression, constitutes action.

"According to Chrysippus, the impulse of man is reason prescribing action to him."[21]

An impulsive impression presents a course of action as something that is to-be-done or something that is appropriate. The Stoics say that the content of the impression here is an incomplete *lekton*, taking the infinitive form of a predicate: e.g. to walk, to eat, to fight. Thus assenting to such an impression is assenting to walk, eat, or fight. But the assent is not separate from the action; the assent constitutes the action insofar as action is carried out in our own minds or souls. Thus the action of drinking my coffee is, for the Stoics, constituted entirely by my assent to the impulsive impression "to drink this coffee" or more explicitly "to drink this coffee is appropriate." Thus I count as having performed the action of coffee drinking even if the cup is stuck to the table and I cannot lift it to my mouth. While this may seem like an odd way to understand an action, Julia Annas points out that it has an advantage in that it "... locates action where responsibility is."[22] Insofar as we want an account of agency to track and explain our intuitions about responsibility, the Stoic picture has an advantage. If I slip and spill my hot coffee all over you, you will not be pleased with me, but you would certainly judge me in a different light than if I had assented to the impulsive impression that "to pour coffee on you is

---

[21] Plutarch, *On Stoic self-contradictions* 1037F (SVF 3.175) in Long and Sedley (1987).
[22] Annas 1992, 100.

appropriate" and poured it intentionally. Thus the Stoic notion of action captures the part of the action that is an expression of our agency and which is to be appropriately evaluated. It brings focus on the part of our action that is up-to-us, the assent to the impulsive impression.

As we grow and mature our impulsive impressions can be improved and honed just as our perceptual impressions are developed. A young child may have an impulsive impression to take candy from others whenever he sees it. As adults we rarely have impulsive impressions of this sort. Just as we can learn to avoid common mistakes in reasoning, we can learn to avoid common inappropriate impulsive impressions. But, as with perceptual impressions, we are not in complete control of our impulsive impressions. Thus, even the sage may feel a pang of jealousy upon seeing a friend's new lavish house.[23] The sage may not be able to stop himself from having this impulsive impression. However it is his reaction to that impression on which he ought to be judged. If he rejects it, and takes no jealous action, then he is acting in the correct and virtuous manner.

By working through the Stoic account of agency in belief and in action we can now see that the two are perfectly parallel for the Stoics. We are responsible for our beliefs and action in the same way; in both cases it is the assent to the impression that is up to us, and on which we ought to be evaluated. This establishes the general claim that we were aiming to provide an argument for: Any group that is organized in such a way that it can take action is in a position to have beliefs. For any group that can take action must have the capacity to assent to an impulsive impression and having that capacity to assent to an impulsive impression must also be able to assent to a non-impulsive impression. In the case of groups those non-impulsive impressions will most likely take the form of assents to non-perceptual impressions (depending on whether groups can have perceptual impressions). But even if we deny that groups have anything like a perceptual capacity, they may still consider and assent to non-perceptual impressions. Thus, even if groups cannot have a sort of perceptual belief, they are still capable of having beliefs in general.

After establishing this general claim, we can also go further and consider the details of the second, third, and fourth grounds on which Wray denies that groups can form beliefs. The second reason given is that unlike acceptances, proper beliefs are not "tailored to our goals." As we have seen above, this is questionable on the Stoic approach; they hold that assent is always given in light of a goal (or goals) so

---

[23] These states are called *propatheiai* to distinguish them from the impulses (particularly the emotional impulses) that we act on. See Annas 1992, 110. See also Gellius 19.1.17–18 (Epictetus fr. 9) in Long and Sedley (1967).

acceptance and belief as distinguished by Wray would have the same goal-directed structure and the distinction between them would evaporate.

If, on the other hand, Wray were to insist that beliefs, in contrast to acceptances, never result from the consideration of our goals (including our epistemic goals) then his conception of belief would be closer to the Stoic's account of an impression than to their account of beliefs. This connection might be further motivated by his identification of belief with that which is involuntary and acceptance with that which is voluntary. On the Stoic view, impressions (particularly perceptual impressions) may arise in us unbidden and in conflict with our considered judgment. Though we can develop our capacities to have more detailed and correct perceptual impressions, we can never develop full control over them. Even the sage has the impression that an attacking army is worthy of fear; the sage simply refuses to assent to that impression. In the perceptual realm this "stickiness" of impressions can be illustrated by perceptual and cognitive illusions. Confronted with the Mueller-Lyer drawing, even the most distinguished psychologist of perception will still have the perceptual impression that the lines represented are of unequal length. However such a psychologist (or anyone who carefully measures the two lines) will not assent to that perceptual impression, and may instead assent to the impressions (here non-perceptual) that the lines are of equal length. This pattern of assent is driven by the goal of obtaining truth and avoiding error. Thus if all goal-directed cognitive activity is to count as acceptance (as per Wray), assent to impressions would count as acceptances while the impressions themselves would count as beliefs, for the impressions are not goal-directed or voluntary.

The important question here is not which state really deserves the title of "belief," but, rather, taking a step back and looking at the larger picture, which cognitive states (of the individual or of the group) are the appropriate target of epistemic evaluation. This is particularly relevant in the context of understanding epistemic virtues, but is also relevant if we limit ourselves to focusing on instances of justified belief and knowledge. Which state then should be the target of evaluation? The Stoics have a clear answer; it must be the assent to the impression, not the impression itself. Even from outside of the Stoic approach, it should be clear that epistemic evaluation should apply to our assents/acceptances rather than to our impressions/beliefs. In the case of visual illusions, we should count as epistemically exemplary a person who, either understanding the mechanism of the illusion or carefully measuring and comparing the lines, rejects the original perceptual impression. It would be excessive to criticize that person or evaluate her as epistemically negligent for not being able to resist the perceptual illusion; it is too much to ask epistemic agents to rewire their perceptual capacities. This is not only true when we are all similarly limited, but also (perhaps even more clearly) when we differ in our capacities. The colorblind person is not to be epistemically criticized for having limited and misleading perceptual impressions; it is the way that he responds to these impressions that should be evaluated. Thus, regardless of how they are labeled, it is assent to an impression that is the proper target of epistemic evaluation and is the state with which we should be concerned. In epistemically evaluating groups we should then be concerned to ask whether groups have the capacity to assent to impressions. As a result, even what Wray calls "acceptance" in a group is sufficient for that group to possess a relevantly epistemically evaluable state.

Turning to the third distinction given by Wray, he claims that belief "results in a feeling...that something is true." Acceptance does not; and this is a further reason to think that groups cannot have beliefs, only acceptances. There are two ways that this "feeling" might be interpreted. It might be closely identified with an impression, or it might be instead identified with a commitment to the content of that impression. If a feeling is simply an impression, then it can easily be accommodated within the Stoic framework. All beliefs are the result of an impression, so they would all involve a feeling; but so too would acceptance of that same impression. If instead we think of feeling as a commitment to the content of an impression, it would require an assent to that impression. But, to qualify as a feeling, over and above our ordinary assents, it would seem to require a kind of commitment that one is reluctant to change in the face of contrary evidence. If so, then this sort of feeling falls into the category of emotions; states which the Stoics warn us against having. The problem with emotions is that they involve an "excessive impulse" such that assent to that impression is disobedient to the dictates of reason.[24] If this is the sort of feeling that Wray is highlighting, then lacking that sort of feeling is a desirable state. Thus, depending on how we interpret Wray's third distinction, either all belief and acceptance results in feeling, or feeling is to be avoided in both. Either way, feeling disappears as a distinction for grounding the denial of beliefs to groups.

The fourth and final distinction in Wray is that "acceptance is voluntary while belief is not." The reasoning behind this claim is presumably that acceptance is more like action than it is like belief. This, taken together with the claim that action is voluntary and belief is not, would lead to the conclusion that acceptance is voluntary (and perhaps explicitly chosen with particular goals in mind, see above). Even if one were to allow that acceptance is distinct from belief, and agree that acceptance is more like action than like belief, the conclusion does not follow unless action is more voluntary than belief. But, on the Stoic account belief and action are equally voluntary. We have seen above how belief and

---

[24] Annas 1992, 105.

action are strongly parallel on the Stoic account. This gives us *prima facie* reason to think that they are equally voluntary. But there are examples that seem to show that this is not the case. If I choose to, I can raise my arm right now. But I cannot similarly bring myself to believe that I am currently dancing the tango (without getting up and dancing the tango). The tension between these two examples seems to show that our voluntary control over our actions is stronger than our voluntary control over our beliefs. Could Wray use examples like this to re-establish the claim that belief is less voluntary than action (specifically the action of acceptance)?

The force of such examples will be undermined, however, if we are careful to consider the degree of voluntary control the Stoics think we have over all our expressions of agency and to compare only those cases that are similarly situated with respect to our moral and epistemic virtues. First, it might be thought that the Stoics ought to allow that belief is involuntary. For they hold that "everything that happens happens through fate."[25] Yet they also hold that assent is "within our power." How then can they reconcile these two claims? This is possible once we see that agency and control are compatible with determinism. For the Stoic version of fate is not a model of an intervening force that interrupts regular causal patterns; rather fate is constituted by that causal pattern. Future events are fated only in the sense that future events are determined by past events. So this is a deterministic conception of fate. The real question then is how it is possible for things to be under our control if we live in a deterministic world. The Stoic answer is best understood through their metaphor of a cylinder rolling down a hill:

"Just as...if you push a stone cylinder on steeply sloping ground, you have produced the cause and beginning of its forward motion, but soon it rolls forward not because you are still making it do so, but because such are its form and smooth-rolling shape—so too the order, rationale and necessity of fate sets in motion the actual types of causes and their beginnings, but the deliberative impulses of our minds and our actual actions are controlled by our own individual will and intellect."[26]

Even though the cylinder cannot begin moving on its own, and, once started, cannot stop itself, the rolling of cylinder is still an expression of its cylindrical nature. The rolling is under the control of the cylinder in the sense that it is determined by the cylinder's nature. Similarly for humans and their natures. The virtuous person who is confronted by someone who needs assistance will (automatically, we say) try to help that person. The action of rendering assistance is thus determined by the impression of the person in need in conjunction with the character of the

---

[25] Cicero, *On fate 20–1*, in Long and Sedley (1987).
[26] Gellius 7.2.6–13 (SVF 2.1000) in Long and Sedley (1987).

virtuous person. Dan, the firefighter, when confronted by the person in the burning house will automatically decide to try to rescue that person. If Dan were not a virtuous person, he might not make that choice. But given that he is virtuous, he could not have done otherwise. It is this tight connection between our character and the actions we take which makes those acts a good indicator of our underlying character. Virtuous people are not free to act viciously, but this is not a freedom or degree of control that would be desirable.

The degree of control granted us by our character is available to us both in the realm of action and the realm of belief. Why then do we see a disparity between common actions and beliefs? The appearance of disparity here is the result of comparing morally neutral actions with epistemically vicious beliefs. The act of raising one's hand is morally neutral; at least it is so in the sort of cases normally considered. Raising one's hand in the circumstances imagined is not in violation of any moral virtue. As a result a person with a virtuous character may choose to perform that action. But the situation is different for actions that are not morally neutral, and specifically those that violate the dictates of the moral virtues. Imagine the virtuous person who has just rushed to the scene of a car accident and is using her hand to apply pressure to a wounded victim who will clearly bleed out if she reduces that pressure. Can this virtuous person choose to raise her hand? The Stoic answer here is that she cannot; her perception of the needs of the victim along with her virtuous character determine that she will keep her had in its position and applying pressure. This limitation should not be surprising when raising one's hand is no longer a morally neutral act.

To properly understand the control we have over our beliefs, we should be careful to compare the neutral with the neutral and the vicious with the vicious. In light of the evidence that I am sitting at my computer, I cannot make myself believe that I am currently tango dancing. If I were able to do so I would be convincing myself to believe in clear violation of the epistemic virtues. Believing against all the evidence is epistemically vicious; so it is no surprise that the epistemically virtuous person cannot do this. But I can easily imagine myself tango dancing. This kind of imagination is no violation of the epistemic virtues (unless I spend all day so imagining and hence miss opportunities to achieve my other epistemic goals). My control over my imagination is then similar to my control over my morally neutral actions. I can do both at will. When we take virtue into account we see that the sort of examples regularly considered do not show any lack of parallel between belief and action. Thus even granting that acceptance is similar to action will give us no reason to draw a sharp distinction between acceptance and belief, and certainly will give us no reason to think that groups may not form beliefs.

5.5. An Objection Concerning the Group *Telos*

Having shown that groups, as well as individuals, may have the epistemic *skopos* of true belief, we can now turn to consider the ways that the group's *telos* may be similar to the *telos* of the individual. Within the ancient Greek approaches to virtue, although there is disagreement about the details of what exactly makes up our *telos*, there is agreement that there is a unified *telos* of human life which is shared between all people. This unity might seem to be in stark contrast with the *telos* of groups if we look for the *telos* of a group in that group's stated purpose. The purposes of different groups are often freely chosen, stated explicitly (e.g. in a mission statement), and can be wildly variable. The purpose of a group can be practical, moral, or epistemic, or a mixture of all these. In addition, groups are formed with the intention of working together for very short or very long durations. As a result it may appear that there is no limit on the purposes for which a group may be formed, and hence no unified *telos* for groups. What *telos* could be shared by a bowling team that meets once a week for years and only aims to win the trophy and an ad hoc committee that meets only once to uncover the truth about whether procedures have been correctly followed? One has a long duration, changing membership, and a practical purpose, while the other has a brief duration, an epistemic purpose, and a determined roster. What can these two groups have in common?

To answer this question about groups we must first specify the degree to which various good human lives must be similar. On an Aristotelian account, there is a high degree of similarity postulated. Despite the apparent diversity of lives discussed in the *Nicomachean Ethics*, in Book Ten Aristotle reveals his conviction that there is a single best type of human life, the life of contemplation. Thus on an Aristotelian account of the virtues, the *telos* of human lives is highly unified. The Stoic conception of the good life, on the other hand, is not one on which there is a single best life for everyone. Rather each person comes to make the choice about how they should live only after they are part of a community and family and often once they have chosen an occupation and taken on other commitments.[27] These commitments influence what a good life for each individual will look like. Epictetus stresses that:

"If, furthermore, you are on the council of any city, you should remember that you are a councilor; if a youth, a youth; if an old man, an old man. For each of these names, if rightly considered, points to the acts appropriate to it." [28]

---

[27] Annas 2002.   [28] Epictetus *Discourses* II.x.

Thus there can be no single good life that is the standard for all people. The good life for a youth will be different from the good life for an old man. The good life for a doctor will be different from the good life for a boat builder. And the good life for an Athenian may be very different from the good life for a Spartan.

But this variety in good human lives does not entail the lack of a unified human *telos* in the Stoic approach. On the contrary, the Stoic account of agency gives us a framework in which to clearly express this unified *telos*. We can first see the unification between the moral and epistemic virtues within a life. The moral virtues, like courage explored above, are constituted by the development and exercise of a disposition to act appropriately in difficult situations. The morally virtuous person will be one who acts well in a variety of circumstances. But acting well on the Stoic picture is just assenting well over the range of impulsive impressions. Compare this to the epistemic virtues. The epistemically virtuous person will be one who believes well in a variety of circumstances. But believing well on the Stoic picture is just assenting well over a range of non-impulsive impressions. Thus the overall virtuous person is simply one who assents well.[29] Since the Stoics hold that virtue is sufficient for both happiness and the achievement of the human *telos*, they will conclude that the human *telos* is being disposed to assent well. This *telos* is perfectly unified across the distinction between the moral and the epistemic and it is also perfectly unified across individuals—the *telos* of all human lives is being disposed to assent well.

The unified *telos* suggested here is still compatible with living a variety of different kinds of lives. The youth will be presented with different situations in which to assent well than those faced by the old man. The Athenian will be assenting well in the context of his Athenian society, while the Spartan will be assenting well in the context of her Spartan society. This contrast can be even more clearly seen in the case of commitments that we have taken on voluntarily. The doctor will focus her assents on impressions dealing with medical topics, while the boat builder will consider, and assent to, impressions about wood types and oar shapes. No one person can assent to every possible impression; to do so would be to believe everything and to do everything. This is not even possible (for humans) if we limit

---

[29] The formulation is, of course, just a place holder for more substantive accounts of exactly what is required acting and believing well. The Stoics will say that acting well is constituted by never choosing a preferred indifferent over virtue and that believing well is constituted by only assenting to what they call "cognitive" impressions (those which cannot be mistaken). This epistemic standard is quite high (in response to skeptical concerns) and I have argued elsewhere (2012, 2013) that a neo-stoic approach should accept a lower epistemic standard. But the details of the standards proposed here are not relevant to this overall approach, so long as the epistemic and moral standards offered for believing and acting well require only that we do what is "in our power."

ourselves to assenting well. Rather, we will all face different impressions (impulsive and non-impulsive) to which we may give our assents, and we each naturally focus our attentions on a different range of impressions in the course of our individual lives with distinct interests. Thus there are a wide range of lives within which people may achieve their shared human *telos* of assenting well.

But the variety of good lives does not entail that just any life is a good life. There are also bad ways to be a youth, doctor, or Athenian, and these will involve assenting poorly. So while our choice of life interests and our socially determined contexts have a degree of variability, we must still assent well within those contexts. Thus the requirement of the human *telos* is not meaningless and will not permit all lives to be equally good. In particular, there may be various life choices and given social roles that cannot be lived well. If one is a thief (even from a family of thieves) the correct course of action is to give up thieving, not to try to live the best life for a thief. Since the very nature of thieving involves unnecessarily harming other people, this social role will require assenting poorly; there is no way for such a life to conform to the human *telos*.

What then of the *telos* of groups? When we look at the stated reason for which groups are convened, it may seem that there can be no unified *telos* for groups. But, as we have seen, diversity is compatible with a unified *telos*. Notice that we have been focusing on groups that are sufficiently organized to take group actions; on the Stoic picture these groups must then be capable of assenting to impressions. (It is from this capacity to assent that we have demonstrated that any group complex enough to act will also be able to believe.) And if a group is capable of assenting to impressions, it must also be capable of assenting well. Thus the *telos* of the group can be identical with the *telos* of the individual; both have the *telos* of being disposed to assent well. Of course assenting well is rarely (perhaps never) the stated aim of a group. But this does not prevent the disposition to assent well from being the *telos* of groups. For a *telos* is not freely chosen, it follows from the possession of particular (and distinctive) capacities. It is for this reason that we can say that the *telos* of a knife is being disposed to cut well, even though there is no sense in which the knife chooses this *telos*. Being constructed so as to cut gives the knife its *telos*. Similarly, being organized so as to assent gives the group its *telos*. Note that this *telos* may (as in the case of the individual person) conflict with the goals that the group sets for itself. A group may come together with the intention of becoming an expert band of thieves. But in forming a group capable of assenting, they have made themselves susceptible to the criticism that they are necessarily assenting poorly in the very act that constitutes the purpose of the group. Thus the group ought to give up its intentions and disband or transform into a group with another (more virtuous) intention. This limitation affects groups whose stated purpose involves (explicitly or tacitly) harming others in any way, morally, practically or epistemically.[30]

Finally, we should note that the group *telos* of being disposed to assent well does not depend on anything outside of the control of the group; this makes it a suitable *telos* in the Stoic framework.[31] At the same time the stated purposes of a group are often outside the control of the group; the bowling team may fail to win their coveted trophy and the ad hoc committee may be misled into believing that procedures are being followed (when they are not). Both of these purposes fail the Stoic criterion for being a *telos*; they are better characterized as the *skopos* of the group. Assent is the only thing that is entirely within our control; as a result so it is the only appropriate *telos* for either the individual or the group.

Thus the final objection to extending the epistemic virtues to cover groups has been dealt with. Both the *skopos* and the *telos* of the epistemic virtues of individuals can be extended to the epistemic virtues of groups. The *skopos* of true belief for the group is one member of the range of self-regarding and other-regarding *skopoi* of the epistemically virtuous group. Since belief, on the Stoic model, is just assent to non-impulsive impressions, any group that is capable of group action (through assenting to impulsive impressions) will also be capable of group belief. These group beliefs will be neither more nor less voluntary than the beliefs of individuals, and will play the same role in the group epistemic virtues as beliefs of individuals play in individual epistemic virtues; true belief is only the *skopos* of the virtuous person or group. The *telos* must be under the control of the individual or group; the only candidate is assents to impressions. Being disposed to believe well (whether for the group individual) will be one part of the general *telos* of being disposed to assent well. Thus all the elements of the Stoic model of the epistemic virtues can be extended to allow for the possibility of epistemically virtuous groups.[32]

References

Annas, Julia. (1994) *Hellenistic Philosophy of Mind*. Oakland: University of California Press.
——. (1995) *The Morality of Happiness*. Oxford: Oxford University Press.

---

[30] The kind of epistemic harm I have in mind here includes the concept of epistemic injustice developed by Miranda Fricker in her (2007).

[31] The requirement that our *telos* not be outside of our control leads to the formulation of *being disposed to* assent well. Even the having of impressions is not required to satisfy this formulation of our overall *telos*, only a disposition to respond appropriately to possible impressions.

[32] My thanks for feedback on this paper from the audience at the 2013 Bled Epistemology Conference, and for the extensive and extremely helpful comments on an earlier draft of this chapter from Jennifer Lackey and an anonymous reviewer.

——. (2002) "My Station and its Duties: Ideals and the Social Embeddedness of Virtue." *Proceedings of the Aristotelian Society 102*: 109–23.
——. (2003) The Structure of Virtue. In *Intellectual Virtue: Perspectives from Ethics and Epistemology*, ed. Michael DePaul, pp.15–33. Oxford: Clarendon Press.
Cicero, Marcus Tullius (1997) *On Moral Ends*, edited by Julia Annas and Desmond M Clarke. Cambridge: Cambridge University Press.
Epictetus. 1995. *The Discourses, the Handbook, Fragments of Epictetus*. Edited by Christopher Gill, Translated by Robin Hard. London: Everyman.
Fricker, Miranda. 2007. *Epistemic Injustice: Power and the Ethics of Knowing*. Oxford: Oxford University Press.
Gilbert, Margaret. (1994) Remarks on Collective Belief, in F. Schmitt (ed.), *Socializing Epistemology: The Social Dimensions of Knowledge*, pp.111–34. Rowman and Littlefield, Lanham, MD
——. (2002) "Belief and acceptance as features of groups." *Protosociology 16*: 35–69.
——. (2004) "Collective Epistemology." *Episteme 1*: 95–107.
Inwood, Brad (1986) "Goal and Target in Stoicism." *Journal of Philosophy 83*: 547–56.
Kawall, Jason (2002) "Other-Regarding Epistemic Virtues." *Ratio 15*: 257–75.
List, Christian and Philip Pettit (2011) *Group Agency: The Possibility, Design, and Status of Corporate Agents*. Oxford University Press
Lackey, Jennifer (2012) Group Knowledge Attributions. In *Knowledge Ascriptions*, edited by Jessica Brown and Mikkel Gerken. Oxford: Oxford University Press.
Long, A. A. (1967) "Carneades and the Stoic *Telos*." *Phronesis, XII*: 59–89.
Long, A. A. and D. N. Sedley. (1987) *The Hellenistic Philosophers: Vol. 1*. Cambridge: Cambridge University Press.
Sherman, Nancy, and Heath White. (2003) Intellectual Virtue: Emotions, Luck, and the Ancients. In *Intellectual Virtue: Perspectives from Ethics and Epistemology*, edited by Michael DePaul and Linda Zagzebski, pp. 34–53. Oxford: Clarendon Press.
Tollefsen, Deborah. (2003) "Rejecting Rejectionism." *Protosociology 18-19*: 389–408.
Wray, K. Brad (2001) "Collective Belief and Acceptance." *Synthese 129*: 319–33.
——. (2003) "What Really Divides Gilbert and the Rejectionists?" *Protosociology 18-19*: 363–77.
Wright, Sarah (2012) "Wisdom, Truth and the Stoics: How Boots Befooled The King." *Acta Analytica 27*: 113–26.
——. (2013) "A Neo-Stoic Approach to Epistemic Agency." *Philosophical Issues 23*: 262–75.

6

Disagreement and Public Controversy

David Christensen

> Unfortunately for the good sense of mankind, the fact of their fallibility is far from carrying the weight in their practical judgment which is always allowed to it in theory; for while everyone well knows himself to be fallible, few think it necessary to take any precautions against their own fallibility, or admit the supposition that any opinion of which they feel very certain may be one of the examples of the error to which they acknowledge themselves to be liable.
>
> —J.S. Mill, On Liberty

J.S Mill's famous defense of free speech makes several arguments, but one of the most interesting springs from his appreciation of human fallibility. This strand of argument is straightforwardly epistemic: Mill would have us treat the opinions and arguments of those who disagree with us as an epistemic resource, which furnishes us with a means for taking precautions against our own fallibility.

More recent discussion of disagreement in mainstream epistemology has not been aimed at drawing conclusions in political philosophy, but at better understanding what sort of purely epistemic role disagreement should play. Most of the debate has revolved around the question of what, if any, effect the disagreement of others should have on the confidence with which one holds one's own beliefs. (Answers to this question may be called "Conciliatory" to the extent that they hold that disagreement often requires us to be less confident in our beliefs than we would be absent the disagreement. They may be called "Steadfast" to the extent that they deny this.) But in this literature, as in Mill, the epistemic significance of disagreement is often tied to considerations of our epistemic fallibility.

Many recent papers on disagreement open by mentioning issues about which there is considerable public controversy; examples from philosophy, morality, politics, and history are commonly cited. But while the epistemic implications of disagreement for issues of public controversy are part of what gives the issue its interest, many papers quickly move on to focus on very simple, artificial cases involving just two people. It's not that participants in the debate are mainly interested in these examples: in fact, people on opposite sides often agree about whether, in a given example, conciliation is called for. What they're interested in, and what they disagree about, is what sort of reasons for changing belief might be provided by the disagreement of others in simple cases. The hope is that by understanding the rational response to disagreement in the simple cases, we'll get some insight into what the rational response is in the more complex ones involving the public controversies among groups that give the issue much of its urgency.

In this chapter, I'd like to focus on a particular theoretical approach to disagreement: a kind of conciliatory approach that sees disagreement as often having important implications for rational belief. And I'd like to look at how this view might apply to public group controversies in philosophy and in politics. It turns out that though this approach springs from the same motivations as Mill's approach to free speech, it yields results in many cases that are opposite to those Mill emphasized. I'll also argue that the appeal of conciliating epistemically will often be stronger for group disagreements than for artificial two-person cases. Finally, I'll look at some ways in which reacting rationally to disagreements of the sort often found in politics can be a particularly difficult and nuanced matter.

6.1. Independence-Based Conciliationism

Having said all that, let me set up the position I want to discuss by reference to a pair of particularly simple artificial examples.

Music Contest: I'm attending a contest for high-school musicians. After hearing all the performers, and becoming quite convinced that Kirsten's performance was significantly better than Aksel's, I hear the man next to me express just the opposite opinion. But then I find out that he is Aksel's father.

Here, it seems that I need not revise my belief much at all.

Mental Math: I've been regularly going to dinner with my friend for many years; we always divide the bill evenly, tip 20%, and figure our shares in our heads. We almost always agree, but when we've differed, we've checked with a calculator, and have been right equally often. Tonight seems typical: neither of us seems especially tired or alert; neither has had more than the usual wine or coffee. I divide the bill and become confident that our shares are $43. But my friend announces that she got $45.

Here, it seems that I should become much less confident of my belief about my share of the bill. And I think this is true even if, this time, I'm the one who happens to be correct.

In the first case, it seems that the reason I need not worry about the other person's disagreement is that I have good reasons for thinking him less likely than I am to have reached the correct opinion on the disputed matter: I know that parents are disposed to overrate the achievements of their children. But, one might ask, don't I also have reason in the Mental Math case to think my friend less likely than I to have come up with the right answer? Why can't I say, "Well, despite our equally good track records, I have reason to think that, on this particular occasion, she's the one who made the mistake. After all, as the evidence shows, my share of the bill is $43, and she believes otherwise!"?

It seems clear that this last sort of response to disagreement is illegitimate. To invoke it would intuitively amount to begging the question—which is raised by my friend's disagreement—of who made the mistake.

But if I cannot downgrade my friend's opinion in the restaurant by relying on my belief about my share of the bill, how could it be reasonable to rely on my (also fallible) belief about parental bias patterns in downgrading the other man's opinion in the Music Contest case? I may, after all, be even more fallible in my opinions on parenting psychology than I am in my opinions on restaurant check division. The answer, it seems to me, depends on the *focus* of the potential doubt about my reasoning prompted by disagreement. In relying on my belief about my share of the bill to dismiss disagreement in the Mental Math case, I rely on the very bit of reasoning—my calculation of my share from the total amount of the check—which the disagreement threatens to cast doubt on. But in relying on my general psychological beliefs to dismiss disagreement in the Music Contest example, I do not rely on my particular assessments of Kirsten's and Aksel's performances.

This suggests that in trying to give a general theoretical account of the rational response to disagreement, we'll need to take into account the extent to which our assessment of the epistemic significance of another's disagreement is *independent* of the reasoning which that disagreement may call into question. The following (admittedly vague) account captures the basic idea. Because I think it has Conciliationist consequences, I'll call it Independence-Based Conciliationism (IBC):

(**IBC**): In responding to disagreement, one should assess the epistemic credentials of the parties involved in a way that's independent of one's own initial reasoning about the matter in question. One should moderate one's (pre-disagreement) belief to the extent that one has epistemically strong, dispute-independent reason to think that those who disagree are well-informed and likely to have reasoned correctly from their evidence, as compared with those who agree.

This formulation is vague and highly simplified, to avoid delving into various complications I wish to avoid here.[1] But to fix ideas, let us interpret it so that in disagreements between equally-confident disputants, when I have very strong dispute-independent reason to think that those who disagree with me are equally well-informed and equally likely to have reasoned correctly as those who agree with me, then I should be much less confident in the disputed proposition than I'd otherwise be, perhaps withholding belief. Note that the view requires conciliation when I have strong positive, dispute-independent reasons for granting epistemic respect to those with whom I disagree, not whenever I lack dispute-independent reasons for thinking less well of them (the importance of this will emerge below).

IBC helps explain why we can dismiss disagreement in the Music Contest case, but not in Mental Math. In prohibiting one from brushing off disagreement by using the very reasoning that's potentially put into question by the others' dissent, IBC seems to capture our sense that in responding to disagreement, we must avoid begging the question of whether we've made a mistake. Obeying IBC thus essentially gives us a way—to use Mill's terms—of taking precautions against our own fallibility.

6.2. IBC and Group Disagreements: Controversies in Philosophy

Naturally enough, many philosophers writing on disagreement are interested in whether the rampant disagreement we seem to see in most areas of philosophy should occasion widespread retreat from confident belief. The "seem" here is to acknowledge that some apparent disagreement in philosophy may be only apparent, the result of people talking past one another (see Sosa (2010), Chalmers (2011)). It seems reasonable to assume, however, that there is enough genuine disagreement in philosophy to make the question of how to respond to real disagreements an important one, even if it will sometimes not be obvious whether a given disagreement is substantive or verbal.[2]

In some ways, the case for conciliation in philosophy seems weaker than the case of conciliation in the Mental Math case. The latter case features exact parity

---

[1] I've tried to do a little better in (Christensen 2011). Some other papers explicitly supporting independence-based responses to disagreement include Christensen (2007), Elga (2007), and Kornblith (2010).

[2] Thanks to an anonymous reader for pointing out the need for making this point.

of informedness: we can both see the total bill perfectly clearly. And it features incredibly strong evidence of equal reliability, in the exact type of reasoning involved in the disputed issue: we have settled a long series of past check-dividing disagreements with a calculator, and we're equally prone to error in scenarios extremely similar to the current one. In typical philosophy cases, by contrast, well-informedness is somewhat amorphous: it typically depends on familiarity with, and understanding of, substantial chunks of the relevant literature, but exactly what literature is relevant is somewhat vague, as are degrees of familiarity and understanding. And of course the group nature of the controversy means, among other things, that I'm unlikely to know all that much about all of the people who disagree with me (or, for that matter, the ones who agree with me). Finally, and perhaps most important, there's nothing remotely like a clear track-record of accuracy for any of us, since there's no philosophical analogue of a calculator to tell us who's been right and who's been wrong in previous judgments. So we lack a clear objective way of measuring an agent's likelihood of reasoning correctly about philosophical matters.

Nevertheless, it seems to me that a strong case can be made, given IBC, that many of us should be much less confident in our philosophical beliefs than we often seem to be. To see why, let us consider a particular example: the status of Multi-Premise Closure (hereafter "Closure") principles for rational categorical belief. When I consider the arguments for and against, it seems to me pretty clear that Closure is false. But many other epistemologists think otherwise. How should I react to these facts? I think three points are worth emphasizing here:

(a) The first is that I *do* have good reason to have as much epistemic respect for my philosophical opponents as I have for my philosophical allies and for myself. Obviously, there's no scorecard I can use to rate the reliability of different epistemologists. But this doesn't mean I have no way (independent of the Closure dispute) of assessing the epistemic credentials of epistemologists.

In some cases, I have specific information about particular people, either on the basis of general knowledge or from reading or talking to the epistemologists in question. This includes information about education; about command of the literature; and about skill in argument and analysis. In some cases, I may even have information about the person's intellectual character (open-mindedness, fairness, intellectual honesty, and so on). These are the sorts of factors that I take to be responsible for a person's ability to reach accurate beliefs about philosophical issues.

Moreover, even where I lack this sort of individualized information about some of the other philosophers in the dispute, it seems that I have strong reason to doubt that, in general, the more honest, or more diligent, or better-read philosophers are the ones who agree with me about Closure. One reason is simply that the individuals I *do* have information about certainly don't fit any such pattern. But another reason derives from the *group* nature of philosophical controversy. It seems clear that the groups of people who disagree with me on various philosophical issues are quite differently composed. Many who are on my side of one issue will be on the other side of different issues. With this structural feature of group disagreement in philosophy in mind, it seems clear that it could hardly be rational for me to think that I'm part of some special subgroup of unusually smart, diligent, or honest members of the profession.

When I think in this way about the people who disagree with me about Closure, I believe that I do get strong, dispute-independent reason to think that those who disagree with me are as well-informed, and as likely to have reasoned correctly from their evidence, as those who agree with me. If that's right, then it would seem that IBC implies that I should not have much confidence at all in the falsity of Closure. Indeed, it would seem that I should probably have few, if any, confident beliefs at all about philosophically controversial matters!

(b) The second point involves a different way in which persistent patterns of disagreement within a group of investigators can pose an epistemic problem. This sort of case for drastically reducing my confidence in controversial philosophical theses has been made by several writers; the version I'll sketch here is perhaps closest to the one developed by Hilary Kornblith (2010).[3] When we look at professional philosophy, its failure to reach consensus on important issues is striking. As Kornblith points out, this lack of consensus indicates that whatever methodology philosophers use is not a reliable way of reaching philosophical truth. And recognition of this, it seems, should make us skeptical of our own applications of that methodology to arrive at confident philosophical conclusions.

The power of this argument also ultimately depends, I think, on an independence principle—on assuming that our evaluation of the epistemic credentials of others, for the purpose of deciding whether to modify our beliefs in response to their disagreement, must be independent of our own reasoning on the disputed matters.[4] After all, I wouldn't have to worry about wide dissensus in philosophy if I could rationally take myself to be special. The independence requirement prevents me from reasoning as follows, even in cases where my original reasoning on the disputed topic happens to be correct: "Well, as the arguments show, Multi-Premise Closure principles are false. And I have come to the conclusion that

---

[3] See also Goldberg (2009, 2013), Christensen (2007), Fumerton (2010), and Brennan (2010) (though Brennan focuses more on whether someone new to philosophy would be justified in studying the arguments and coming to hold philosophical opinions).

[4] Kornblith (2010) does endorse an independence requirement.

they're false. So, whatever general problems there are with philosophical methodology, they apparently haven't led me astray in this case!"

Disallowing this sort of response makes sense precisely because it would beg the question to answer doubts about the cogency of a certain bit of reasoning I did by relying on that very bit of reasoning. I would not really be taking seriously the possibility that my reasoning, rather than that of the other philosophers, was faulty. Thus it seems that taking ourselves to be fallible in the same way we see others as fallible is all we need to argue for severe limitations on the rational confidence we can have in controversial theses in philosophy.[5]

c) The third reason that conciliatory pressure may be greater in group disagreements concerns the unavailability, in group contexts, of a particularly nice way of rationally dismissing disagreement in certain two-person cases.

Some critics of IBC have argued that it gives the wrong results in cases where one starts off with extremely high rational confidence. Jennifer Lackey (2010) gives examples of beliefs about elementary math and about the location of a favorite restaurant. Suppose I've been frequenting My Thai for many years, and I am extremely confident that it's on Michigan Avenue. One day my friend, who's just as familiar with the city, and also a frequent My Thai patron, tells me he's extremely confident it's on State Street instead. Lackey argues that in this sort of disagreement, there's an *asymmetry* that makes it rational for me to conclude that it's my friend who's wrong in this case. In situations of this sort, it seems likely that one of us is badly malfunctioning. She points out that I may know full well that I'm not drastically sleep-deprived, that I don't remember taking drugs or drinking a lot recently, or having psychotic hallucinations. I would add to Lackey's list that I also know I'm sincere: I'm not lying or joking about what my belief is about My Thai's location. But I have much less firm reason to believe these things about my friend. So insofar as I have very good justification for my initial belief, the right thing to conclude in such a case is that it's highly likely that my friend is badly malfunctioning (or insincere). The same response can be made, even more persuasively, for cases like 2+2=4, where one starts out with even greater rational confidence in one's opinion. Lackey calls the considerations I use here to break the symmetry and resist the undermining power of disagreement "personal information".

---

[5] This is not to deny that in philosophy, it is good to take positions, and defend them as if I believe them. If there's some hope of making progress in philosophy, it's not implausible that we need people vigorously defending positions in a way that people wouldn't if they didn't have more confidence in their positions than is rationally warranted. There may be some good—even epistemic good—in our epistemic hubris. It also may be argued that the sort of assertion typically involved in philosophical debate need not be based in justified belief to be legitimate; see Frances (2010), Goldberg (2013).

Lackey and I disagree about whether this invocation of personal information is consistent with IBC.[6] But I won't pursue that question here. Instead, I want to note that this sort of response, which ameliorates the corrosive power of disagreement so nicely in certain two-person cases involving extremely high rational credence, seems to be much less applicable in the context of disagreements among groups.

Now even before considering features characteristic of group disagreement, I should note that one might reasonably hold that personal-information-based dismissal will rarely be appropriate in philosophical disagreements anyway. After all, the personal-information-based argument for steadfastness in the elementary math case depends crucially on the subject's initial extremely high level of rational confidence in her belief—this is required to support the claim that the disagreement is likely due to severe malfunction or insincerity. But group disagreements in philosophy tend not to revolve around issues as obvious as the sum of two and two, so it's not clear that the personal-information-based argument will often get off the ground. I think this point is basically right. But I suspect that we've all had conversations with colleagues who seem to regard their own takes on some issue as being about as obvious as two plus two—or at least as if their takes should be that obvious to anyone who bothered to think the issue through. And many philosophers seem as confident in their philosophical views as they are about the location of their favorite restaurants. So I want to put this point aside. It seems to me that even if one does take one's initial view on, say, free will to be overwhelmingly obvious, one cannot use this high level of initial confidence, in combination with personal information, to resist the undermining power of disagreement among large groups of philosophers.

The reason for this is explained nicely by Maja Spener (2011), in discussing uses of controversial introspective reports in the philosophy of perception. As Spener argues, even if it makes sense to use asymmetry of personal information to conclude that one's friend is malfunctioning in cases like Lackey's, the asymmetry diminishes drastically in the group context. Clearly, one lacks personal information about all the other people on one's own side of the dispute, as well as about all the people on the other side. Moreover, in order to explain the disagreement by reference to the sort of insincerity or malfunction that can be eliminated by personal information in one's own case, one would have to suppose that it affected all of one's opponents, and not one's allies. As Spener puts it, "[i]t would be ridiculous to claim that all the disagreeing partners happened to be intoxicated, cognitively malfunctioning, joking or inattentive at crucial junctures" (2011, 278). So it seems

---

[6] See Christensen (2011) for an argument that this sort of resistance to conciliating is consistent with evaluating my friend's epistemic credentials in a way that's independent of our dispute.

that in the group context, the power of personal information to defuse disagreement is diluted to the point of washing out.

Now it should be made clear that the point here is not that severe malfunction or insincerity cannot occur at the group level, or that there's no asymmetry at all in the group situation. It's that in the vast majority of such cases, one's own personal information will not be of *significant* use in selectively attributing malfunction or insincerity to one's opponents. Consider a disagreement in a field with 10 professors at various institutions claiming that P, and 10 others claiming that ~P, and suppose I'm in the former bunch. I can, of course, rule out insincerity and particular sorts of severe malfunction for myself, and not for any of the others. So there is at least a bit of asymmetry. But can I credibly explain the group disagreement by reference to the sort of insincerity or malfunction that I can rule out in my own case? This would involve (1) believing the 10 philosophers on the other side were insincere or malfunctioning in some way such that if I were malfunctioning in that way, I'd be able to detect it; and (2) not believing this about the 9 other philosophers on my side of the dispute. This is not impossible, but it strikes me as highly implausible—much more implausible than selectively believing that my single friend is insincere or malfunctioning in one of those ways in a two-person disagreement. It's worth noting that there are many other explanations for the group disagreement, including our general unreliability on the issue in question, biases, influences from our education, and more severe malfunctions that don't reveal themselves to their victims in any way. But those are factors I can't eliminate in my own case by personal information, so they are of no use in selectively downgrading the opinions of those who disagree with me.[7]

One can, of course, imagine disagreements between two groups where personal information would be effective. Suppose, e.g., that one has good reason to believe that every member of one group or the other has been paid to express a certain opinion, and one also knows about oneself that one has not been paid. But such examples are contrived, and don't affect the point that the sort of disagreements we see in philosophy, or in other disagreements involving large groups, will not in general be dismissible on personal-information grounds.[8]

---

[7] Thanks to Jennifer Lackey for prompting me to make this case more carefully. (Of course this should not be taken to imply that she is convinced.)

[8] It also should be noted that some features of philosophical disagreements which help block the personal-information-based argument for steadfastness can occur outside the group context. For example, philosophical disagreements often persist over long periods of time. If a two-person disagreement persisted over a long period of time, many of the malfunction-related explanations for the disagreement would be less plausible, so the power of personal information to support steadfastness would be reduced. (Thanks to an anonymous reader for making me see this; I should note that Spener makes a related point.) That said, it remains true that the group nature of many disagreements

In sum: the example of philosophical disagreement provides a nice illustration of some ways in which the group nature of certain disagreements can present a stronger case for reduced confidence than is present in the two-person toy cases on which the literature tends to concentrate. True, in many such cases, we will lack the sort of clear track-record evidence we have in the Mental Math case. But we may yet have good reasons to believe that those who disagree with us are just as likely to get things right as are those who agree, especially when the claim that we are part of some especially reliable sub-group is implausible.

Moreover, if we set up the argument for reducing confidence as Kornblith does, it doesn't rest on commitment to any very specific identification of what makes one good at ferreting out truth in the relevant domain. And persistent disagreements among group members provide track-record-style reason to worry about the relevant methodology—a reason that doesn't depend on a referee scoring individual judgments right or wrong. Insofar as we take the controversial questions in a domain to have objectively right and wrong answers, persistent widespread disagreement of group members is enough to show that the methods the group employs are not generally reliable.[9]

Finally, insofar as one is tempted to resist conciliatory views of disagreement on the grounds that personal information can license steadfast responses to certain cases, it seems clear that one's reasons for resisting conciliation will not apply to the cases many of us cite as motivating our interest in the epistemology of disagreement: well-known disagreements about philosophy, politics, morality, history, and so on. The fact that the disagreements occur in the context of large groups makes personal information largely irrelevant. The group nature of certain sorts of disagreement thus turns out, on balance, to strengthen the case for conciliation significantly.

6.3. Fallibility and the Epistemic Value of Disagreement: Mill vs. IBC

As noted earlier, Mill's position also stems from a concern with our epistemic fallibility. Mill points out quite convincingly that fallible thinkers are prone to rely on false beliefs, and end up suppressing true beliefs. But he argues that we should not take acknowledgment of our fallibility to paralyze us—to prevent us from taking

---

is by itself sufficient to preclude significant reliance on the personal-information-based argument for steadfastness.

[9] Of course, this would seem to apply to the methods I'm employing here. For some discussions of the self-undermining problem for conciliatory views of disagreement, see Elga (2010), Frances (2010), Christensen (2013), and Weatherson (2013).

any actions at all based on our beliefs. So then why not act on our beliefs by suppressing beliefs we take to be false? According to Mill, it is precisely by allowing one's beliefs to confront vigorous dissent that one can achieve the level of rational certainty that would justify acting on one's beliefs. So this argument for free speech rests on the epistemic benefits of confronting disagreement:

> Complete liberty of contradicting and disproving our opinion is the very condition which justifies us in assuming its truth for purposes of action; and on no other terms can a being with human faculties have any rational assurance of being right. (1859, 24)
>
> In the case of any person whose judgment is really deserving of confidence, how has it become so?... Because it has been his practice to listen to all that could be said against him; to profit by as much of it as was just, and expound to himself, and upon occasion to others, the fallacy of what was fallacious.... The steady habit of correcting and completing his own opinion by collating it with those of others, so far from causing doubt and hesitation in carrying it into practice, is the only stable foundation for a just reliance on it: for, being cognizant of all that can, at least obviously, be said against him, and having taken up his position against all gainsayers—knowing that he has sought for objections and difficulties, instead of avoiding them, and has shut out no light which can be thrown upon the subject from any quarter—he has a right to think his judgment better than that of any person, or any multitude, who have not gone through a similar process. (1859, 25)

Thus, for Mill, it seems that exposure to dissent is epistemically valuable because it can help us compensate for our fallibility, thus allowing us to become more rationally confident in our opinions.

This account of the epistemic importance of disagreement presents a stark contrast with the account which IBC gives in the case of public disagreements in philosophy. Consider what Mill might say about my opinion on Closure. I have read and thought more carefully about this issue than I have about most others. I've studied arguments from the literature on both sides, and talked the issue through with epistemologists of both persuasions. I've published my own anti-Closure arguments. And I've read and thought carefully about responses from those who are thoroughly unconvinced by my arguments. When I consider all these arguments, as carefully and honestly as I can, it still seems to me pretty clear that Closure is false. And it seems to me that I can see the problems in others' arguments for Closure, and in their criticisms of my arguments against Closure; indeed, I have expounded the fallacies of such arguments to myself, and, upon occasion, to others. So it would seem that, on Mill's account, my encounters with articulate, well-informed and intelligent defenders of Closure have actually put me in a position to be more rationally confident of my position.

Not so, according to IBC; in fact, quite the reverse. For I do have a great deal of epistemic respect for many Closure-supporters. When I bracket their misguided views on Closure (and closely-related matters), I see many of them as my philosophical equals or betters: at least as likely as I am to succeed in getting at truths in philosophy. For reasons rehearsed in the previous section, obeying IBC would mean my reducing my confidence in the falsity of Closure way below what it would be absent the disagreement of those fellow epistemologists. Given the distribution of opinion on the topic among philosophers I have every reason to respect, I should probably withhold belief on the topic.

Clearly, IBC embodies a more radical way of reacting to our fallibility. In philosophy, we've all paid at least lip service to the injunction that one must read and take seriously the arguments and opinions of others, as a condition of responsible belief. We pride ourselves in this sort of open-mindedness or epistemic modesty, even as we take strong positions on controversial issues. [10] But the degree of epistemic modesty supported by IBC is far less comfortable.

Yet it also bears noticing that the fundamental motivation behind IBC is not far away from Mill's. Mill's position stems from the realization that we often err by overlooking, or failing to attend carefully to, arguments opposing what we're inclined to believe. And engaging carefully and honestly with those who disagree is the natural precaution against this sort of fallibility. IBC flows from the realization that our fallibility runs a bit deeper than Mill suggests: we also often err in coming to settled, all-things-considered judgments, *even after the most careful reflection and conscientious engagement with our opponents.* This is obvious, when one looks at all the mutually incompatible opinions stably held by various groups in philosophy—it seems undeniable that a lot of us have failed to reach the truth on a lot of the issues we study. To my mind, the more radical-seeming consequences of IBC simply represent the natural precautions suggested by this more thoroughgoing acknowledgment of our fallibility.[11]

Fortunately, little of practical importance depends on whether one or another epistemologist arrives at the truth about Closure. Even if most of us have irrational amounts of confidence in our own pet views, this does not seem likely to do anyone serious harm. Unfortunately, analogous claims cannot be made for controversial political issues. So it is worth asking: do the sorts of considerations which argue for widespread belief-withholding about the positions debated in academic

---

[10] I of course would not claim that all those who profess to take seriously the opinions of others actually do so. But I think that most philosophers at least make some steps in this direction in mostly good faith.

[11] As Nathan Ballantyne has pointed out to me, one might actually take Mill's position to require substantial withholding of opinion on controversial matters, in a quite different way. On many issues, I have not seriously engaged all (or even most) of the detailed arguments advanced by those holding contrary views. If serious engagement with "all that can...be said" against my opinions were necessary for rational belief, I would fail to meet this standard pretty frequently. But the contrast remains between this reading of Mill's position and IBC. On the former, the reason I fail to meet the standard for rational belief is that I've not engaged sufficiently with those who disagree. Disagreement remains a source (albeit untapped) for increasing rational confidence, not a source of its undermining.

philosophy carry over to recommend a similar amount of withholding with respect to positions that are subject to political controversy?

Trying to give a blanket answer to that question at this point strikes me as unpromising, since political controversies differ from one another in ways that seem to me to have important epistemic implications. Instead, I'd like to look at some particular examples, with an eye towards identifying the sorts of factors that would help us arrive at reasonable answers in particular cases.

6.4. IBC and Public Controversies in Politics: Evolution

One thing that makes the Conciliationist argument so strong in philosophy is that I think of my opponents as being just as fair-minded, unbiased, honest, and well-informed as I am. Of course, there may well be arational factors influencing most philosophers' beliefs: where a given philosopher went to graduate school, which views she happened to latch onto early in her intellectual development, etc. But it does not seem that I can cite these sorts of factors *selectively* to downgrade my philosophical opponents; my views are equally a product of such arational factors. In a general sense, I think I have very good reason to think of my philosophical opponents as my peers with respect to aptitude, informedness, and intellectual virtue.

It goes without saying, I suppose, that people in political controversies do not standardly regard one another this way. This may be particularly true in moral controversies. But let us put aside controversies over purely moral matters. At this point in our understanding of morality, it's unclear whether moral judgments express straightforwardly factual claims, non-cognitive attitudes, or something in between. Since there are plenty of straightforwardly factual claims that are subject to political controversy, we may avoid some complications by focusing there.

I should emphasize that I'll have to work with example controversies in artificially simplified form. For each example I'll discuss, people accept or deny significantly different versions of the central claim, and for significantly different reasons. The complexity of the evidence and arguments relevant to the issues, and of the social facts about the distribution of opinions on these issues, make a serious, detailed treatment of any of them well beyond what I could attempt here. Instead, I'll work with fairly crude caricatures of the debates, in order to illustrate some general patterns of argument.

One example of a factual claim that's politically controversial and subject to widespread disagreement in the U.S., is:

Evolution: Humans arose by evolution from earlier life forms.

Now I happen to be a firm believer in Evolution, but I know that many people—some of them very intelligent—disagree. In this case, I not only don't find my confidence shaken by the dissent of Evolution-deniers, but I also don't think my confidence should be shaken. Is this position consistent with IBC?

It seems to me that it is. Even though close to half of my fellow U.S. citizens disagree with me[12], IBC does allow me to give a steadfast response to this case. Looking at the reason why will, I think, begin to reveal the complexities involved in applying IBC to certain sorts of politically-charged matters.

One might think that I have an easy answer to the evolution-deniers. After all, I take the question of human origins to be a biological/historical question, to be approached through an understanding of how biological forms arise in nature, study of the fossil record, etc. And it's clear that the vast majority of experts on this—paleontologists and evolutionary biologists, that is—believe that humans arose through evolution. This does not seem to be a question like the status of Closure principles for rational belief, where the expert opinion is much more evenly divided. And this near-unanimity of paleontological/evolutionary biological opinion is a fact quite independent of the matter under dispute; everyone acknowledges it. So it can figure in the dispute-independent evaluation of the Evolution-deniers' epistemic credentials that IBC asks me to perform.

But things are not quite this simple. There is a common sort of Evolution-denier who poses a challenge to the Evolution-believer that cannot be answered this way. The theory of evolution conflicts with certain fundamentalist religious views that many Americans subscribe to. Some such fundamentalists deny that science has any purchase at all when it conflicts with certain ancient texts. This sort of Evolution-denier holds that the ancient texts, taken literally, reveal truths, and that science can at best fill in gaps left open by the texts. Some advocates of this position hold, for instance, that the Earth is less than 10,000 years old, basing this claim on a literal interpretation of certain ancient religious writings. On this sort of view, adherence to the correct version of the correct religion is a prerequisite to arriving at accurate beliefs about the world. Paleontologists who reject the literal truth of the ancient texts are, on this view, no experts at all. So it looks like I cannot after all take these people's disregard for expert opinion as a *dispute-neutral* way of negatively assessing their epistemic credentials.

Now my strong instinct is to see such people's strong emotional attachments to their religious views as irrational influences which interfere with their ability to

---

[12] A 2012 Gallup poll showed 46% believing that "God created human beings pretty much in their present form at one time within the last 10,000 years or so" <http://www.gallup.com/poll/155003/Hold-Creationist-View-Human-Origins.aspx,> accessed 6/12/12.

let their beliefs be guided by the evidence. In this respect, I regard their judgments about human origins in much the way I regard Aksel's father's judgments about Aksel's musical talent. But my attitude here brings up a difficult question concerning IBC. In the case of Aksel's father, it's unlikely that he'd dispute my general belief that parents overrate their own children, even if he didn't believe that his own judgment of Aksel's performance was a product of this sort of distortion. So this general fact about parental bias can figure in a dispute-independent evaluation saying that I am more likely to reach the correct conclusion from the evidence that Aksel's father and I share. Does the same apply to my view that religious attachments distort good reasoning? Clearly, this belief of mine would be rejected by the Evolution-deniers in question; in effect, it's part of what's in dispute between us. So it does not seem to be a dispute-neutral claim that I can use in the sort of evaluation mandated by IBC.

What, then, does IBC say about my disagreement with such people? I think it's not at all clear that I can treat their disagreement the way I treat my disagreement with Aksel's father. The issues in dispute between us do not obviously provide for a strong dispute-neutral assessment to the effect that they're less likely to get at the truth. After all, the scientific method, which I take as my fundamental standard for forming beliefs about the world, is treated by them as secondary, to be violated whenever its deliverances conflict with certain texts. So no ordinary empirical argument challenging the inerrancy of the texts will count as neutral.

On the other hand, it's also not at all clear that I should treat my disagreement with these Evolution-deniers like I treat my disagreement with those who believe in Closure. The Closure fans and I share the basic assumption that factors such as intelligence and familiarity with the literature are what, if anything, would allow a person to form accurate beliefs about epistemology. So my epistemic respect for Closure fans is founded on my own dispute-neutral positive reasons for granting them that respect. But that's not at all obviously present in the case of the Evolution-deniers: I don't seem to have a strong dispute-independent basis for taking them as peers—to be equally likely to get at the truth.

To see what IBC—as formulated above—says about this sort of case, it's important to recall a key structural aspect of the view. It does not say that I must revise my belief whenever I *lack* dispute-independent reason to think myself more likely to get it right than my opponents. It says (roughly) that I must revise my belief when I *have* strong dispute-independent reason to think that my opponents are equally (or more) likely to get it right. So the idea is not that others, simply in virtue of having beliefs, are granted some sort of default status as my epistemic peers, status that they retain absent independent reason to demote them. The epistemic respect I owe to other believers must be earned. In cases where the beliefs of others undermine my initial confidence in some matter, the undermining is ultimately based on my own positive (dispute-independent) reasons for thinking the others likely to get the disputed matter right. If that is lacking in the case of certain Evolution-deniers, IBC does not recommend a conciliatory attitude toward their beliefs.[13]

So here we seem to get a clear contrast between standard disputes in academic philosophy, and at least one sort of political controversy. In the case of this sort of political disagreement, it does not seem that much conciliation is required by IBC. (Of course, Mill's argument will still tell us to confront their arguments; but if my confidence emerges from that encounter unshaken, so much the better for my opinion.)

6.5. IBC and Public Controversies in Politics: Economics

I would not want to suggest, however, that all politically charged controversies involve challenges to my most basic assumptions about how to form beliefs about the world. Many political disputes, for example, turn in large part on economic questions. In the U.S., disputes often trade on questions about the differential effects that policies have on different economic strata. Progressive income tax rates, on which the wealthy pay a greater percentage of their income than poorer citizens, seem to benefit the poor. But some argue that cutting taxes on the wealthy will actually stimulate the general economy to the extent that the poor will end up benefiting. So there's controversy about:

Tax Cuts: Cutting taxes on wealthy Americans will benefit poor Americans.

For another example, minimum-wage laws are designed to protect the lowest-paid workers. But some argue that they increase unemployment to the extent that they end up hurting those they're intended to help. So there's controversy about:

Minimum Wage: Raising the minimum wage will benefit poor Americans.

---

[13] I should note that not all Conciliationist writers who invoke independence requirements see things this way. It is natural to state the Conciliationist position by saying that revision is required when we lack independent reason for downgrading those who disagree. (And of course lacking independent reason to downgrade and having independent reason for respect will typically coincide.) But it seems to me that the negative formulation leads to skepticism, and misses the point that the mandate to revise in clear cases like Mental Math rests on one's own strong positive reasons for thinking the other person reliable. See (Christensen 2010) for more detail on this.

In these cases, none of the disputants are challenging the claim that the questions are to be settled by empirical means. So how should one's beliefs be affected by this sort of controversy?

We should first notice that the sort of empirical arguments that bear on these economic questions are well beyond the reach of most Americans. So it's not clear that the opinions of ordinary Americans are the most relevant epistemically; most Americans are simply not well-informed.

It might seem that politicians and government officials responsible for economic policy would be well-informed, and hence that I should give epistemic respect to their opinions. And it is true that many such people have access to economic experts, even if they know relatively little economic theory themselves. Even so, there are reasons to be careful here. It's far from clear that the opinions many such people announce actually express their own views. Politicians say what they need to say to please their voters and financial backers. And appointed government officials avoid saying things that their politician bosses will fire them for saying. So while it may be that many politicians and government officials are relatively well-informed about economic matters, it is less clear that I have very strong reason to take their *expressed* disagreement with my opinions as a reason for revision. In political disputes, much more than in disputes within academic philosophy, we often have reason to suspect the honesty of the disputants.

Of course, there are economic experts whom I have more reason to take as being sincere. For example, senior academic research economists occupy protected positions, and can generally say what they like. So I cannot dismiss their pronouncements as easily as I might dismiss those of the politicians and government officials.

In some cases, positions which are controversial politically may not be nearly as controversial among academic economists. Suppose, for instance, that while American politicians are divided on the question, the vast majority of research economists agree that cutting taxes on the wealthy will end up hurting lower-income Americans. If I'm initially inclined toward this position, the wider political controversy may not provide much reason for me to revise my belief. (Of course, if my initial belief is opposite to that of the research economists, I may be under rational pressure to revise.) But the wider political controversy per se may not be all that epistemically significant.

In other cases, though, controversy may penetrate to the academic economists themselves. Consider the claim that raising the minimum wage would benefit lower-income Americans. Let us suppose that in this case, the experts are roughly evenly divided, and that I have dispute-independent reason to accord economists on both sides a high degree of epistemic respect. And let us suppose that I'm inclined to believe the liberal side of the debate, and vote for, and maybe give money to, politicians who would raise the minimum wage. Should I revise my belief in light of the disagreement?

In this case, the disagreement does seem to provide me with a reason to moderate my opinion. On the assumption that I have reason to identify a certain group of people as highly intelligent and knowledgeable, and to think them honest in expressing their opinions, it seems that disagreement among them may well put a limit on the rational confidence I can have on the relevant issues. My initial inclination to believe the liberal position that raising the minimum wage would benefit the poor may be no more rationally sustainable, once I'm aware of expert disagreement, than my inclination to reject Closure principles for justification. If that's right, then perhaps I shouldn't be spending much of my money or political energy trying to support politicians who would raise the minimum wage.

But even here, there are more complications. Suppose I'm initially inclined toward the liberal position on minimum wage laws, and suppose I think as follows: "Economists are humans, and so subject to non-rational influences on their beliefs. In general, unconstrained employment benefits the better-off, and economists tend to be well-off. One might predict that, when the empirical evidence is somewhat open to interpretation, self-interest will tend to lead some economists to reach conclusions in line with their self-interest, in effect creating a bias toward conservative conclusions. Since I have dispute-independent reason to expect economists' beliefs to be biased in this way, I may correct for this expected bias, and give less weight to the opinions of conservative economists."

On the other hand, suppose I'm initially inclined toward the conservative position on minimum-wage laws, and think like this: "People's beliefs are often influenced by the group with which they identify—for instance, the liberal group or the conservative group. It's well-known that university faculty in the U.S. tend to have more liberal views than the population at large. And people will be more likely to hire members of their own group. So universities are subject to systematic bias against conservative views. Since I have dispute-independent reason to expect academic economists' beliefs to be biased in this way, I may correct for this expected bias and give less weight to the opinions of liberal economists."

Both of these trains of argument are, of course, gross caricatures. But I think that they do represent *types* of argument that are not uncommon in politically charged disputes. And without going into the details or merits of either one, I think that we can see something important about the *structure* of this sort of argument. In both cases, the arguer presents reasons for discrediting those with whom she disagrees, and the reasons are—at least at first blush—independent of the matter under dispute. Thus this sort of argument presents another possible way that the rational pressure for belief-revision generated by IBC may be reduced in politically-charged controversies.

Of course, it's one thing to point to the possibility of offering dispute-independent rational grounds for discrediting one's political opponents, and another to say in a given case that one has really done so. Whether one has or has not will of course vary widely across examples, and we shouldn't expect there to be some simple recipe for generating this sort of argument, or for assessing the cogency of particular examples. The present point is that this sort of response is much more natural in thinking about politically important issues than, say, in thinking about Closure in epistemology.

I suspect that discrediting one's opponents' opinions in this way is more natural in politics, at least in part, because it's more often legitimate. Political controversies involve matters of great practical importance. The high practical stakes raise the emotional temperature, and thus invite bias, through self-interest, group-identification, and other emotionally powerful distorters of rational thought.[14]

So we've seen a way in which the political nature of certain disputes can make it more likely that one has grounds for selectively discrediting one's opponents. And when that discrediting is independent of the matter under dispute, it may reduce the IRC-mandated pressure to revise one's beliefs. But one final point about this sort of maneuver deserves noticing. And that is that it will often be unclear to what extent one really has strong independent reasons for discrediting one's opponents.

Consider the liberal who believes that conservative economists are biased by self-interest. She is relying on unquantified common-sense psychology in supposing that self-interest plays a large enough role in conservative economists' thinking to produce a significant bias in favor of policies that benefit the wealthy. Now there's nothing wrong with common-sense psychology: it seems quite legitimate when I use it to discredit the opinion of Aksel's father. But here's another bit of common-sense psychology: people tend to interpret evidence in a way that supports beliefs they already have, especially when those beliefs are important to them. And we can see that discrediting our opponents is an indirect way of supporting our initial beliefs. This suggests that we are likely to be prone to overestimating the degree to which our independent evidence supports downgrading the epistemic credentials of those with whom we disagree.

---

[14] Of course, beliefs in philosophy are hardly immune from irrational influences. And some of these may even be emotionally powerful—for example, if a philosopher has a long history of supporting a certain position, it could be painful to admit that he was wrong when he encountered strong arguments pointing in that direction. (Thanks to Nathan Ballantyne for emphasizing this to me.) That said, I think it will be relatively rare that this sort of distortion can be cited *selectively*, to discredit one's opponents but not those with whom one agrees.

The problem is exacerbated by the complexity of our epistemic task in applying IBC. As hard as it is to arrive at rational all-things-considered judgments about complex matters in general, here our task is a bit more complex: we must arrive at judgments about what's supported by that subset of our reasons that are independent of the reasoning under dispute. We must focus on the dispute in order to judge how strongly our dispute-independent reasons speak for according epistemic respect to those on the other side.

The difficulty of doing this is, of course, yet a further facet of our fallibility, against which we should take precautions. In applying IBC, we must beware of letting ourselves off the hook too easily. We probably should often be more generous in our epistemic assessments of our opponents than we might otherwise be inclined to be, especially when we're emotionally invested in our side of the dispute. And this argues for expanding the amount of conciliation we do beyond what might seem to be required by a naive application of IBC to many political controversies.

6.6. Conclusion

IBC, like Mill's argument, makes the disagreement of others an important tool to be used in taking precautions against our epistemic fallibility. IBC stems from seeing that fallibility goes well beyond our failure to notice or respond carefully to considerations which count against our beliefs. It extends to our failure to reason reliably, even when we take all available considerations into account as carefully and conscientiously as we humanly can. Unlike Mill's argument, IBC will often push us toward reduced confidence in disputed matters.

We have seen some ways in which, when we scale up IBC from toy cases to actual cases of widespread group disagreement, the pressure towards conciliation is increased. That's in part because the argument for reducing confidence in the products of our investigative methods need not depend on scoring individuals' track-records, or even identifying very specifically the factors which allow people to arrive at accurate beliefs. And it's in part because the asymmetries of personal information that allow us to dismiss disagreements in some two-person cases disappear in group disagreements. We can see these points in the case of philosophical controversy.

When we move to political controversy, though, things get more complicated in some ways that reduce the pressure towards conciliation. With respect to many issues of political controversy, dispute-independent epistemic evaluation of the parties to the disagreement is particularly difficult. In some cases (such as those involving religious fundamentalism) there may be too little material that's independent of the dispute to provide strong reason for granting epistemic respect to those with whom one disagrees. In such cases, there may be very little reason, even given IBC, for reducing confidence in one's beliefs.

In other cases of political controversy, one may have dispute-independent reason to think less well of one's opponents. One may have reason to believe that they're ill-informed; that their pronouncements don't reflect their true opinions; or that their thinking is distorted by self-interest, group-identification, or other biasing factors. To the extent that such reasons are strong, the IBC-based mandate for reducing confidence is weakened.

But these cases, which I suspect are very common in political disputes, present special difficulties. For a thorough acknowledgment of our fallibility surely includes acknowledging fallibility in assessing the degree to which dispute-independent factors favor our own reliability over that of our opponents. And once this is taken to heart, the confidence-lowering effects of conscientiously applying IBC in cases of political disagreement become more severe than one might have hoped they would be.

To the extent that this means that our political decisions will inevitably depend on a less secure picture of what the world is like, this is bound to be frustrating, as it is in philosophy. But surely we should remain mindful of the downside of taking bold actions based on mistaken confidence in politically important matters. Given the unfortunate fact of our fallibility, we should take Mill's advice, and avail ourselves of such precautions against it as we can find. Even if, in the end, confronting disagreement reduces, rather than bolsters, our rational confidence about important matters, disagreement is a valuable epistemic resource. We should be grateful that diversity of opinion can serve us as a warning sign, indicating issues on which our thinking is especially likely to have gone astray.

Acknowledgments

For helpful discussion or comments on drafts, I'd like to thank Nathan Ballantyne, Jennifer Lackey, Andrew Rotondo, Maja Spener, Henry Swift, an anonymous referee for Oxford University Press, and audiences at the Second Copenhagen Conference in Epistemology, the Brandeis Graduate Student Brown Bag series, and the Conference on Epistemology of Groups at Northwestern University.

References

Brennan, J. (2010), "Scepticism about Philosophy." *Ratio 23*, 1–16.
Chalmers, D. J. (2011), "Verbal Disputes." *Philosophical Review 120*: 515–66.

Christensen, D. (2007), "Epistemology of Disagreement: the Good News." *Philosophical Review 116*: 187–217.
——. (2011), "Disagreement, Question-Begging and Epistemic Self-Criticism." *Philosophers' Imprint*: 1–22.
——. (2013), "Epistemic Modesty Defended," in Christensen and Lackey.
Christensen, D. and J. Lackey, eds. (2013), *Disagreement: New Essays* (Oxford: Oxford University Press).
Elga, A. (2007), "Reflection and Disagreement." *Noûs 41*: 478–502.
——. (2010), "How to Disagree about how to Disagree," in Feldman and Warfield.
Feldman, R. and T. Warfield, eds. (2010), *Disagreement* (Oxford: Oxford University Press).
Frances, B. (2010), "The Reflective Epistemic Renegade." *Philosophy and Phenomenological Research LXXXI*, 2: 419–63.
Fumerton, R. (2010), "You Can't Trust a Philosopher," in Feldman and Warfield.
Goldberg, S. (2013), "Disagreement, Defeaters, and Assertion," in Christensen and Lackey.
——. (2009), "Reliabilism in Philosophy." *Philosophical Studies 124*: 1, 105–17.
Kornblith, H. (2010), "Belief in the Face of Controversy," in Feldman and Warfield.
Lackey, J. (2010), "A Justificationist View of Disagreement's Epistemic Significance", in A. Haddock, A. Millar, and D. Pritchard (eds.), *Social Epistemology* (Oxford: Oxford University Press).
Mill, J. S. (1859), *On Liberty* (Indianapolis: Bobbs-Merrill, 1956).
Sosa, E (2010), "The Epistemology of Disagreement," in A. Haddock, Millar, A. and Pritchard, D. (eds.), *Social Epistemology* (Oxford: Oxford University Press).
Spener, M. (2011), "Disagreement about Cognitive Phenomenology," in T. Bayne and M. Montague (eds.), *Cognitive Phenomenology* (Oxford: Oxford University Press).
Weatherson, B. (2013), "Disagreements, Philosophical and Otherwise," in Christensen and Lackey.

PART III

Individual and Collective Epistemology

7

Social Roots of Human Knowledge

Ernest Sosa

What follows offers an account of human knowledge and belief as constitutively social. Social factors affect epistemology in at least two ways. They bear on an important sort of belief, and also on a corresponding sort of epistemic competence. This concerns both a kind of value that knowledge has, and also how the pragmatic can properly encroach on epistemology. We begin with this latter issue and circle back to our main theme, that of epistemology's social roots.

7.1. Pragmatic Encroachment

7.1.1. *The risk of pragmatic encroachment*

What *sorts* of factors bear on the hunting-relative evaluation of an archer-hunter's shot? This involves how well that shot contributes to the overall hunting-relevant objective: say, a good afternoon's hunt. One way it can contribute is by being successful, by aptly hitting a target of high (hunting) value, and killing that prey. Such aptness does not require that the shot be also meta-apt. A shot can aptly kill its prey, manifesting archery skill, even though it was too risky a shot, and betrayed poor judgment by the hunter. An apt shot can thus fail to be meta-apt. On a meta-level we ask whether the risk undergone is appropriate. What might this involve? How can we understand a way of managing and assessing risk while bracketing such practical objectives as how much it matters to that hunter or to his tribe that he not misuse his energy, time, and resources?

Suppose *a successful hunt* to be the primary objective in the domain of hunting, and the correspondingly primary value in the critical evaluation proper to that domain. Yes, of course, but what constitutes "success," i.e., *hunting* success? As it stands this objective is formal and must gain content with the specifics of the particular hunt. What is the size and character of the hunting party (down to the limiting case of an individual)? What is the sort of prey involved? Is it a sporting event or is it a hunt for needed food? For present purposes, however, let us abstract from all such detail and focus on the formal objective. The hunter's assessment of proper risk will then plausibly depend on how taking his shot with its chance of success is combined with other shots one might take, and what shots others in the hunting party might take, and also on the resulting pattern's likely contribution to a successful hunt.[1] The evaluation hence needs to go beyond the single probability assessment, to the assessment of patterns containing that shot. A low-probability shot *can* still be meta-apt, if it contributes appropriately to an overall total pattern that, while containing some such shots, still probably enough results in a successful hunt. (That can still be so, even if what is involved in a hunter's successful hunt is not sharp and determinate, especially if she is part of a hunting party. Each hunter might then aim to attain a successful hunt, which might involve either the hunt of the individual hunter or that of the hunting party.)

The like is found across otherwise disparate domains. Take a tennis champion in the heat of an important match. Gathering up all his might at a crucial point, he blasts a very flat, extremely low-percentage second serve past his opponent. An excellent serve, of course, on one dimension: a successful ace owed to the champion's skill. His shot has a 15 percent chance of success, let us say, while a hacker who tried a flat serve hit so hard would have a nearly 0 percent chance. Nonetheless that shot may show extremely poor *tennis* judgment. He should never have taken such a risk at that crucial juncture, judged by the tennis-relative objective of winning the match.

Here is something that does not help: that the champion noticed his girlfriend entering the stands and wanted to impress her. The shot did impress her, but that fact does not make it *a better tennis shot*. Another serve would have been more appropriate: a high-percentage spin serve kicking high to the opponent's weaker backhand side. This would have been a more appropriate shot even if it had just missed the service court, thus losing the point.

Not that the flat hard serve is never relevantly appropriate. It might be appropriate despite being low-percentage. This will depend for one thing on how it fits within a pattern of shots over the course of the match. (It might unnerve the opponent, for example, or lead him to receive farther back).

Something similar is true of the archery hunt. The average reliability required for archery competence in a hunt will depend, for example, on the hit/miss

---

[1] We must be flexible on how, in a given context, the proper ultimate hunting-relative aim is set: whether, for example, the good hunt is relative to an afternoon, or relative to a days-long hunting trip. Either way, the aim will be domain specific; it will not vary generically over the full range of aims that a subject or a community might have.

differentials compatible with a successful hunt. But a shot can still be apt by manifesting a competence that is not reliable outright, and even when its reliability is quite low, so long as it is reliable *enough*. What matters is how the shot, with its individual reliability, fits within some broader pattern that coordinates with the agent's past and future selves, and with other agents altogether.

We turn next from performance normativity in general to virtue epistemology more specifically.

7.1.2. *Pragmatic encroachment through norms of assertion and belief*

When we are told that knowledge is the norm of assertion, this can be understood as advocating a necessary condition for *proper* assertion, namely knowledge.[2] What is this propriety? Arguably, it involves social epistemic norms. These may or may not derive from human convention. They may rather be norms set, not by arbitrary convention, but by the needs of an information-sharing social species. Leaving open the exact source, content, and nature of such norms, I rely only on the plausibility of their existence.

Without going further into the source and objectivity of epistemic norms, we can still wonder: What sort of thing determines their correctness? Let's suppose for the sake of argument that in some important sense knowledge *is* a norm of assertion, that one falls short if one affirms, whether publicly or privately, what one does not know. Such affirmation can be an act either of thought or of speech. *Judgment* in particular is an affirmative act of thought.[3] Knowledge then is a norm of judgment. And this is of course compatible with knowledge being apt belief, or belief whose correctness manifests (sufficient) competence and not (too much) luck. The conclusion to draw is then that aptness is a norm of belief. And this fits our picture platitudinously. A belief does surely fall short if it fails to get it right through competence. It falls short in the way any performance with an aim falls

---

[2] This is then defended as a way of explaining how repugnant we find certain Moore-paradoxical claims, such as "p but I don't know that p" or "p but I don't believe it" or "p but I'm not justified in believing it." What makes knowledge *the* norm as opposed to, say, truth, or belief, or justified belief? Arguably, what is distinctive is that knowledge is the most general such norm that explains the others. Yes, truth, belief, and justified belief, are also norms in that it would be incorrect to assert when one lacks any of truth, belief, or justification, but that is plausibly because in lacking any of these one lacks also knowledge. So it is knowledge that thus unifies the relevant set of norms. However, if this is the argument, then knowledge that one knows may be a more plausible candidate for being thus *the* norm of assertion. This is because there are several Moore-paradoxical claims covered not by the knowledge norm but only by the knowledge-that-one-knows norm, notably the following: "p but I'm in doubt as to whether I'm justified in thinking this to be something I know." But these issues are peripheral to our present concerns.

[3] This is a temporary expedient for expository purposes; in due course we will find reason to distinguish more elaborately between the state of believing and the assertive act of judgment.

short if it fails to secure its aim through competence. That knowledge is a norm of belief is then a special case of the fact that *aptness*, success that manifests *competence*, is a norm of *performance*.[4]

What, however, does such competence require? Core epistemic competence is a dispositional ability to discern the true from the false in a certain domain. Infallibly so? Surely not: that is asking too much. Reliably? Well, yes, reliably *enough*. What then is the standard? How much reliability is required for it to be, epistemically, reliability enough?

But is it really appropriate to require a precise specification of a threshold? Is this not as inappropriate as it would be to insist on an exact threshold for justification enough to constitute justification, or an exact threshold for confidence enough to constitute belief? We are content to assume that *there are* such thresholds (or twilight zones) for justification and for belief. Why can't we extend that tolerant attitude to the supposed threshold of reliability for epistemic competence? Can't we just assume that there is such a threshold, even if we cannot specify it more precisely?

Fair enough. But we might still wonder about the dimension of epistemic justification and that of epistemic competence (whether these are different or at bottom the same), and even about the dimension of confidence. All three are magnitudes, each plausibly involving a threshold. We might still wonder as to how such a threshold is set. What *sorts* of considerations determine it? In particular, is the epistemic threshold invariant across the practical situations of both subject and attributor?

How reliable is reliable enough? Will this vary depending on how much is practically at stake for the subject? For the attributor? Take a fact that p. Earlier we distinguished (a) the degree of reliability required for an appropriate public assertion of that fact (or for the *claim* to know it) from (b) the degree required for the subject to just know it, regardless of whether he claims to do so, and also from (c) the degree required even just to believe *competently* that p, to manifest in so believing a reliable enough competence. These degrees may well coincide, determined as they all are by what we can appropriately store for later retrieval even when the original basis is gone from memory. If we put aside pragmatic concerns such as whether a

---

[4] This provides an understanding of the knowledge norm of assertion different from that found in Timothy Williamson's *Knowledge and Its Limits* (OUP, 2000). See especially Chapter 11, "Assertion," where the knowledge rule is understood as governing *assertion* constitutively, by analogy with the ways in which the rules of chess constitutively govern the pieces and how they may and may not be moved in the game. Our account is in terms of the constitution of judgment and assertion as actions, but the constitution is teleological rather than normative.

check will bounce, or whether one will be late for a meeting in another city, what then determines whether a competence is epistemically reliable *enough*?

How can we assess risk of failure (false belief) once practical concerns are set aside? The concerns that remain would be cognitive or theoretical. Using a catchall label, let's call them '(purely) epistemic'.[5] What is distinctive of these? They presumably involve truth, and its reliable acquisition. A competence is epistemic only if it is an ability, a disposition, to discern the true from the false in a certain domain. But infallibility is too much to require, which triggers once again our persistent question: How reliable is reliable "enough," and is this something that varies from subject to subject, or from attributor to attributor, or both?

When we bring in extra-epistemic concerns about physical safety, or bouncing checks, or importance of timely arrival, in the *epistemic* assessment of a belief, are we proceeding as inappropriately as when we assess the tennis appropriateness of a serve by how well it impresses a friend entering the stands? There appear to be domain-internal standards that determine proper risk in tennis. And the same seems true of hunting, and of indefinitely many other domains of human performance. These admittedly resist precise formulation. They presumably concern how success is assessed internally to the domain. Domain-internal standards of such success would help determine domain-internal standards for "reliability enough." For a hunt we have the successful hunt, for tennis the winning match. Whether a particular performance is appropriate within either domain depends on how appropriately that performance is meant to contribute—and how appropriately it does contribute—to a pattern of activities with enough probability of attaining domain-internal success, such as that of the hunt or of the match.[6]

As humans and as fellow members of our communities and of our species, we depend crucially and variously on the acquisition and sharing of information. The epistemically successful life is a difficult thing to define in general terms, as is the epistemically successful history of a community or species. It seems a matter of collectively attaining and sustaining a picture of the surrounding world that enables a level of prediction, control, and understanding within an acceptable range, given the possibilities and trade-offs proper to the constitution and situation of

---

[5] In a fuller account we may need to rule out other concerns besides the prudential and moral, such as perhaps the aesthetic. I leave that open for now, and assume for simplicity that any other such concerns fall in with those I am gathering under the title of the "practical or pragmatic."

[6] And we will need to allow also a derivative sort of appropriateness for performance under simulation, as when a device is tested without being properly situated. Through similar flexibility we can also assess how good a *practice* serve is, one that is not part of a match; its quality is presumably correlated with how hard it would have been for an opponent to handle it in a match.

the subject and/or his group.[7] Here non-epistemic factors do plausibly bear. What determines the acceptable range depends on the needs of that life and community, and on the range of possible success allowed by the constitution and situation of the participants.

Epistemic competences are analogous to tennis and hunting competences. The latter abilities or dispositions attain their status as competences by how they bear on the proper objectives of tennis and hunting respectively. Whether a tennis or hunting ability is reliable enough depends on whether its exercise can sufficiently further the relevant objectives over the span of a match or of a hunt. This is compatible with the failure of many instances of that exercise. And assessment of proper performance must also take into account how effectively that particular performance joins how successful a pattern by that subject or group over the span of a match or hunt.

7.1.3. Competence and reliability

In our two comparison cases, hunting and tennis, an *unreliable* ability can still be reliable enough to constitute a competence. Despite its low reliability, such an ability can be manifest in the success of the hunter's kill or the champion's winning ace, making this an apt performance. But it seems quite otherwise in the epistemic domain; or at least so it seems initially.

A speculative hypothesis that a detective, or a lover, or a meteorologist feels in his bones to be correct, can be based on a considerable ability that nevertheless falls well short of being reliable, far short of 50 percent. An affirmation on such a basis is thus analogous to the long shot by the hunter-archer or the blasting serve by the tennis champion. These latter seem properly assessable as apt, so long as they succeed within the hunt or the match. Suppose the long shot does kill the prey and the blasting low-percentage serve does win the point, and suppose these performances to be part of a pattern reliably predictive of success over the course of a hunt or of a match. That particular hunting shot, and that particular serve, would then each be assessed as both apt and meta-apt, as one whose success manifests a domain-specific competence of the performer, and one that runs appropriate risk (perhaps when viewed as part of a relevant overall pattern), even if the risk of failure for that isolated performance is quite high.

It seems otherwise, however, in the domain of knowledge. Take the speculative belief-in-one's-bones based on an ability to discern with very low reliability. That belief will not be considered an instance of knowledge, surely; nor will it be

---

[7] This is success on a basic level, one analogous to the shot's hitting its target; or, more directly relevantly, to a belief's hitting the mark of truth.

thought to hit the mark of truth through a reliable enough epistemic competence exercised by the believer. If that ability falls very far short of reliability, if it falls near the server's 15 percent rate of success, then it will not be granted the status of a knowledge-level epistemic competence; when taken at face value, its deliverances will provide neither knowledge nor reliably enough apt belief.

Why is a batter's 15 percent competence deemed outstanding, as is a basketball player's 40 percent three-point percentage, while an epistemic ability at those levels is dismissed as subpar and inadequate to provide knowledge? True, those athletic percentages top the relevant distributions among humans and even among players. Suppose however that the ability to speculate correctly on the part of the detective or the lover or the meteorologist also tops its relevant distribution. All three of them are as good at such risky, speculative, thought as is anyone, and far better than most. Nevertheless, this would not make their pertinent competences reliable enough to give them knowledge of the truth. Even if we did not always require epistemic reliability above 50 percent (as we apparently do), still 15 percent would hardly suffice. The correctness of unreliable speculation cannot manifest epistemic competence sufficient to constitute knowledge.

Take a thought that manifests a disposition with low reliability. Why might such a thought be deemed insufficiently reliable? Should this be explained through our membership in an information-sharing species, and in more specific epistemic communities? Why does apt belief and judgment require more reliable competence than the baseball hit or the basketball field goal? At least in part, I suggest, the answer is that epistemic competences are relevant not only to the attainment of a good picture of things for the believer, but also to informing others, enlarging thereby the pool of shared information. Risky informed guesses do not pass muster as objectively endorsable apt attainments of the truth, properly stored for later use, and transmissible to others through public assertion.

Why not? Why would our need to inform others explain more here than our need to know things ourselves? Why might the social dimension of epistemology import a requirement of reliability higher than seems proper in other domains, where performance is recognized as apt despite the low reliability of the competence manifest? What follows will gradually develop an answer to these questions.

Take a Hail-Mary shot by a player in the last seconds of a basketball game. The shot goes through the hoop and earns credit through the player's apt performance, even though this long shot had a very low chance of success. A social entity, the team, is involved, and the player's performance is assessed as part of the team's performance. Nevertheless, his unreliable shooting competence (from that far out) might still be manifest in an apt performance, his game-winning field goal. That shot can manifest competence, even if from that distance his percentage is quite low, say 10 percent. The percentage of the average player, after all, even the average pro, may fall well below that.[8] Even if his relevant competence is not at all remarkable, moreover, it does involve some skill. He at least threw in the right general direction. In addition, there was no alternative play that would have had greater chance of success, as there was no time to pass to a teammate. The team-involving social dimension of basketball hence does not preclude apt performance that manifests very unreliable competence. Why not allow similarly that aptness of belief might be based on unreliable competence?

The foregoing suggests a distinction between:

sheer *apt thought*, whose correctness manifests the believer's competence, which is above average, on the matter at hand and in the circumstances,

and

reliably enough apt thought, above a threshold of reliable competence set by the needs of human flourishing in information-sharing communities.

Given this distinction, we might well allow that a thought can attain a kind of aptness without amounting to knowledge. Thus the well-informed hypotheses of a self-confident Sherlock Holmes or Albert Einstein can amount to apt thoughts (affirmative thoughts), while falling short of knowledge. In a way they *are* apt affirmations, whose correctness does manifest competence far above the average for the sort of question and the circumstances involved. Nevertheless, they are not *reliably enough* apt affirmations. They need to be confirmed—in some cases through more pedestrian, reliable ways—before they can attain the status of outright knowledge. Only through such confirmation could they finally attain the status of reliable-enough apt belief.

Note further how this might help explain the standing of norm-requiring competence (or epistemic justification) for assertion. There is a norm of assertion that derives from a default reliability requirement imposed on members of human communities. We are accordingly required to assert only what manifests reliable enough competence. What is properly asserted is only what is underwritten thus reliably. The standing of this norm derives in turn from the requirements for *appropriate* sharing of information, conducive to human flourishing through mutual reliance. So, the explanation of the norm's standing will derive

---

[8] Note also that the per-swing success ratio of a good baseball hitter (as opposed to the per-at-bat ratio) is similarly low.

from the requirement of reliability if sharing is to conduce properly to such flourishing.

7.1.4. A better solution: we must understand judgmental belief properly

When I go for my yearly eye exam, I am asked to read the lines of a chart with letters that shrink line by line from a huge single letter at the top, to those barely visible at the bottom. At some point I start to lose confidence that I am getting the letters right, but I keep going until the technician tells me to stop and then records some result. At that point there are many cases where I am quite unsure as to whether it is an 'E' or an 'F', say, or a 'P' rather than an 'F', etc. Suppose, however, it turns out that I am in fact infallibly right year after year at a line where I am thus unsure. At that point I am in effect "guessing." I do affirm, to myself in private and to the technician in public, and I do so in the endeavor to get it right. And surely we can stipulate that I thereby manifest a competence that I do not recognize as reliable enough. That is why I resort to guessing, when I affirm as I undergo the eye test. Unbeknownst to me my affirmations are surprisingly reliable, as it turns out. How then do we assess my performances? We are here conflicted. In a way I *do* know those letters, as shown by my impressive reliability. But there is also a pull to say that I do not *really* know. What accounts for this? Quite plausibly, what is missing is my assessing my "guesses" as reliable enough.

That being so, we can draw a distinction concerning the first-order act or attitude involved in one's question as to whether the letter is an 'E' (or an 'F'). The act or attitude that we retain even once our confidence wanes sufficiently is the affirmation, or the willingness to affirm, that the letter is indeed an 'E', where one affirms in the endeavor *to get it right on that question*. The act or attitude that we no longer perform or host is the affirmation, or willingness to affirm accordingly, in the endeavor to get it right *reliably enough*.

Accordingly, we can distinguish two sorts of affirmation. Affirmation in the endeavor to get it right *reliably enough* on a certain question is *judgment*—let us call it that. To affirm in the endeavor to get it right, *without* affirming in the endeavor to get it right *reliably enough* is, by contrast, only to *guess*. (This leaves it open that you can also guess in other ways: for example, by merely *supposing* or *assuming* in the endeavor to get it right, without so much as affirming.) Of course, either a judgment or a guess can in fact get it right, and if it does get it right, the judgment or guess might or might not get it right reliably enough. Either of them can thus amount to an apt intellectual performance, a performance that attains its aim in a way that manifests the performer's competence.

As a result, we now have a better way to account for our reluctance to attribute knowledge to the guesser in the eye exam. The knowledge that we are reluctant to attribute requires full-fledged judgment, not just a guess. Compatibly with that, we can allow a lower grade of "knowledge," whether metaphorically or literally, one that requires only apt guessing, and not apt judging. Apt judging, moreover, requires that the performer attain his aim, and do so in a way that manifests relevant competence. Accordingly, to really know (judgmentally) one must affirm in the endeavor to get it right reliably enough, and one must attain *that* objective in a way that manifests one's relevant competence. The guesser in the eye-exam does not even judge, so he cannot know.[9]

7.1.5. Encroachment and invariantism: what is reliability "enough"?

Aptness then is success through competence, where the competence must be reliable enough. This enables a distinction between the things we know full stop, and the things we know well enough. One might know something, after all, even though in a special context, e.g., where one's expert opinion is required, one does not know it well enough. Just think of the stakes involved in the context of a nuclear reactor, or a law court, or a surgery room. How more specifically do we understand this variation?

We might try saying that to know well enough in a high stakes situation is to have a reliable-enough apt belief. If we applied our earlier formula, then, we would have to say that as the stakes rise, the subject's knowledge dwindles or even disappears, provided his competence does not rise.

More plausibly, however, there is no such outright loss of knowledge; what changes is only whether the subject knows well *enough* in the new context, with its higher stakes, whether he knows well enough to enable proper reliance on that belief as a premise in practical reasoning. *This* threshold does rise: reliability enough for deciding about something unimportant need not be enough when the stakes rise. (The Appendix goes further into this.)

The following example might help make plausible how the standard for knowledge can remain stable through variation in the stakes.

Suppose that H(igh) is in a high stakes situation and has excellent evidence for his belief that p, but not good enough to give him knowledge that p. L(ow) for his part also has good evidence for believing that p, but not nearly as good as H; yet L's evidence is good enough to give L knowledge that p, since the stakes are so low in his context. Suppose H and L both store their beliefs in the normal way we do all the time. Weeks later they both believe the same thing based just on their retentive memory, now while asleep and quite removed from

---

[9] Although we have focused on judgmental belief, with its constitutive aim, functional belief might also aim at getting it right reliably enough, so that there are functional correlates of judgment and of judgmental belief, correlates that require only functional aimings, and not intentional and conscious endeavorings.

any high stakes situation. Should we now say that L knows while H does not, even though L's evidential basis is weaker than that of H, and there is no other relevant difference beyond the different stakes at the time of acquisition of the respective beliefs? Take someone who acquires knowledge that p, and retains his belief that p through excellent retentive memory, and acquires no defeaters in the meantime. When later still he believes that p, very plausibly he still knows that p. And this verdict then applies to L with comparable plausibility.

That strikes me as quite a motivating reason in favor of invariantism. But here we may just find ourselves conflicted.[10] If we still find remaining plausibility in subject-sensitivity and variantism, we need to reconsider how best to accommodate whatever makes these as plausible as they are.

My suggestion is that "human knowledge" is not tied to the stakes at the time of acquisition, nor at the time of evaluation. What we "know" period is a matter of what we believe with reliable enough aptness for storage of that belief. And the reliability required for such storage is the reliability pertinent to belief and assertion by members of our information-sharing social species. Asserting things that you do not believe with enough reliability would thwart human communities, since we cannot possibly keep track of the evidential aetiology of people's beliefs. So, we need some agreed measure for assessing how much weight to place on the *testimony* that crosses from one subject to another, and on the *retention* that crosses from our past selves to our present selves.

According to the present suggestion, then, one "knows that p" period if and only if one aptly believes that p reliably enough for storage of the belief even after the loss of the original basis for its acquisition. No mere guess is good enough to be stored, so as to remain in place even once its initial credentials are gone; only knowledge is suitable for such storage.

That, moreover, is compatible with the fact that what you know well enough for storage may *not* be something you know well enough for it to provide a proper practical basis for action when the stakes are high. So you might know something "flat out" even if you do not know it well enough to act on it when the stakes are high.

On the flip side is the apt Hail Mary shot, or its intellectual correlates in the beliefs of our imagined Holmes or Einstein. Your affirmative thought might be apt even when it is not even flat out knowledge. It might still admirably get it right

---

[10] Wouldn't the proponent of pragmatic encroachment simply deny preservationism about memorial knowledge? True, proponents of pragmatic encroachment already seem implicitly committed to denying preservationism, but that seems prima facie not just a feature of the view, but an intuitive problem. To fully resolve the conflict, we would of course need to consider any independent arguments against preservationism, but I myself know of none that seem convincing against a properly formulated preservationism.

through competence, with a competence reliable enough for speculative thought, or thinking in the dark. Your thought might still fall short: it might not be reliable enough for storage, or, accordingly, for human knowledge, plain and simple.

7.2. Knowledge and Judgment

7.2.1. *Belief and its relation to judgment*

I have elsewhere distinguished two varieties of belief: first, credence above a certain confidence-threshold; second, affirmative judgment or the corresponding disposition.[11] This latter "affirmative" variety is belief as a kind of disposition to affirm in the endeavor to answer the pertinent question correctly, and reliably enough. Such affirmation is an all-or-nothing act of judgment that takes place in the privacy of the subject's mind. Denial is then affirmation of the negation, and suspension is the intentional omission both of affirmation and of denial, an omission that can be either provisional (while one deliberates or ponders) or else conclusive, settled.

Why however should we think that there is any such all-or-nothing act of affirmative thought? If only we could make sense of this act, related acts could then be explained in terms of it. (Thus, denial of <p> is affirmation of <not-p>, and suspension on the question whether p is intentional omission of affirmation that p, along with intentional omission of denial that p.) How then should we make sense of the supposed act of private, mental affirmation? How more fully and explicitly should we understand this supposed act? Why should we so much as allow that there is or might be any such?

Undeniably, there is of course the all-or-nothing act of public assertion performed through the use of a natural language. Through assertion we can endeavor to attain one or another of a vast number of aims, including pragmatic aims divorced from disinterested intention to inform. Fortunately, there *is* very often the intention simply to inform—to inform and not to misinform—as a dominant aim in human communication. Given our capacity for strategic self-deception, a similar distinction seems in order for judgment and belief as for assertion. Despite how susceptible we can be to epistemically irrelevant pragmatic factors, there is such a thing as disinterested belief influenced purely by the aim to get it right, to believe correctly.

---

[11] In *Knowing Full Well* (Princeton University Press, 2011). One side of this is developed earlier in our text. My forthcoming papers on epistemic agency and the epistemology of judgment go into it more fully.

Consider the importance of proper assertion for an information-sharing social species. A newscaster or a teacher might assert with testimonial propriety even when they do not voice their own beliefs.[12] If the speaker plays no role in any such epistemic institution, however, no such role as that of newscaster or that of teacher, then their assertion is epistemically proper only when it voices their own belief. Otherwise it would be improperly insincere. But what sort of belief is at issue here? Is it belief as confident enough credence or is it rather *judgment*, an act of judgment or a disposition to judge with the aim of judging correctly, with truth, reliably enough? Note the difference here between act and disposition. It can be true of someone asleep that *in his judgment* we ought to proceed a certain way, even though he is at the time performing no *act* of judgment.

Suppose such judgment to be what most directly determines proper, sincere affirmation. A speaker's assertion of what he does *not* in this sense judge to be true would then involve an epistemically improper clash: what he is willing to say publicly then clashes with what he says to himself *in foro interno*. In order to avoid such impropriety, what the speaker asserts publicly must comport with what he would affirm to himself in the privacy of his own mind. Otherwise there would be either some speech flaw, or some failure of sincerity. Fully epistemically proper assertion requires the avoidance of any such flaw or failure. It must express in unflawed speech what the speaker thinks (in act or disposition). The speaker speaks with epistemic propriety only if he speaks as he thinks, with sincerity and without linguistic flaw.

Is there an account in terms of credential threshold that rivals our account in terms of judgment? According to such a rival account what assertion requires by way of sincerity and avoidance of flaw would perhaps be *proper expression of a credence above a certain threshold of confidence*. But what will set that threshold? Would it not be the threshold at which the subject is willing to affirm to himself in the endeavor to answer correctly? Maybe so, but why the privacy restriction, why the restriction to what the subject affirms to himself? Why not just understand belief as a disposition to assert publicly when one faces the corresponding question and one endeavors to answer it with the aim of answering correctly? Well, for one thing, no-one mute could then hold any beliefs. Moreover, our answer in terms of private affirmation is unaffected by the fact that epistemically irrelevant pragmatic factors might so easily influence what one is willing to say in public. And, finally, ours is the account of belief that will most smoothly bear on the subject's conscious reasoning, as he invokes premises in his practical deliberation or theoretical pondering, all of which can take place in the privacy of his own thought.

---

[12] As Jennifer Lackey has made clear, in her book *Learning From Words* (Oxford University Press, 2008) and in earlier papers cited in the book.

7.2.2. When is a belief sufficiently reliable to constitute knowledge?

Consider a stream of thought or speech on which pragmatic factors are not allowed to encroach. The subject perceives that p, stores that belief, and when later he fields a relevant question, his answer is in line with his stored belief. Consider next the reasons, perceptual or otherwise, that prompted the initial storage of that belief, which is then retained long after the lapse from memory of the basis on which it was formed. After that point our accessible basis will be reduced to whatever still supports our continuing to so believe, often just the fact that we do still believe as we do, along with whatever we can properly assume as to our trustworthiness on the subject matter involved.

Although we may have acquired the belief with a very high degree of confidence, this confidence will fade in tandem with our dwindling awareness of our original basis for believing as we do. In fact, our confidence will align not with the original confidence and its basis but rather with our synchronic confidence in our present reliability on the subject matter of our belief. What is the degree of reliability that is appropriate for retention of a belief? This can differ crucially from the degree of reliability later required for reliance on that belief either in the subject's private conscious reasoning or in his public assertion. What one is later justified in premising privately or asserting publicly will of course depend on the question at hand and on the amount at stake for the subject or his community in the correctness of his so premising or asserting. But our question abstracts from such special contexts, where the risk exceeds what is normally at stake in conveyance of information or reliance on a premise. Indeed, our question applies even when the subject is just asleep, or unconscious altogether. At that point he is still storing immensely many beliefs. What determines whether a belief is thus stored with epistemic propriety?

What is the use, the epistemic use, of such stored beliefs? Largely it is the use they still have even when the subject has forgotten the bases on which they were initially stored, or retained over time. However, we do want our beliefs to be reliable beyond some minimum. We want to be able to appeal to them properly at any arbitrary later time when the belief may become relevant. So, we are allowed to store a belief when its basis endows it with at least that minimum level of reliability. Moreover, we want to store potentially useful beliefs when they do reach that level, to the extent possible, without overloading our memory banks. We are now considering the subject and his indefinite future, and the uses he may find for his stored beliefs. Even just for an arbitrary subject in isolation from his group, some level of reliability is required if he is to store a belief with epistemic propriety. This is a level that he wants in his stored beliefs, so that he can in the indefinite future trust those stored beliefs to have that level given just their storage in his memory. Of course, what is pragmatically at stake in a particular situation can vary enormously, and the degree of reliability required in a belief if it is to be worthy of trust *as a basis for action* will depend on the stakes in that particular situation. Consider extraordinary situations where the stakes are abnormally high and where reliability is at a premium. Such high-stakes situations must be distinguished from ordinary situations where the stakes are normal. A reasonable degree of reliability is required for such normal questions in ordinary situations of quotidian interest. This is the degree of reliability that is required for ordinary human knowledge. As the stakes rise, we need knowledge that rises above those ordinary levels of epistemic quality. We now need knowledge for sure (or for more sure). And now of course we cannot just draw a belief from storage and trust it simply on that basis. Now we are in a context in which we need additional reason for trust. These special reasons could take either of two forms. They could amount to first-order reasons synchronically in view for a certain answer to our high-stakes question, or they could amount rather to special reasons for believing that we are particularly reliable on such subject matter, when situated as we are when we then consider our question.

Such contexts, we say, require abnormally high reason for trust. But what is this "trust"? How do we manifest our trust in a high stakes situation? Do we manifest it by what we are willing to judge affirmatively even to ourselves in the privacy of our own thoughts? If so, then the stakes *do* after all affect what we know, for they affect what we relevantly believe. They affect how we are willing to think affirmatively, what we are willing to affirm to ourselves. And this affects what we believe in the sense of judgment, or affirmative belief.

There is however an attractive alternative option. We might deny that the mere heightening of the practical stakes affects what we are willing to affirm to ourselves, or how we are willing to judge. And this is so for more than one reason. First of all, the stakes may not affect what we are willing to affirm to ourselves in the simple endeavor to get it right on that question. Not even what we are willing to guess in *foro interno* is affected that way. Even more plausibly, moreover, we might deny that the mere heightening of the practical stakes affects what we are willing to affirm in the endeavor to affirm correctly *and reliably enough, above the threshold set by our social epistemic norms*. This is because the social epistemic norms pertain to what judgmental beliefs we can properly store for appropriate later retrieval and sharing, in quotidian contexts with normal stakes. What the stakes may happen to be at that moment is hence not relevant to our willingness to judge, therefore, not if judgment is defined as affirmation in the endeavor to affirm reliably enough for normal stakes.

What is affected instead by rising stakes, we might counter, is how we are willing to *choose* on a given basis. Thus, we might feel confident enough to judge and even to affirm publicly that the ice is solid enough to bear our weight. But we might still hesitate to step on it, if the water is too cold and we fear for our lives or even just for our comfort. On this view, we are still willing to think, and even to say, that the ice is solid enough, but unwilling to add that this is certain enough to justify relevant action. What is more, our judgment might even constitute ordinary, common sense knowledge, even though this knowledge is not relevantly "actionable."

The considerations bearing thus on the mnemonic channel from one's past self to one's present self, apply similarly to the testimonial channel from one subject to another. When we take at his word someone else who speaks in his own person, we can very often believe accordingly with epistemic propriety, and we can reason practically on that basis, and we can assert thus in turn when speaking in our own person. When all of this happens, it is often because the testifier is voicing his stored belief, one that was stored and retained reliably enough, and the speaker communicates competently vis-à-vis the hearer. However, one cannot *always* take a speaker's say so on trust so that the knowledge that we obtain thereby is actionable. It depends on the question and situation, and what is at stake. As the stakes rise, so do the requirements properly imposed on speakers in determining how worthy they are of our trust in the specific situation, and whether their testimony yields knowledge that is relevantly actionable. The normal human reaction is to accept testimony at face value, even without special knowledge of the speaker's credentials. Compare how memory operates unimpeded, properly so, even once the subject's awareness of the initial basis fades and disappears. This is how it is for the great bulk of our body of beliefs. This is how it must be, given human limitations. It would be cognitively disastrous always to relinquish beliefs as soon as our awareness of their source dwindled, or to reject all testimony unsupported by known credentials. We are built to retain beliefs even after we have lost awareness of their initial basis and of how reliable that basis may have been. And we are built to trust testimony absent special reasons for distrust.

A further interesting question concerns the degree of confidence that attaches to a belief when it is initially acquired. When that belief is stored and retained, what exactly is retained? Is it a credence *with its initial degree of confidence*? Not so, I argue, and properly not so, at least in most cases. A high degree of confidence will be retained only so long as one retains awareness of the belief's excellent enough basis. On pain of vicious regress, however, this meta-awareness must be a kind of pseudo-retention. What "remains" is rather a related but fresh belief, of some degree of confidence, that one's synchronic first-order belief is properly based on some reliable basis. Confident enough endorsement from one's I-now perspective is required for proper retention of a first-order belief with a corresponding degree of confidence. Any reduction of your ability to endorse that first-order belief, from your synchronic I-now perspective, is correlated with a corresponding reduction of your ability to retain your high degree of confidence in it. The retained belief now remains only as a belief once acquired. Only through features of one's synchronic I-now perspective, can one now sustain it with a corresponding degree of confidence. So, the credence's degree of confidence will fade in tandem with any reduction in the subject's ability to endorse that credence properly from his ongoing second-order perspective. And it will eventually dwindle below the degree of confidence required to sustain the subject's first-order belief. But what is that degree of confidence? Plausibly, it is the degree of confidence required for proper synchronic affirmation.

What then is the degree of confidence epistemically required in a normal context for such affirmation? What is required at least for affirmation to oneself? Is the degree of confidence required for proper synchronic affirmation to oneself the same as the degree required for proper synchronic affirmation to an interlocutor? This is not so plausible, simply because public assertion can be misleading if speaker and hearer each knows that the other knows the stakes to be high. In such a case, confident assertion is likely to convey not just where one takes the truth to lie, but also where it lies surely enough as to make our knowledge relevantly actionable.

Consider the need to guide oneself individually with proper allowance for one's cognitive and mnemonic limitations. Consider also our need to guide ourselves cooperatively, with proper allowance for those same individual limitations. Some threshold of reliability is thus required for storing our guiding beliefs, so that our continuing disposition to affirm will satisfy that minimal degree of reliability. This requires the subject's ability to remember without undue distortion. We must guard against a memory that reduces reliability below the required minimum when the belief is later drawn from storage in a normal setting. We need a store of beliefs, of stored dispositions to affirm to oneself or to others in normal settings: i.e., in ordinary settings of human reasoning or communication. Given human storage limitations, we cannot always or even often store awareness of how our beliefs are initially acquired, nor can we retain a running awareness of their continuing basis. Moreover, what is most relevant to our epistemic cooperation is the act of assertion, normally just flat-out assertion. This is how propositions can figure as premises of reasoning, practical or theoretical. Proper cooperation requires sincerity, moreover, sincerity to oneself (avoidance, for example, of wishful thinking) and sincerity to interlocutors.

In sum, there is a minimum level of reliability that is required in the epistemic deliverances that we trust in our daily lives. This includes the many gauges that we go by in a technological civilization. We do not require infallibility, since little if anything could then be trusted. But we do require a high level of reliability. We are ourselves among our main sources of information. This includes not only our fellow human beings but also our own past selves. Just the fact that such a source delivers a proposition is a good reason to believe that proposition, absent special reasons for mistrust. If we could not trust in that way the testimony of our neighbors or our own memories, we would be greatly reduced epistemically, well below the level of an isolated Robinson Crusoe, who must trust his memory at every turn. Indeed it is hard to see how any human could live once so radically reduced epistemically. But for this to be feasible there must be some consensus, whether natural or conventional, on what is a minimum level of confidence (and corresponding reliability) required for storage of a belief (making allowance for the inevitable dampening of reliability that will come with later reliance on memory). *This*, I submit, is the level that comports with what we are willing to recognize as *human knowledge*, the level that is required for proper assertion, and for properly endorsed synchronic judgment (absent special reason for mistrust).

That is all compatible with heightened requirements for trust when the stakes rise. This is perfectly in line with the similar rise in our requirements for trust in any relevant gauge when the stakes rise. Ordinary gauges may not suffice in a nuclear plant, in a surgery room, or in a Formula One car. Much higher reliability may well be required for our trust in such special contexts. Someone who uses an ordinary gauge in some such special context may still know what his gauge delivers, even if he should not there guide his conduct by what he knows. He needs not just such ordinary knowledge but knowledge *for sure*, or for *more* sure. He might have knowledge all right, while still lacking *actionable* knowledge.

7.2.3. Communication and the value of knowledge

A crucial component of our collective epistemic life is the act of sincere affirmation, which could take the form of either sincere private affirmation to oneself, or sincere public assertion to others, in the endeavor to affirm with epistemic correctness, with truth.

Two critical domains are here important. First, there is the domain of epistemic communication. Acts of communication are subject to epistemic assessment in various respects. They are assessable in respect of clarity, of conciseness, and also of audibility or legibility (and even of readability), and more. When we speak we often aim to communicate information, to convey it from speaker to hearer, so that what the speaker knows becomes thereby knowable to the hearer. This knowledge involves belief in the sense of disposition to affirm. What is affirmed becomes thus available to others, and perhaps usable in their own reasoning, and as a basis for their rational action, provided the stakes are appropriate. Various features of the act of communication become relevant to this aim to communicate. Communicative acts are subject to such varied assessment concerning the appropriate conveyance of information. They can be better or worse in these various respects. This fact teaches something important for the study of the value of knowledge, to which we turn next.

We have taken note of the fact that an intended act of communication can be assessed in various ways: in respect of clarity, for example, or if aural in respect of audibility; and so on, and so forth. This does not require that acts of communication must have some objective final value. Not even successful acts of communication need have any such value. I may write in my diary in beautiful cursive "Today I had eggs for breakfast," or I may twitter this to the world at large. My act can then be assessed in various communicative respects: legibility, for example, spelling, grammar, and so on. One such act can certainly be *better* than another. But none of this requires that there be some distinctive, objective *communicative value* that constitutes a distinctive sort of final value, not even one that is prima facie or pro tanto.

The same is true, of course, for critical domains generally. There is no distinctive final archery value, or chess value, even though archery and chess performances can be assessed as better or worse *as performances of the relevant sort*. It might be replied that there is a crucial distinction between archery shots and chess moves, on the one hand, and beliefs on the other hand. Archery and chess are just invented domains of amusement for human beings. The domain of beliefs is not at all like that. Beliefs and the broader epistemic domain are unavoidable for human beings, and crucial for our individual and collective success. Our participation in that domain is crucial for the flourishing of our lives individually and in society.

Compare however the domain of speech. Utterances in speech can of course be assessed. Some are better than others in a great variety of respects. Most of these respects of evaluation do not require any consequentialist understanding according to which there would be some distinctive communicative final value, some final value that successful communicative utterances would need to have. There is no such distinctive final speech value any more than there is a distinctive chess final value or archery final value. Nor is any such communicative final value made any more plausible by the fact that communication is not optional for humanity, unlike chess or archery. True, without communication there would be no humanity. Communication in fact seems barely less important to our social species than is knowledge. Yet we can still assess human communicative acts without committing to any distinctive final communicative value. So we should similarly consider whether epistemic assessment of beliefs requires any distinctive final doxastic or epistemic value.

Why not think of it instead as follows? Human communication is important for human flourishing, for the flourishing of individual lives and for the flourishing of human groups. This does not require that there be any distinctive communicative final value. It requires only that communication be an important component of enough human ways of flourishing, which can take many and various forms. It is hard to imagine a flourishing human life that will not involve communication in some important ways at some stages at least of that life. Moreover, communication enables flourishing not only instrumentally, but even constitutively, as shown by the place of communication in human relationships. And it is nearly impossible to imagine a flourishing human society deprived entirely of communication. So, communication of various sorts will figure as a component of human flourishing individually or socially. But from this it hardly follows that so much as a single act of communication need have any final value distinctively its own, or indeed any final value of its own at all. Much less does it follow that all successful acts of communication must have some such final value.

Just so, human knowledge is at least as important for human flourishing as is communication, both for the flourishing of individual lives, and for the collective flourishing of groups. But this no more requires any distinctive epistemic final value than does the importance of communication require any distinctive communicative final value. It is required at most that knowledge be an important component of enough human ways of flourishing, which can take many and various forms. We have found it difficult to imagine a flourishing human life or society that will not involve communication in some important ways. Similarly, it is hard to imagine a flourishing human life or society deprived entirely of knowledge. Knowledge of various sorts will surely figure as a component of the flourishing of individual lives and of the flourishing of human beings in groups.

But is it really true that human flourishing requires knowledge in the ways suggested? We face the *Meno* problem and its variations. Why is knowledge better than merely subjectively competent belief? Why is knowledge better than merely true belief? Well, compare this: Why is well-based happiness or pleasure better than the equally subjectively pleasant tone of the subject in an experience machine victimized by a controlling demon? The life of such a hedonic victim is no more a flourishing human life than is the illusory life of a Matrix dweller, which indeed can itself include much illusory or false pleasure. The subjective character would be real enough, of course, but its content would be illusory nonetheless. Victims of experience machines and Matrix frameworks would have subjective enjoyment, true enough, but their lives would fall short nonetheless, as is revealed by our preferences when a choice is forced. Better truth than falsity in a human life, better competence than incompetence, yes, but better yet what is required for the full human flourishing of that life, which is incompatible with the various illusions canvassed.

Appendix

Actionable knowledge

If one knows that ø-ing is the best thing for one to do now (out of its relevant reference class of options), does one act wrongly if one does not ø? What if one *also* knows that there is a non-zero objective chance (relative to one's basic evidence) that ø-ing is not best, and indeed that there is a non-zero objective chance that ø-ing will be horrendously bad. What if, by comparison, what one knows is that only a miniscule margin of value is secured by ø-ing? By hypothesis one knows that ø-ing is best, so ø-ing is of course best, and in fact those horrendous consequences will not ensue upon one's ø-ing. It might still be appropriate for one to hedge one's bets, however, by not ø-ing. Just consider the enormous risk that one runs by ø-ing, when this risk is assessed relative to one's basic relevant evidence.

Suppose for example that one knows one's ticket to have lost, even without having seen the lottery results. Is it now appropriate for one to sell one's ticket for a penny, since this will mean a net gain over the other relevant options? But what if one knows that one's irascible partner will react very badly if in fact one's ticket has won and one has sold it for a penny. Or suppose one knows or believes justifiably that God would punish with eternal damnation those whose actions turn out so badly? Would one act appropriately by disregarding the objective chance (relative to one's basic evidence) of such untoward results? Suppose one acted in accord with what one knows to be best, however small may be its margin of positive value. Would that be appropriate? Surely not.

We are thus prompted to take a closer look at the argument that runs as follows:

1. My ticket has lost.
2. If it has lost, it is worthless.
3. If it is worthless, it is best for me to sell it, even for a penny.
4. It is best for me to sell my ticket, even for a penny.

It may be thought that this argument is bad, and that it is bad simply because one does not know its first premise. After all, only what one knows can properly be used as a premise in such practical reasoning. So that's why the argument is bad. Its first premise cannot properly be used in reasoning well in accord with that argument.

We are supposed thereby to have a reason to reject that a lottery proposition such as 1 can be known. However, consider the practical syllogism that continues the argument as follows.

5. If it is best for me to sell my ticket for a penny, then I shall so sell my ticket.
6. I shall sell my ticket for a penny.

And suppose the further conclusion of this practical syllogism is my selling of my ticket for a penny.

This argument might now be put in question through the sorts of considerations adduced above. Whether it is appropriate for one to reason in accord with the practical syllogism, and even to act accordingly, would seem to depend on what other information is at one's disposal, including the relevant objective chance that selling the ticket for a penny might have disastrous consequences. So, one can reject the full practical reasoning involved without questioning whether premise 1 is known. That premise might or might not be knowable. This argument would seem to leave that question unaffected.

8

Belief, Acceptance, and What Happens in Groups
Some Methodological Considerations

Margaret Gilbert and Daniel Pilchman

Introduction

The vast majority of the discussions in epistemology have focused on the epistemic states of human individuals.[1] Those discussions consider, for example, what it is for individual human beings to believe that such-and-such or to know that such-and-such. For present purposes we will call the inquiry in question *individual epistemology*.

Individual epistemology leaves outside its purview a whole range of everyday ascriptions of epistemic states. For in everyday thought and talk ascriptions of belief and other epistemic states commonly include ascriptions both to human individuals and to groups made up of individuals.

Thus we might speak of Jones's belief that the team will win, or of the team's belief that it will win. We might speak of Smith's belief that there is an after-life, or of her bible-study group's belief in an afterlife. Robinson might say that she believes her country is the best in the world, or she might say, in reference to the relevant citizen body, "We believe this is the best country in the world".

Ascriptions of epistemic states to groups raise the question of what it is for a group to have beliefs, knowledge, and so on. We shall call the inquiry that focuses

---

[1] Here we use "states" in a broad non-technical sense to include e.g. episodes and dispositions.

on these questions *collective epistemology*.[2] This inquiry is by now well under way with a rapidly growing literature.[3]

The broadest concern of this paper is the relation between individual and collective epistemology.[4] It approaches this relation by considering some prominent contributions to collective epistemology. These include a relatively long-standing debate that invokes a distinction between "belief" and "acceptance" in specified senses of these terms. Among other things we shall argue that these contributions to collective epistemology throw into high relief an important methodological caveat that is often ignored: One should not assume that accounts and distinctions arrived at within individual epistemology are appropriately applied within collective epistemology, however central they are to individual epistemology.

8.1. Cohen on Belief and Believers

Twenty years after its publication, L. Jonathan Cohen's *An Essay on Belief and Acceptance* is still one of the most cited sources for authors engaged in collective epistemology. Cohen has made his own contributions to the subject. In addition, his accounts of the nature of belief and acceptance have heavily influenced the continuing debate in collective epistemology that we shall discuss. We start, therefore with some discussion of Cohen's work. We focus, first, on his ideas about belief.

On Cohen's view, "belief that p is a disposition, when one is attending to issues raised, or items referred to, by the proposition *p*, normally to feel it true that *p* and false that *not-p*."[5] This account of belief, as Pascal Engel points out, has much in common with Hume's conception of belief as belonging to the passive side of the human mind.[6] At some length, Cohen situates "credal feelings" within the realm of sentiments when, on his use of the phrase, he writes:

What is important here is not to provide a phrase that is a synonymous equivalent for the word 'belief', but to place belief in its right conceptual category. Specifically, it is classifiable as a disposition to have a certain kind of mental feeling, not as a disposition to perform a certain kind of action.[7]

---

[2] Cf. (Gilbert 2004). We allow that either collective epistemology or individual epistemology could in principle have one or more skeptical outcome. Some have argued that individuals are not knowers; some have argued that they are not believers. As we discuss later, some have argued that groups are not believers.

[3] See, e.g. (Gilbert 1987; Gilbert 1989; Tuomela 1992; Clark 1994; Schmitt 1994; Cohen 1995; Tuomela 2000; Wray 2001; McMahon 2002; Tollefsen 2002; Bouvier 2004; Mathiesen 2006; Pettit 2010).

[4] We take *social* epistemology to be something of a mongrel category depending on how it is interpreted. In any case, it is not our specific focus here. For a classic source see (Goldman 1999).

[5] (Cohen 1995, 4).   [6] (Engel 2000, 11); echoing (Cohen 1989, 20).

[7] (Cohen 1995, 11).

While the ability to believe, on this view, is inextricably linked to feelings, what Cohen refers to as "acceptance" is not. In his words,

> To accept that *p*, is to have or adopt a policy of deeming, positing, or postulating that *p*—i.e. of including that proposition or rule among one's premises for deciding what to do or think in a particular context, whether or not one feels it to be true that *p*.[8]

Cohen holds that the distinction between belief and acceptance is significant because it makes an important difference to human life that we are able both to believe and to accept propositions and that we understand that this is so.[9]

8.1.1. Cohen on groups and belief

Given his understanding of belief it is no surprise that Cohen was skeptical about group or collective belief.[10] Focusing on organizations, he says:

> When we look closely enough, and get behind the metaphor or the accidents of vocabulary, we find that organizations are typically engaged in accepting premises or pursuing goals, not in experiencing beliefs or desires. No doubt this is for two main reasons. First, organizations share with human adults the ability to formulate what they accept or decide in language... Secondly, an organization is not exposed at all to the chemical or physiological stimulation of feelings.[11]

This suggests the following general argument. Groups are incapable of having or being disposed to have feelings; believing involves having or being disposed to have feelings, in particular credal feelings; so groups are incapable of belief.

In assessing that argument, let us assume, first, that groups cannot be *disposed* to have feelings if they cannot *have* feelings, and, second, that groups are indeed incapable of having feelings in the sense at issue here. The second assumption would seem to be true, if feelings are understood essentially to involve *subjective experiences*. We shall so understand feelings here.[12] It follows from these assumptions that groups cannot be disposed to have feelings. Given these assumptions, then, we must allow that *if* any believer must be disposed to experience credal feelings,

---

[8] (Cohen 1995, 4).
[9] (Cohen 1995, 61) Cohen maintains that the distinction between belief and acceptance also gives us important insights into questions about the epistemology of animals, infants, and artificial intelligences as well as into persistent philosophical problems including Moore's paradox and self-deception. Compare (Engel 2000, 11).
[10] We use the phrases "group belief" and "collective belief" interchangeably in what follows.
[11] (Cohen 1995, 55)
[12] Cf. Cohen's phrase "mental feeling" in one of the above quotations. It is of course common in everyday speech to refer to the emotions of groups as in "The team was furious with its manager" and "We just loved the opera". One can take these seriously without allowing that groups have subjective experiences of their own. For detailed discussion of a particular ascription of collective emotion see (Gilbert 2001). Gilbert (2014) discusses collective emotions generally.

then groups are not believers. This argument, however, does not clinch the case against group belief.

For one thing, Cohen's account of belief has not generally been accepted, and a variety of criticisms have been made of it. Raimo Tuomela, for instance, argues that, when distilled, Cohen's credal feelings are little more than "the thought that the content of the belief is true."[13] In other words, so-called credal feelings are not really *feelings* at all. Leslie Stevenson criticizes Cohen's appeal to credal feelings in another way. Stephenson identifies examples that one might very naturally call credal feelings—like the feeling that one's spouse is in the house despite knowing that he or she is dead—but that do not intuitively seem like beliefs. So credal feelings may not, after all, be the mark of *belief*.[14]

Irrespective of the correctness of Cohen's account of belief, there is another reason for thinking that the above argument does not clinch the case against group belief. The argument relies on Cohen's account of belief. That account, however, was based on the individual human case.[15] A plausible way of seeing Cohen's account, then, is as an account of belief *as it occurs in individual human beings*. If Cohen's account of belief is seen in this way, then, even if it is correct, it leaves open the nature of belief in the *collective* case.

8.2. Methodological Remarks: With Reference to Plato's Approach to Justice

The point just made suggests some important methodological points. We preface our discussion of them by recalling Plato's methodology in the *Republic*. Though he is primarily concerned with justice, as opposed to belief, his procedure is instructive.

Plato's overarching aim is to understand what it is for an individual human being to be just. Early in his discussion, however, he notes that justice is commonly ascribed both to individual human beings and to political societies (poleis). He then suggests that an inquiry into the nature of justice in the individual case may benefit from an inquiry into the nature of justice in the collective case. Presumably justice in the one case and justice in the other will have something in common. Both, after all, are cases of *justice*.[16]

---

[13] (Tuomela 2000, 128).   [14] (Stevenson 2002, 111).

[15] That this is so is clear enough from his discussion in, say, (Cohen 1989) where all of the initial expository examples concern individual human beings. He is, of course, operating in the context of a long epistemological tradition in philosophy and cognitive science that betrays no interest in the collective case. Cohen is an exception here but his discussion of the collective case is relatively cursory and comes after the main expository work has been accomplished.

[16] (Plato, Grube, and Reeve 1992 Bk II, 368 b–e).

Plato investigates the collective case first. Taking account of some of the salient features of this case he goes on carefully to probe the individual case, an inquiry that proceeds to a large extent in its own terms.

For present purposes the main point about Plato's procedure is not his starting with the collective case. His stated reason for doing so is not, indeed, particularly convincing. The main point is that Plato clearly sees it as both possible and appropriate to engage in *two distinct inquiries* in relation to justice: an inquiry into the nature of justice in the collective case, and an inquiry into the nature of justice in the individual case. Though he believes the results of the former may be expected to help with the investigation of the latter, he also believes that, by and large, each should be investigated on its own terms.

There are several lessons for epistemology here. In contemporary epistemology inquiries into the nature of belief and so on have started with the individual case. The results of these inquiries may well help to throw light on the nature of the collective case. Nonetheless caution is required with respect to the use of results deriving from the individual case in approaching the collective case. There may be significant disanalogies between these cases, despite their having some features in common. Careful, independent investigation of the collective case—as of the individual case—is required in order properly to understand it. Quite possibly, such careful investigation of the collective case will help to throw light on the individual case as well.[17]

Let us return for a moment to the argument, drawn from Cohen's work, to the effect that groups are not believers. A proponent of this argument may be ignoring the methodological points just made. For he (or she) may be adopting uncritically a concept of belief developed within individual epistemology—the concept articulated in Cohen's credal feelings account—when approaching the collective case.

Whether or not application of a given concept is warranted in relation to the collective case can only be decided given the details of that case. We take it that a full appreciation of this will involve an inquiry into the intended referents of those everyday statements that, on the face of it, ascribe beliefs to groups—an inquiry central to collective epistemology.

Later we shall argue that the methodological points made in this section are apt to help us to understand the stalemate that has arisen in a current debate in collective epistemology. This debate owes much to Cohen though its proponents generally do not accept all of the particulars of his account of belief. The debate focuses

[17] See e.g. (Priest ms).

on a particular account of the referent of those everyday statements that appear to ascribe beliefs to groups, an account whose accuracy it does not dispute.

Before turning to that account, and the debate it has prompted, we briefly note some of the problems associated with a different type of account. This is the account that may first come to mind, and that Cohen, for one, appears to espouse. It is the failure of this type of account, among other things, that has led theorists to focus on something different.[18]

8.3. Collective Belief Ascriptions: The Failure of Summativism

Although Cohen doubts that there are collective beliefs—in light of his understanding of belief—he is aware of the prevalence in everyday life of what are, on the face of it, ascriptions of beliefs to groups: utterances such as "The team believes it will win", "My bible study group believes in an afterlife", and so on. We shall refer to all such statements as *collective belief ascriptions*. We include under this label statements such as "We believe that. . ." where no established label for a type of group is at issue. In such cases it may be clear both to the speaker and the audience that the speaker's words are not simply elliptical for "We all believe that. . ." or "We both believe that. . ." Rather a belief is here ascribed to *us* as opposed to each one of us.

This is what Cohen says about collective belief ascriptions:

When a community or nation is said to believe or desire that p this is normally a figurative way of saying that most of its individual members or most of its official representatives believe or desire that p.[19]

He suggests, then, that when someone appears to be ascribing a belief that p to a group he (or she) is really ascribing that belief to most of the group's members or most of its official representatives.

Years earlier, Anthony Quinton had written something similar:

Groups are said to have beliefs, emotions, and attitudes...But these ways of speaking are plainly metaphorical. To ascribe mental predicates to a group is always an indirect way of ascribing such predicates to its members. With such mental states as beliefs...the ascriptions are of what I have called a summative kind. To say the industrial working class is determined to resist anti-trade union laws is to say that all or most industrial workers are so minded.[20]

---

[18] The next section covers ground familiar to those specializing in collective epistemology, and is intended largely for non-specialists.

[19] (Cohen 1989, 383).

[20] (Quinton 1975, 9) cited in (Gilbert 1987; Gilbert 1989). Since then Quinton has become the poster-philosopher for views of the kind he expresses here.

We shall call an account of the referent of everyday collective belief ascriptions an account of *collective belief*. One can think of Quinton and Cohen as offering such an account. It may be tempting to accept their proposals since irrespective of these authors' contributions, one's initial attempt at providing an account of collective belief is likely to take the following form:

A group G believes that p if and only if all or most of the members believe that p.

Borrowing Quinton's term, we shall refer to this as a "summative" account of collective belief. *A summative account of collective belief,* by definition, places at its core the condition that *all or most members of the group in question have the belief that is ascribed to the group.* We shall refer to this as the *summative condition*.[21]

More complex summative accounts than the one just formulated are possible. For instance, one might add to the above the condition that everyone in group G knows that all or most members of G have the pertinent belief.[22] We shall therefore refer to the account consisting of the summative condition alone as the *simple summative account* of collective belief.[23]

The simple summative account clearly has its attractions. For one, it appeals only to the beliefs of individual human beings, an appeal with which we can assume most theorists are comfortable. Further, it makes no allusions, implicit or explicit, to a "group consciousness" or the subjective experiences of groups. It is, one might say, completely realistic. As Margaret Gilbert has argued for some time, however, there are good reasons to reject the simple summative account and, indeed, to reject all summative accounts of group belief.[24]

The following simple example may help to make the point. Joe meets Karen and, wanting to say something pleasant, comes out with "Lovely day!" Karen, wanting to be agreeable says "Yes, indeed!" Joe and Karen then come across Fred, who grumbles about the day's weather. Karen confidently responds, on behalf of Joe and herself "We think it's a lovely day!" Karen's statement seems to be on target, as a statement of collective belief, irrespective of any personal beliefs of the parties regarding the weather.[25]

---

[21] Call an account of collective belief "correlative" if, according to that account, a group cannot believe that p unless at least one member of the group believes that p. All summative accounts are correlative, but not vice versa.

[22] An account discussed in (Gilbert 1989, ch. 5) and elsewhere adds a more complex, "common knowledge" condition to the summative condition. The initial philosophical discussion of "common knowledge" is in (Lewis 1969).

[23] For presentation of several different summative views see (Gilbert 1989). For a smaller range see (Gilbert 1987).

[24] (Gilbert 1987; Gilbert 1989; Gilbert 1996) and elsewhere.

[25] Cf. (Gilbert 1989, 288f,).

This is not the place further to discuss this example. For present purposes the important point is as follows: this and related examples strongly suggest that what is properly acknowledged to be "our" belief may not be the opinion of all or most— or, indeed, any— individual group members. If, indeed, a group G can believe that p without any of its members believing that p, no form of summativism, however complex, can be right.

8.4. Collective Belief Ascriptions, Belief, and Acceptance

Suppose that no summative account of collective belief is correct. The question remains: to what exactly do everyday collective belief statements refer? In what follows we shall not pursue this question for its own sake. Rather, we focus on a debate that has arisen in connection with a particular non-summative account of collective belief, the joint commitment account of Margaret Gilbert.[26]

As a way into this debate we return briefly to Cohen's discussion. Cohen denies that groups have or, indeed, can have beliefs, and offers a summative account of the referents of collective belief ascriptions. He does not deny that groups can *accept* propositions in his sense. Indeed, he asserts that they can and sometimes do accept propositions in that sense.[27] Cohen's openness to the idea of a group's being able to accept propositions may prompt the following question: Is the phenomenon to which collective belief ascriptions refer a matter of acceptance in Cohen's sense?

In the years following Cohen's publications on belief and acceptance several authors have considered an analog of this question with respect to collective belief according to Gilbert's joint commitment account of it.[28] More specifically, they have considered Gilbert's account in light of distinctions between belief and acceptance that to some extent echo Cohen's distinction, though the pertinent accounts of belief generally either ignore or fail to give a central role to credal feelings.[29]

---

[26] We explain "joint commitment" and what we are calling the joint commitment account later in the text.

[27] As far as ordinary language use is concerned, to say that someone "accepts" a certain proposition is at least sometimes to say that he believes it. For instance, were X to say "Jack will not be elected." and Y to reply "I accept that." a reasonable gloss on what Y says may well be "I believe that". Evidently Cohen would not agree that groups accept propositions in this vernacular sense.

[28] These authors include (Meijers, 1999; Tuomela 2000; Wray 2001; Gilbert 2002; Tollefsen 2003); Hakli (2006) continues the discussion with reflections on the foregoing material. We say more about the belief-acceptance distinction as it tends to figure in the debate shortly.

[29] (Wray 2001) is one who does include credal feelings in his account of belief.

Before focusing on these discussions, we need to explain Gilbert's joint commitment account. This was developed in order to account for a range of contexts in which everyday collective belief ascriptions are made, with further reference to important aspects of the situation once a collective belief was formed. With respect to the latter, Gilbert focused in particular on the fact that parties to an established collective belief take themselves to be in a position to rebuke one another for denying the truth of the proposition in question in certain contexts—though they may choose not to issue such rebukes, which may be the right decision all things considered.

8.5. Gilbert's Joint Commitment Account of Collective belief

As the label we are using for it suggests, joint commitment in Gilbert's sense is central to her account of collective belief.[30] The account runs roughly as follows:

The members of a population, P, *collectively believe that p* if and only if they are jointly committed to believe that p as a body.

This formulation involves several technical terms that will now briefly be explained.

First, what is it for two or more individuals to be *jointly committed* in some way?[31] We can answer this question by starting with the more familiar idea of the personal commitment of a given individual.

If Jake decides to go to the store, then there is a sense in which he has *committed himself* to going to the store. He now has, if you like, a commitment of the will. A commitment in the sense we have in the mind is a normative constraint on behavior. Roughly, all else being equal, the committed person ought to conform to his commitment, in a sense of "ought" that is not specifically moral.[32]

Through Jake's decision he accrues a personal commitment. By definition, when there is a *personal* commitment the committed person has unilaterally brought his commitment into being and can rescind it unilaterally by changing his mind.[33]

---

[30] In prior work Gilbert has referred to this and related accounts of other collective phenomena as "plural subject" accounts. In her technical terminology, those who are jointly committed with one another in some way constitute, *by definition*, a plural subject. Since some have tended to read more than was intended into the phrase "plural subject", we have avoided that phrase here.

[31] For a longer treatment see e.g. (Gilbert 2006 ch. 7). See also the introduction and chapter 2, in particular, in (Gilbert 2013a).

[32] (Gilbert 2013b).

[33] There are richer notions of commitment, but we are operating with a simpler, yet important, notion. See (Gilbert 2013b).

In order for two or more people jointly to commit them all, it is neither necessary nor sufficient for each of those involved to make an appropriate personal commitment. That would indeed involve all of their wills. For joint commitment, however, their wills must be involved in a different way.

In the basic case of joint commitment, on which we shall focus, all of those involved must openly express their readiness together to commit them all in a specified way.[34] This suffices jointly to commit them all: they are now jointly committed in the way specified.

Once they are jointly committed the concurrence of each is required for the joint commitment to be rescinded, absent special background understandings. Thus one cannot unilaterally free oneself from its constraints. Things would be different if, rather than jointly committing them all, each had made a personal commitment of some kind. In that case each would be in a position to free himself from his personal commitment, without any input from the others.

In non-basic cases there are special "authorizing" joint commitments such that, for example, one person can bring it about that a given plurality of persons are jointly committed in a particular way. For instance, the members of a given group may be jointly committed to believe as a body whatever proposition their leader expresses belief in, in a particular context. So, if the leader, in the right context, says "Eating meat is wrong," the members are now jointly committed to believe as a body that eating meat is wrong. In this kind of case the jointly committed persons may in principle be unaware of the content of their joint commitment. Cases involving special background commitments of the kind in question are, evidently, special cases, though they may be common. We set them aside here.

What is it to be jointly committed to believe *as a body* that p, for some proposition p? Roughly, the parties are jointly committed to emulate, in relevant contexts, a single believer—a single party who believes that p—by virtue of the actions, including the verbal utterances, of each. In order to conform to the commitment so understood, an individual member of P must act, or refrain from acting, in certain ways. For instance, she must not express beliefs contrary to or inconsistent with p in relevant contexts—not in an unqualified manner. It may be unproblematic for her to express such contrary beliefs when she is not speaking as a party to the joint commitment. But when she is, she must keep to "the company line." Alternatively, she must qualify her statement as in "*Personally*, I doubt whether p."

---

[34] "Openly" will suffice for present purposes. See (Gilbert 1989, ch. 4) for a more detailed discussion of the requirements of joint commitment formation that appeals to a particular account of "common knowledge".

On this account, certain collective beliefs, such as those about the repugnance of an activity, will be more demanding than others, strongly impacting as they do our actions other than our verbal utterances. If we collectively believe that it is bad to smoke cigarettes, then I am not only constrained with respect to my speech, I am also constrained with respect to my cigarette smoking. If we collectively believe that everyone should do what they can in favor of energy conservation, I am constrained in my decision as to what car to buy, and so on. In contrast, if we collectively believe that the universe came into being with a big bang, while this may restrict my liberty to publicly doubt the theory, our joint commitment is unlikely to affect the way each of us goes about his daily round.

Gilbert has argued elsewhere for an important aspect of joint commitment that goes beyond anything that is involved in a concatenation of personal commitments. If Jake and Sue have jointly committed one another in some way then by virtue of that joint commitment and that alone, Jake is *obligated to* Sue to act in a way that conforms to the joint commitment, and the same goes for Sue.[35] Each has the correlative right against the other. In other terms, each owes the other conforming action.

This feature of Gilbert's account counts in its favor, she argues, since it provides an explanation for central aspects of the way people behave in the context of what they take to be a collective belief. These include something mentioned earlier: the parties to an established collective belief take one another to be in a position to rebuke one another for denying the truth of the proposition in question in certain contexts. One whose right to an action has been violated has the standing to rebuke the person who has offended against them.

The simple summative account favored by both Cohen and Quinton lacks this advantage. More generally, the prevalence of a particular belief among the members of a given population does not suffice to endow them with obligations towards each other to express, or at least not outwardly deny, the belief in question.[36]

Note that there is nothing in the joint commitment account of collective belief that entails that all, most, or, indeed, any of the members of the relevant population personally believe what they believe *collectively*, either before or after the collective belief is formed. Prior to its formation, people can be ready, and express their readiness, together to commit one another to believe that p as a body without believing that p themselves. Of course all or most of them may believe that p, and this may be a common situation. It may also be the most desirable situation from a

---

[35] See e.g. (Gilbert 2006, ch. 7).
[36] See (Gilbert 1987; Gilbert 1989, ch. 5). For further discussion of the relevant notions of right and (directed) obligation, see e.g. Gilbert (2013a, ch. 13).

variety of points of view. In principle, however, one or more or even all of the parties may fail to have any personal views on the matter, or themselves think that not p. Nonetheless each one may be ready to join with the others to commit them all to believing that p as a body, as explicated here. Their motives may vary: one may wish to be done with discussion, one may be deferring to a more powerful person or wish to curry favor with him, and so on.[37]

Once the collective belief is formed, there may be a tendency on the part of the people involved to form the corresponding personal belief. After all, they are committed to expressing that belief when acting as members of the group, and owe such expression to the other parties. It is plausible to suppose that one with no prior personal view on the relevant matter is likely to form the corresponding personal belief. Here too, however, it is not logically necessary that the personal views of any of the members will come to align themselves with the collective view.

Clearly, then, the joint commitment account is not a summative account. It neither states nor logically implies that all or most members of the population in question themselves believe what the group believes in a given case.

Plausibly, conversations, whether brief or extended, are a primary context for the formation of collective beliefs. Gilbert has argued elsewhere that this idea fits well with her account of collective belief: one can interpret what happens in a typical conversation, short or long, as at least in part a matter of collective belief formation according to her account.[38] In a conversation, propositions are proposed for collective belief by one participant and accepted or rejected by the other or others. If the proposal is accepted the interlocutors are jointly committed to believe the pertinent proposition as a body.

One further aspect of Gilbert's account should be mentioned here. She has argued that a central type of collective or social group is constituted by one or more joint commitments. Thus, for example, two or more people who previously did not together constitute such a group constitute one by virtue of the emergence among them of one or more collective beliefs.[39] Examples of groups of the kind in question include typical families, teams, clubs, and associations of various kinds. They also

---

[37] See (Gilbert 1989, ch. 5) for further discussion. In arguing for her account of collective belief, including the radical conceptual disjunction between a collective belief and the beliefs of the people involved, Gilbert has tended to focus on cases in which a group belief emerges in informal discussion or on the basis of a simple majority voting procedure. More recently, drawing on work of Laurence Sager and Lewis Kornhauser, and often in conjunction with Christian List, Philip Pettit has discussed various formal procedures for "aggregating" the personal beliefs of group members such that the resultant belief is distinct from that of any of the members. See e.g., (Pettit 2010).

[38] See (Gilbert 1989, ch. 5); for a more recent, extended discussion see (Gilbert and Priest 2013).

[39] For detailed discussion, see (Gilbert 1989; Gilbert 2006).

include relatively transient groups such as two people playing an impromptu game of catch.

Generally speaking, the authors we primarily engage with here—the "rejectionists"—do not question the accuracy of Gilbert's account of the referent of at least some collective belief ascriptions. That is not their central concern. Rather, assuming that Gilbert's account more or less accurately describes a real phenomenon, they argue that—whatever people may call it in everyday speech—the phenomenon in question is not belief, but acceptance.

To keep things clear and avoid prejudging the issue, we shall refer to the phenomenon Gilbert's account describes as collective belief*. Here the asterisk after "belief" is intended to imply agnosticism on the question whether the phenomenon in question is belief or not. The previously mentioned authors have become known as *rejectionists*, then, on account of their rejection of the idea that collective belief* is belief.[40]

Although our primary interest in the debate between rejectionists and their opponents is methodological rather than substantive, our methodological points will usefully be made in light of a relatively detailed focus on the substance of the debate.

8.6. Belief and Acceptance after Cohen

The following accounts of belief and acceptance are representative of those appealed to by rejectionists.[41] Notably, these accounts are quite complex: both acceptance and belief are characterized in terms of as many as six features.

Acceptance is: (1a) voluntary, (2a) aimed at utility, (3a) shaped by pragmatic goals, (4a) not subject to the ideal of integration, (5a) context-dependent, and (6a) does not come in degrees. Belief, in contrast, is (1b) involuntary, (2b) aimed at truth, (3b) shaped by evidence, (4b) subject to the ideal of integration, (5b) context-independent, and (6b) comes in degrees.[42]

These accounts and others much like them may be found appealing for several reasons. One is descriptive efficacy. These theoretical distinctions between belief and acceptance seem at least roughly to track a significant distinction that is

---

[40] (Gilbert 2002) introduced the label "rejectionist"; (Tollefsen 2003) labeled those who argue that collective belief is belief as "believers". We shall refer to those who oppose rejectionists simply as their opponents for reasons that will emerge.

[41] There are some exceptions including (Hakli 2006), and (Wray 2001), who, as noted earlier, associates belief with credal feelings. In order to keep our discussion to manageable proportions we shall work with these representative accounts.

[42] See (Mathiesen 2007, 209–16).

represented in everyday speech. Thus we might say that a philosopher accepted that moral statements are truth-evaluable for the sake of a particular argument though he did not believe that moral statements are truth evaluable. Or we might say that a scientist provisionally accepted a hypothesis he knew to be unproven while working out how to test it experimentally. We might also say that in constructing his closing argument a trial lawyer did not accept his client's guilt, though he believed his client was guilty. Finally, we might also say that a philosopher accepted God's existence for the purposes of a proof of some kind, while acknowledging that, at the same time, the philosopher believes in God's existence. Thus, depending on the context one may be said to accept a proposition one does not believe, not to accept a proposition one does believe, or to accept a proposition that one does believe.

8.7. The Rejectionist Credo (1): Collective Belief* is Acceptance

We now turn to the debate between rejectionists and their opponents. Rejectionists agree with Wray when he asserts that " ... the phenomenon that concerns Gilbert is a species of acceptance" and not a species of belief.[43] They have put forward a number of arguments for rejectionism which, evidently, has two distinct parts. First, in brief, collective belief* is not belief. Second, collective belief* is acceptance.

Gilbert countered the rejectionists' conclusions in her paper "Belief and acceptance as features of groups".[44] She argues, for one, that collective belief* is not acceptance, as the rejectionists claim.[45]

In so arguing she focuses on what rejectionists say about the relationship of the will to acceptance, as opposed to belief. According to rejectionists a belief cannot be voluntary. That is, I cannot bring a belief of mine into being by an act of will, or not directly. Acceptances, in contrast, are directly willed into being: in order for me to accept some proposition I must directly will this acceptance into being.[46]

The identity of the agent who wills the acceptance and the agent who thenceforth bears the acceptance is important in this connection. It seems that, without special authorization, no person or group can accept a proposition on the behalf of another person or group. Rather, acceptances must be willed *by the relevant agent*. That is, they must be willed into being by the one who thereafter accepts the proposition in question. In the case of my acceptances, then, I am the relevant agent. In the case of your acceptances, you are the relevant agent. In the case of collective

---

[43] (Wray 2001, 319). See also (Wray 2003).
[44] (Gilbert 2002).
[45] (Gilbert 2002, 59–63).
[46] In this discussion, Gilbert focuses on (Meijers, 1999).

belief*, if it really is acceptance, as the rejectionists claim, the social group whose acceptance is in question is the relevant agent—the social group itself, and not its members taken one by one.

If there can be a collective belief* that is not willed into being by the relevant agent, however, then it is not a case of acceptance, since acceptances, by their nature, are willed into being by the relevant agent. It follows that collective beliefs* as such are not, of their nature, acceptances.

In support of this general conclusion Gilbert argues that there are cases of collective belief* such that those who jointly commit one another to believe as a body that such and such have not previously together constituted a social group or collective. Rather, it is this very joint commitment, the commitment to believe as a body, that constitutes them as a collective.

Consider the following case: Six unrelated people are sitting in the same compartment of a train.[47] Each is minding his or her business, reading, staring out of the window, talking on a cell phone, and so on. None of them has yet made eye contact with any of the others. We take it that they do not together form a collective at this time. After a while one of them says, "Phew! It's far too stuffy in here." There is a general murmuring of assent as each person says something like "Yes indeed" or "Agreed!" Let us assume that the collective belief* that it is far too stuffy in the carriage has now been established among the six people in question, as is plausible given no special background circumstances.[48] Assuming, with Gilbert, that the parties to any joint commitment constitute a collective, then, at the moment their collective belief*—with its constitutive joint commitment—is formed, and not before, these six people constitute a collective, if only one whose central feature is its believing* that it is too stuffy in the carriage.[49]

This example shows that, at least in some cases, collective beliefs* are not willed into being by the social group to whom the belief* is subsequently attributed. The relevant group simply did not exist, qua social group, at the time. Since any acceptance is only appropriately attributed to the agent that willed it, such collective beliefs* cannot be acceptances.

Examples like the one above suffice to reject the central tenet of rejectionism: that collective belief* as such is a species of acceptance. Moving to a different

---

[47] This example draws on (Gilbert 1989, 310).
[48] This assumption in no way disputes the possibility that, at the same time, all of the six personally believe that the compartment is too stuffy. The point relates only to generation in this context of the applicable collective belief*. The conditions described suffice for this.
[49] On the possibility of groups whose central feature is a particular belief, consider, for instance the Flat Earth society. Cf. (Gilbert 1989, ch. 5).

example allows us to consider the question of collective belief* and acceptance in a different, more familiar, context, that of an already existing collective.

Suppose the faculty members of a philosophy department gather for their weekly meeting. After the meeting has gone on for many hours, one professor says, "This meeting has gone on long enough." There is a general murmur of assent. Absent any special background considerations, this has the character of a non-controversial case of collective belief* formation. Unlike the previous case, however, the relevant group—the group of department faculty—predates the collective belief* in question, so it could in principle have willed the belief* into being.

Did the group will its collective belief* into being in this situation? We would say not. The wills of the members, qua members, even when publicly expressed, do not suffice to constitute the will of the group itself. They do, of course, establish a new feature of the group: the group has a new collective belief*. A group will, however, must be established as such by the group, however informally.

We take the following to be an example of the formation of a group will. Before they tired, the same faculty members were discussing the dwindling morale in the department. Students are disaffected, faculty do not talk to each other outside department meetings, and so on. A professor who has studied the way in which morale is kept high in athletic teams says "We faculty need [collectively] to believe[*] that this department is one of the best in the world."[50] The others concur.

We take it that this interchange establishes a resolution of the group of department faculty and to that extent represents the will of that group. Indeed, it is the group' will that it have a certain belief*, namely, that it is one of the best departments in the world.[51]

We do not deny, then, that there is a sense in which a group can will that it believe* something. We take it, however, that in many cases, even when the individual wills of the group members, qua group members, are involved, a group believes* something without first willing that it believe* it, let alone willing the collective belief* in question into being.

With respect to the rejectionist claim that collective belief* is acceptance, then, there are humdrum cases of collective belief* that do not bear the relationship to the will of the collective that would required for these to be cases of acceptance. More precisely, the collective with the belief* did not *itself* will the belief* into being, though that belief* came into being as a result of the exercise of its members'

---

[50] The square parentheses are intended to indicate what he means; were he to have written out his statement, he would not have included any such parentheses, but rather understood it (we are assuming) in the terms indicated by the parentheses.

[51] Note that we do not say that the group has *willed a belief* into being*. Rather it is the group's will that it have a particular belief*. We consider the former possibility in due course.

wills. Contrary to the rejectionists, then, collective belief* is not acceptance. If it were, it would always be a creature of the group's will.

8.8. The Rejectionist Credo (2): Collective Belief* is Not Belief [52]

Rejectionists argue that collective belief* is not belief. This may seem to be a doubtful conclusion, if one allows that collective beliefs* are what everyday collective belief ascriptions refer to. Everyday collective belief ascriptions are, after all, ascriptions of so-called beliefs to collectives. Setting that consideration aside, we shall consider a particular segment of the debate over this part of the rejectionist credo.

Gilbert argued at length in "Belief and acceptance as features of groups" that rejectionist arguments to the effect that collective belief* is not belief are not as strong as might be thought. In this vein she has addressed both the rejectionists' claim that beliefs "aim at truth", and their claim that a belief cannot be willed into being, or, in the terms we used above, the claim that belief is involuntary.[53] Here we continue the discussion with a focus on the latter claim, with special reference to an article by Raul Hakli that responds to that part of Gilbert's material.[54] For the purposes of our discussion here we shall accept the rejectionists' assumption that there is a sense in which belief cannot be willed into being.[55]

A central premise in the rejectionists' argument is that whereas belief is such that one *cannot* will one's belief into being, collective belief* *can* be willed into being.[56] Following Gilbert, we have so far shown that there are collective beliefs* that are not willed into being—not by the group itself. The examples of the people on the train and the faculty members, which were offered in order to argue that collective belief* is not acceptance, both speak to this point. We now address the question: Is it *possible* for a group to will its collective belief* into being, even if collective beliefs* are not always generated this way?

---

[52] If rejectionists constitute a collective then they would seem to be a collective whose credo is that they have no credo—given that a credo is a matter of what is believed.

[53] (Gilbert 2002) discusses the issue of "aiming at truth" at pages 51–9, and the issue about the will at pages 59–64.

[54] (Hakli 2006).

[55] The extent to which this is true in the individual case has itself been a matter of some debate, a debate we shall not enter here.

[56] At issue here is directly willing a belief into being. A typical case of willing a belief *indirectly* would be such as this: a husband wishing to believe his wife does not flirt with other men on social occasions deliberately turns away when a man approaches his wife on such an occasion. He thus deliberately precludes himself from confronting evidence contrary to his desired belief. No one disputes that people can will their beliefs into being indirectly in this way.

In discussion of this question Gilbert focused on an example akin to one in the last section, an example we develop a little further for present purposes. Fran and her partner Trudy explicitly adopt as their collective goal their collectively believing* that their future is bright.[57] Perhaps Fran says to Trudy "We need to believe[*] that our future is bright" and Trudy agrees. The setting of such a collective goal can, we have allowed, be seen as a case of a group's willing that it believe* something.

Gilbert observes that the setting of this collective goal—this instance of group willing—does not *immediately* produce the desired collective belief* of Fran and Trudy. A new joint commitment must be made, a joint commitment constitutive of the collective belief* in question. Thus, after a pause, Trudy might say, in a cheerful tone, "Our future is indeed bright!" and Fran concur, thus establishing their collective belief* that their future is bright. It seems, then, that the pertinent collective belief* may yet count as a belief, granted the rejectionists' assumption that beliefs cannot be willed into being.

Reflecting on Gilbert's discussion, Hakli disputes her judgment that the relevant collective belief* in this case is not willed into being. He writes "Granted that a new joint commitment must be made, nothing special is required for that."[58] He concludes that "there is no necessary or conceptual obstacle for the group to form a view according to its will".[59]

One might agree with the point about the lack of necessary or conceptual obstacles while wondering if that is sufficient to refute Gilbert. After all, there are many humdrum ways in which some kind of slippage might have occurred between the formation of the group's will to believe* and the formation of the collective belief* itself. For instance, the conversation might have been interrupted, the parties thereby losing the opportunity to make the crucial joint commitment. Or one party might have rethought the matter and told the other that she is not sure, after all, if a belief that their future is bright is what is needed, thus stalling or possibly aborting the process of collective belief* formation. Or the parties might simply have lost interest in the whole business and failed to make the necessary final move.

One sympathetic to Hakli's position might respond that, in spite of this, it is relatively easy for a group to bring a collective belief* into being after resolving to do so. He might, indeed, aver that when Judy and Fran move from setting their collective goal to forming the desired collective belief* without a hitch, this is direct

---

[57] (Gilbert 2002) notes that there may be something off-color about the adoption of precisely such a goal in both the collective and the individual case.
[58] (Hakli 2006, 296). [59] (Hakli 2006).

enough a connection between the group's will and the collective belief* to deny to it the name of belief—assuming, of course, that belief is such that it cannot be willed into being directly.

At this point we want to step back from the discussion of collective belief* and belief and note the following: Suppose that, when Judy and Fran do proceed to form their desired collective belief* without a hitch, it *has* been willed into being in such a way that it cannot be belief. Then the result of this and the last section taken together would be this: collective belief* is neither acceptance, nor belief.

8.9. Further Methodological Observations

We shall not pursue further the debate between rejectionists and their opponents. Nor shall we attempt a final conclusion on that debate. Suffice it to say, here, that even if the rejectionists' claim that collective belief* is not belief as they understand it is sustainable, there is reason to reject their claim that collective belief* is acceptance as they understand that.

We want to emphasize the following two observations. First, the disagreements within the debate over rejectionism are about categorization. They concern, more specifically, whether or not certain concepts of acceptance and belief apply in a particular context. Neither side questions that collective belief* happens. Second, in the work of both Cohen, discussed earlier, and those who largely follow him, the relevant articulations of the concepts of belief and acceptance derive from the individual case. The debate over rejectionism concerns the application of these concepts, so articulated, to the case of collective belief*, the details of which are agreed upon by all parties.

This brings us back to the methodological points we brought up in relation to Cohen's rejection of group beliefs, citing Plato's procedure in the *Republic*. These points are clearly pertinent to the debate over rejectionism, in relation both to the account of belief and to the account of acceptance at issue.

We now briefly develop this observation. In order to mark the fact that the basis for the relevant articulations of the concepts of acceptance and belief lies in the individual case, we shall in what follows refer not simply to belief and acceptance but rather to belief-i and acceptance-i.[60] With some development, the points made in our earlier discussion suggest that though there is some interest in asking

---

[60] Cf. the use of the phrase "individual belief" in Gilbert (2002).

whether collective belief* is belief-i, or, rather, acceptance-i, this is not the most important question to be asked. Indeed, these points recommend an alternative approach to collective epistemology.

For the purposes of the following discussion we shall assume that collective belief* is the referent of everyday collective belief ascriptions. Our points apply to any relevantly similar phenomena that may be invoked as the referents of everyday collective belief ascriptions. We shall also assume that belief-i and acceptance-i—belief and acceptance roughly as characterized by the rejectionists and others influenced by Cohen—are the referents of everyday ascriptions of belief and acceptance to individual human beings.

As illustrated earlier, someone may doubt that either the concept of belief-i or the concept of acceptance-i applies to the case of collective belief*. Suppose we assume, finally, that, indeed, though collective belief* is rampant in groups, groups neither believe-i nor accept-i.

This might tempt us to reconsider the articulated concepts of belief-i and acceptance-i themselves, thinking that collective belief* needs to be accommodated by one or the other—in particular the former, given that it is labeled "belief" in everyday life. So long as we are interested in individuals, however, these concepts and the distinction they mark, or something close to them, may be fine as they are.

Conversely we might be tempted to use the fact that collective belief* is not belief-i as evidence that it is not the referent of everyday collective belief ascriptions. Collective belief ascriptions could just be a *facon de parler* whose real target is some fact about the beliefs-i of individuals. The problem here is that, as discussed earlier, there are arguments against both summative and, indeed, correlative accounts of the target of such ascriptions.[61]

We advocate a third response. The concepts of belief-i and acceptance-i, roughly following Cohen's work, were developed from considerations about individuals. But groups are not individuals, and it is unclear why we would expect concepts and distinctions designed to characterize the cognitive states of the latter to apply cleanly to the former, as the rejectionists, for instance, seem to do.[62]

Indeed we can see the concepts of belief-i and acceptance-i, on the one hand, and collective belief*, on the other as belonging to two distinct inquiries. The concepts of belief-i, and acceptance-i, roughly following Cohen, are primarily concepts for individual epistemology. The concept of collective belief* is a primarily a concept

---

[61] For concordant remarks see (Tollefsen 2003, 401–4). For the term "correlative" see footnote 21.
[62] Cf. Gilbert (2002: 49) with special reference to the rejectionist use of an account of belief derived from the individual case.

for collective epistemology. This being so one should not be surprised if collective belief* fails clearly to be belief-i, let alone acceptance-i. Indeed, though the relations between collective belief*, belief-i, and acceptance-i are of some interest, the question "Is collective belief* belief-i or acceptance-i?" insofar as it presupposes that collective belief* must be one of these, appears to be misplaced.

8.10. Generic Epistemology

Supposing that collective belief* is neither belief-i, nor acceptance-i, what is it? If we want a parallel label, we could reasonably call it belief-c. Here we are assuming, as before, that it is collective belief* to which everyday collective belief ascriptions refer.

The naturalness of this labeling suggests that our discussion should not end with the distinction between collective and individual epistemology. Even if we understand that these are separate inquiries, there will be important questions that straddle the two. For instance: what are the analogies and disanalogies between belief-i and belief-c? What, for that matter, are the analogies and disanalogies between acceptance-i and its opposite number, acceptance-c?[63] How can these analogies and disanalogies be explained?

Answers to such questions are likely to throw into better relief the cognitive characteristics of both individuals and groups.[64] From this perspective, then, there is considerable value in the debate over rejectionism, which has occasioned much consideration of analogies and disanalogies between belief-i and acceptance-i and belief-c.

The pursuit of such questions can be part of either collective or individual epistemology. It can also be part of a third inquiry, which may be labeled *generic epistemology*. The questions of generic epistemology will include such questions as: what—if anything—is common to belief-i and belief-c? What, for that matter, is common to belief *whatever it characterizes*, whether human individuals, groups of human individuals, animals perhaps, or other beings?

With reference to our discussion of Plato's methodology earlier in this essay, it may be noted that the author the *Republic* does not attempt to formulate a general characterization of justice. His main target, as noted, is what we may now call justice-i. He works towards an account of that by a careful examination of what we may call justice-c. He does not, however, go further than these two accounts, or advance to a further inquiry, beyond both the theory of individual justice and the

---

[63] See (Gilbert 2002); (Tollefsen 2003) on acceptance when "said of" groups.
[64] See (Tollefsen 2003; Hakli 2006).

theory of political justice, an enquiry that might be referred to as generic justice theory. To use his own terms, he does not attempt to come to grips with the *form* of justice, the *idea* of justice itself, justice as it pertains both to polities and to human beings.

Plato does not explain why he does not pursue a theory of justice in general. Whatever his reasons, and they may be good ones, it is not clear that epistemologists should follow his lead. There may well be merit in pursuing generic epistemology.[65] At least part of the basis for this would presumably be the combined results of individual epistemology on the one hand and collective epistemology on the other.

In that case there are surely some good pointers already in the literature, features of both belief-i and belief-c. For instance, the idea of belief "aiming at truth", when suitably articulated, could be a central characteristic of belief in general, something possessed by both individual and collective believers.[66] This is not the place for an extended foray into generic epistemology.

8.11. Concluding Summary

We first distinguished between the projects of individual and collective epistemology. The former is concerned with the cognitive states of individual human beings and the latter with the cognitive states of collectives. We then argued that those engaged in one of these projects should not rely on accounts and distinctions developed specifically for the other, though they may find much of interest in the results obtained by those engaged in the other project.

As we explained, this methodological point has not generally been respected by researchers in collective epistemology. The opposite methodology is exemplified in influential work by L. Jonathan Cohen, in which he denies that groups have beliefs, as opposed to acceptances, as he understands these states. It is exemplified further by a recent debate in which revised versions of Cohen's distinction have been brought into play. This is the debate between "rejectionists" and their opponents with respect to whether or not the phenomenon Margaret Gilbert has argued to be the referent of standard everyday ascriptions of collective belief is belief—or acceptance.

The debate over rejectionism has reached something of a stalemate. After reviewing some of its central features, we argued that though important points

---

[65] (Gilbert 2002 esp. 47–9).
[66] See (Gilbert 2002) on the relation of collective belief* to various ideas, from individual epistemology, of belief as having the aim of truth. Also relevant to generic epistemology is Gilbert (1989: 313).

have been made on both sides, there is reason to think that the debate itself is misguided. For, although the collective case is at issue, the debate operates with accounts and distinctions tailored specifically to the case of the individual. This is surely the wrong procedure. Though individual and collective epistemology will doubtless have related results, neither one should rely on accounts and distinction tailored specifically for the other. Rather, those working on either one of these projects should develop concepts of belief and acceptance appropriate to the particular project at hand, without being constrained by the results of the other, however helpful these results may be from a heuristic point of view.

With respect to collective epistemology, then, supposing for the sake of argument that Gilbert's account of collective belief is correct, the collective epistemologist needs primarily to be concerned with the particular features of collective belief*—its relation to truth, the will and so on. The same goes, *mutatis mutandis*, for whatever account of collective belief the collective epistemologist prefers.

In concluding, we briefly argued for the interest of generic epistemology. This is an inquiry that, while paying attention to the results of both individual and collective epistemology, can be seen as a subject in its own right.[67]

References

Bouvier, Alban. 2004. "Individual Beliefs and Collective Beliefs in Sciences and Philosophy: The Plural Subject and the Polyphonic Subject Accounts." *Philosophy of the Social Sciences* 34 (3): 382–407.
Clark, Austen. 1994. "Beliefs and Desires Incorporated." *The Journal of Philosophy* 91 (8): 404–25.
Cohen, L. Jonathan. 1989. "Belief and Acceptance." *Mind* 98 (391): 367–89.
———. 1995. *An Essay on Belief and Acceptance*. Oxford: Clarendon Press.
Engel, Pascal. 2000. *Believing and Accepting*. Dordrecht; Boston: Kluwer Academic.
Gilbert, Margaret. 1987. "Modelling Collective Belief." *Synthese* 73 (1): 185–204.
———. 1989. *On Social Facts*. Princeton: Princeton University Press.
———. 1996. *Living Together*. Lanham, MD: Rowman & Littlefield.
———. 2001. "Collective Remorse." In *War Crimes and Collective Wrongdoing: A Reader*, edited by A. Jokic. Rochester, NY: Blackwell Publishing.

---

[67] Margaret Gilbert would like to thank all of those who have taken account of her work on collective belief and contributed to the discussion of it both formally and informally, including the rejectionists. Thanks also to Aaron James for discussion of aspects of the present paper. Daniel Pilchman would like to thank Amanda Trefethen for helpful conversation, and to personally thank Alban Bouvier for introducing him to the rejectionist debate in a graduate seminar on Social Epistemology during the 2008-9 academic year at UC Santa Cruz. Both of us would like to thank Alban Bouvier, Raul Hakli, Jennifer Lackey, Daniel Siakel, K. Brad Wray, and an anonymous referee for this volume, for their comments on a late draft, and Boaz Miller for related discussion. We have done our best to respond to all of the comments while keeping within the time and space available.

———. 2002. "Belief and Acceptance as Features of Groups." *Protosociology* 16: 35-69.
———. 2004. "Collective Epistemology." *Episteme* 1 (02): 95-107.
———. 2006. *A Theory of Political Obligation: Membership, Commitment, and the Bonds of Society*. Oxford: Oxford University Press.
———. 2013a. *Joint Commitment: How We Make the Social World*. New York: Oxford University Press.
———. 2013b. "Commitment." In *International Encyclopedia of Ethics*. Blackwell.
———. 2014. "How We Feel: Understanding Everyday Collective Emotion Ascriptions." In *Collective Emotions*, edited by Mikko Salmela and Christian van Sheve. Oxford University Press.
Gilbert, Margaret, and Maura Priest. 2013. "Conversation and Collective Belief." In *Perspectives on Pragmatics and Philosophy*, Capone, Alessandro; Lo Piparo, Franco; Carapezza, Marco (eds.). Perspectives on Pragmatics, Philosophy, and Psychology 1. Springer.
Goldman, Alvin I. 1999. *Knowledge in a Social World*. Oxford: Clarendon Press.
Hakli, Raul. 2006. "Group Beliefs and the Distinction Between Belief and Acceptance." *Cognitive Systems Research* 7 (2-3): 286-97.
Lewis, David K. 1969. *Convention: a Philosophical Study*. Oxford: Blackwell.
Mathiesen, Kay. 2006. "The Epistemic Features of Group Belief." *Episteme* 2 (03): 161-75.
———. 2007. "Introduction to Special Issue of Social Epistemology on 'Collective Knowledge and Collective Knowers.'" *Social Epistemology* 21 (3): 209-16.
McMahon, Cristopher. 2002. "Two Modes of Collective Belief." *Protosociology* 18 (19): 347-62.
Meijers, A.W.M. 1999. "Believing and Accepting as a Group." In *Belief, Cognition and the Will*, 59-73. Tilburg: Tilburg University Press.
Pettit, Philip. 2010. "Groups with Minds of Their Own." In *Social Epistemology: Essential Readings*. Alvin Goldman and Dennis Whitcomb (eds.). New York: Oxford University Press.
Plato, G. M. A Grube, and C. D. C Reeve. 1992. *Republic*. Indianapolis: Hackett.
Priest, Maura. "Doxastic Voluntarism: From the Collective to the Individual."(unpublished ms.).
Quinton, Anthony. 1975. "Social Objects." *Proceedings of the Aristotelian Society* 76: 1-27.
Schmitt, Frederick F. 1994. "The Justification of Group Beliefs." In *Socializing Epistemology*, F. Schmitt (Ed.), Lanham: MD: Rowman & Littlefield.
Stevenson, Leslie. 2002. "Six Levels of Mentality." *Philosophical Explorations* 5 (2): 105-24.
Tollefsen, Deborah. 2002. "Organizations as True Believers." *Journal of Social Philosophy* 33 (3): 395-410.
———. 2003. "Rejecting Rejectionism." *Protosociology*, 18 (19): 389-405.
Tuomela, Raimo. 1992. "Group Beliefs." *Synthese* 91 (3): 285-318.
———. 2000. "Belief Versus Acceptance." *Philosophical Explorations* 3 (2): 122-37.
Wray, K. Brad. 2001. "Collective Belief And Acceptance." *Synthese* 129 (3): 319-33.
———. 2003. "What Really Divides Gilbert and the Rejectionists." *Protosociology* 18 (19): 363-76.

PART IV

Collective Entities and Formal Epistemology

9
Individual Coherence and Group Coherence

Rachael Briggs, Fabrizio Cariani, Kenny Easwaran,
and *Branden Fitelson*

9.1. Individual Coherence[1]

9.1.1. *Deductive consistency: the recent dialectic*

It is often assumed that an epistemically rational agent's (full) beliefs ought to be deductively consistent. That is, the following is often taken to be a (synchronic) epistemic coherence requirement for individual agents.[2]

(CB) **Consistency Norm for Belief**. Epistemically rational agents should (at any given time) have logically consistent belief sets.

One popular motivation for imposing such a requirement is the presupposition that epistemically rational agents should, in fact, obey the following norm:

(TB) **Truth Norm for Belief**. Epistemically rational agents should (at any given time) believe propositions that are true.

These two norms differ in one fundamental respect: (TB) is *local* in the sense that an agent complies with it only if each particular belief the agent holds (at a given time) has some property (in this case: truth). On the other hand, (CB) is a *global* norm: whether or not an agent's doxastic state (at a given time) is in accordance

---

[1] This section is an abridged version of a much longer story we have written about individual coherence (Easwaran & Fitelson 2013). In that longer paper, we lay out the philosophical and formal framework in greater detail. Specifically, see that longer paper for a detailed discussion of the various idealizations that are involved in the present framework.

[2] Notable advocates of (CB) include Pollock (1990), Ryan (1991, 1996), and Kaplan (2013). Christensen (2004), Kolodny (2007), Foley (1992), Klein (1985), and Kyburg (1970) all reject (CB). See (Easwaran & Fitelson 2013) for an extended discussion of the recent dialectic concerning (CB), as well as a more in-depth discussion of the present alternative(s) to (CB).

with (CB) is a more holistic matter, which trades essentially on properties of their entire belief set. While these two epistemic norms differ in this respect, they are also intimately related, logically. We may say that one norm n *entails* another norm n' just in case everything that is permissible according to n is permissible according to n'. In this sense, (TB) *asymmetrically entails* (CB). That is, if an agent is in accordance with (TB), then they must also be in accordance with (CB), but not conversely.

Although (CB) accords well with (TB) there is a strong case to be made that (CB) conflicts with other plausible local norms, in particular:

(EB) **Evidential Norm for Belief**. Epistemically rational agents should (at any given time) believe propositions that are supported by their evidence.

It is plausible to interpret preface cases as revealing a tension between (EB) and (CB). Here is a rendition of the preface that we find particularly compelling:

Preface Paradox. Let **B** be the set containing all of S's justified first-order beliefs. Assuming S is a suitably interesting inquirer, this set **B** will be a very rich and complex set of judgments. And, because S is fallible, it is reasonable to expect that some of S's first-order evidence is misleading. As a result, it seems reasonable to believe that some beliefs in **B** are false. Indeed, we think S herself would be justified in believing this very second-order claim. But, of course, adding this second-order belief to **B** renders S's total belief set inconsistent.

We take it that, in suitably constructed preface cases (such as this one), it would be epistemically permissible for S to satisfy (EB) but violate (CB). That is, we think that some preface cases are counterexamples to (CB). It is not our aim here to investigate whether this is the correct response to the preface paradox.[3] Presently, we simply take this claim as a *datum*. In this sense, our response to the preface is similar to the recent responses of Christensen (2004) and Kolodny (2007).

However, our approach to individual coherence diverges from Christensen's and Kolodny's. Christensen and Kolodny (and almost everyone else in this literature) would be inclined to accept the following conditional:

(†) If there are any (synchronic, epistemic) coherence requirements for full belief, then (CB) is among them.

Christensen (2004) urges his readers to focus on partial belief (*viz., credence*). He suggests that all epistemological explanations (worth having) can be couched solely in terms of credences. In other words, Christensen seems to think that epistemology can (in some sense) do without full belief. As such, Christensen

---

[3] We think Christensen (2004) has given compelling arguments for the epistemic rationality of certain preface cases (*i.e.*, for the rationality of some inconsistent belief sets).

would be inclined to deny the antecedent of (†), which is a (trivial) way of accepting (†).[4]

Unlike Christensen, Kolodny does not think we can do without full belief (in epistemology). On the contrary, Kolodny thinks full belief is indispensable in epistemology (for proper accounts of practical and theoretical reasoning). However, Kolodny thinks that the only (synchronic) epistemic requirement on full belief is (EB). That is, Kolodny argues that there are no coherence requirements for full belief *per se*, and he offers a sophisticated error theory to explain away our intuitions to the contrary. As a result, Kolodny would also deny the antecedent of (†), but for different reasons than Christensen.

Our response to preface cases (and other epistemic paradoxes involving deductive consistency) differs from both Christensen's and Kolodny's. Whereas they would both abandon the idea that we should bother trying to articulate (synchronic, epistemic) coherence requirements for full belief, we would be inclined to say that (†) is false. Having said that, we do think there is a kernel of truth in each of Christensen's and Kolodny's responses. Unlike Kolodny, Christensen thinks there are coherence requirements for credences (*i.e.*, requirements of probabilistic coherence). We agree. In fact, our approach to grounding new coherence requirements for full belief was inspired by an existing approach to grounding probabilism as a coherence requirement for credences. Indeed, one of the main virtues of our approach is that it gives a unified framework for grounding both quantitative and qualitative coherence requirements. Unlike Christensen, Kolodny thinks that full belief is indispensable (in epistemology), and that (EB) is a *bona fide* epistemic requirement for full belief. We agree. And, this is why we think it's important to try to articulate and defend an alternative to (CB), which is consonant with (EB).

1.2. A Principled Alternative to Deductive Consistency

Our alternative to (CB) was not motivated by thinking about paradoxes of deductive consistency (like the preface). It was inspired by some recent arguments for probabilism as a (synchronic, epistemic) coherence requirement for credences. James Joyce (1998, 2009) has offered arguments for probabilism that are rooted in considerations of accuracy. We won't get into the details of Joyce's arguments here.[5]

---

[4] Here, we are going beyond what Christensen explicitly says in his book. He doesn't explicitly endorse an eliminativist stance regarding full belief (in epistemology). But, he does seem to imply that (*qua* epistemologists) we don't need to invoke coherence requirements for full belief *per se*. That is, he seems to think epistemology only requires coherence requirements for credences.

[5] There are some important disanalogies between Joyce's argument for probabilism and our analogous arguments regarding coherence requirements for full belief. See (Easwaran & Fitelson 2012) for discussion.

Instead, we present a general framework for grounding coherence requirements for sets of judgments of various types, including both credences and full beliefs. Our unified framework constitutes a generalization of Joyce's argument for probabilism. Moreover, when our approach is applied to full belief, it yields coherence requirements that are superior to (CB), in light of preface cases (and other similar paradoxes of consistency).

Applying our framework to judgment sets J of type $\mathfrak{J}$ only requires completing three steps. The three steps are as follows:

Step 1. Say what it means for a set J to be *perfectly accurate* (at a possible world w). We use the term "vindicated" to describe the perfectly accurate set of judgments of type $\mathfrak{J}$, at w, and we use the abbreviation $\overset{\circ}{J}_w$ to denote the vindicated set of judgments of type $\mathfrak{J}$, at w.[6]

Step 2. Define a *measure of distance between judgment sets*, $d(J, J')$. We apply this measure to gauge the distance between a given set of judgments J of type $\mathfrak{J}$ and the vindicated set $\overset{\circ}{J}_w$.

Step 3. Adopt a *fundamental epistemic principle*, which uses $d(J, \overset{\circ}{J}_w)$ to ground a (synchronic, epistemic) coherence requirement for judgment sets J of type $\mathfrak{J}$.

This is all very abstract. To make things more concrete, let's look at the simplest application of our framework—to the case of *opinionated full belief*. Let:

$$B(p) =_{df} S \text{ believes that } p.$$
$$D(p) =_{df} S \text{ disbelieves that } p.$$

For simplicity, we suppose that S is opinionated, and that S forms judgments involving propositions drawn from a finite Boolean algebra of propositions. More precisely, let $\mathcal{A}$ be an agenda, which is a (possibly proper) subset of some finite boolean algebra of propositions. For each $p \in \mathcal{A}$, S either believes p or S disbelieves p, and not both.[7] In this way, an agent can be represented by her "belief set" **B**, which is just the set of her beliefs (B) and disbeliefs (D) over some salient agenda $\mathcal{A}$. More precisely, **B** is a set of proposition-attitude pairs, with propositions drawn from $\mathcal{A}$ and attitudes taken by S toward those propositions (at a given time).

---

[6] As a heuristic, you can think of $\overset{\circ}{J}_w$ as the set of judgments of type $\mathfrak{J}$ that an omniscient agent (*i.e.*, an agent who is omniscient about the facts at world w) would have.

[7] The assumption of opinionation results in no loss of generality for present purposes. This is for two reasons. First, as Christensen (2004) convincingly argues, suspension of belief is not a plausible way out of the preface paradox (or other similar paradoxes of consistency). Second, in the context

Similarly, we think of propositions as sets of possible worlds, so that a proposition is true at any world that it contains, and false at any world it doesn't contain.[8]

Step 1 is straightforward. It is clear what it means for a set **B** of this type to be perfectly accurate/vindicated. The vindicated set $\overset{o}{\mathbf{B}}_w$ is given by the following definition:

$\overset{o}{\mathbf{B}}_w$ contains $B(p)$ $[D(p)]$ just in case p is true [false] at w.

This is clearly the best explication of $\overset{o}{\mathbf{B}}_w$, since $B(p)$ $[D(p)]$ is accurate just in case p is true [false]. So, in this context, Step 1 is uncontroversial.

Step 2 is less straightforward, because there are many ways one could measure "distance between judgment sets". For simplicity, we adopt perhaps the most naïve distance measure, which is given by:

$d(\mathbf{B}, \mathbf{B}') =_{df}$ the number of judgments on which **B** and **B**′ disagree.[9]

In particular, if you want to know how far your judgment set **B** is from vindication (at w) just count the number of mistakes you have made (at w). To be sure, this is a very naïve measure of distance from vindication. In this chapter, we will not delve into the various worries one might have about $d(\mathbf{B}, \overset{o}{\mathbf{B}}_w)$, or the plethora of alternative distance measures one could adopt. Here, our aim is primarily to explain the ramifications of our new approach to individual coherence for the existing dialectic concerning group coherence and judgment aggregation.

Step 3 is the philosophically crucial step. Given our setup, there is a choice of fundamental epistemic principle that yields (CB) as a coherence requirement for full belief. Specifically, consider the following principle:

Possible Vindication (PV). There exists *some* possible world w at which *all* of the judgments in **B** are accurate. Or, to put this more formally, in terms of our distance measure d: $(\exists w)[d(\mathbf{B}, \overset{o}{\mathbf{B}}_w) = 0]$.

---

of judgment aggregation, it is typically assumed that judges are opinionated (at least, with regard to the agendas on which they are jointly making judgments). For exceptions, see, e.g., Dietrich and List (2008, 2007b). In general, we would want to be able to model suspension of judgment in our framework (Friedman 2013). See (Easwaran 2012) for just such a generalization of the present framework.

[8] It is implicit in this formalism that agents satisfy a weak sort of logical omniscience, in the sense that if two propositions are logically equivalent, then they are in fact the same proposition, and so the agent can't have distinct attitudes toward them. However, it is not assumed that agents satisfy a stronger sort of logical omniscience — an agent may believe some propositions while disbelieving some other proposition that is entailed by them (*i.e.*, our logical omniscience assumption does not imply closure).

[9] This is called the *Hamming distance* between the binary vectors **B** and **B**′ (Deza and Deza 2009). On distance measures between judgment sets, see, *e.g.*, Pigozzi (2006); Miller and Osherson (2009); Duddy and Piggins (2012).

Given our setup, it is easy to see that (PV) is equivalent to (CB). As such, a defender of (TB) would presumably find (PV) attractive as a fundamental epistemic principle. However, in light of preface cases (and other paradoxes of consistency), many philosophers would be inclined to say that (PV) is too strong to yield a (plausible, binding) coherence requirement for full belief. Indeed, we ultimately opt for fundamental principles that are strictly weaker than (PV). But, as we mentioned above, our rejection of (PV) was not (initially) motivated by prefaces and the like. Rather, our adoption of fundamental principles that are weaker than (PV) was motivated (initially) by analogy with Joyce's arguments for probabilism as a coherence requirement for credences.

In the case of credences, the analogue of (PV) is clearly inappropriate. The vindicated set of credences (*i.e.*, the credences an omniscient agent would have) are such that they assign maximal credence to all truths and minimal credence to all falsehoods (Joyce, 1998). As a result, in the credal case, (PV) would require that all of one's credences be extremal. One doesn't need preface-like cases (or any other subtle or paradoxical cases) to see that this would be an unreasonably strong requirement. It is for this reason that Joyce (and all others who argue in this way for probabilism) back away from the analogue of (PV) to strictly weaker epistemic principles—specifically, to accuracy-dominance avoidance principles, which are credal analogues of the following fundamental epistemic principle.

Weak Accuracy-Dominance Avoidance (WADA). **B** is *not weakly*[10] *dominated* in distance from vindication. Or, to put this more formally (in terms of d), there does *not* exist an alternative belief set **B'** such that:

(i) $(\forall w)[d(\mathbf{B'}, \overset{\circ}{\mathbf{B}}_w) \leq d(\mathbf{B}, \overset{\circ}{\mathbf{B}}_w)]$, and

(ii) $(\exists w)[d(\mathbf{B'}, \overset{\circ}{\mathbf{B}}_w) < d(\mathbf{B}, \overset{\circ}{\mathbf{B}}_w)]$.

(WADA) is a very natural principle to adopt, if one is not going to require that it be possible to achieve perfect accuracy. Backing off (PV) to (WADA) is analogous to what one does in decision theory, when one adopts a weak dominance principle rather than a principle of *maximizing (actual) utility*.

Initially, it may seem undesirable for an account of epistemic rationality to allow for doxastic states that cannot be perfectly accurate. But, as Richard Foley (1992) explains, an epistemic strategy that is guaranteed to be imperfect is sometimes preferable to one that leaves open the possibility of vindication.

---

[10] Strictly speaking, Joyce *et al.* opt for *strict* dominance-avoidance principles. However, in the credal case (assuming continuous, strictly proper scoring rules), there is no difference between weak and strict dominance (Schervish *et al.* 2009). So, there is no serious disanalogy here.

...if the avoidance of recognizable inconsistency were an absolute prerequisite of rational belief, we could not rationally believe each member of a set of propositions and also rationally believe of this set that at least one of its members is false. But this in turn pressures us to be unduly cautious. It pressures us to believe only those propositions that are certain or at least close to certain for us, since otherwise we are likely to have reasons to believe that at least one of these propositions is false. At first glance, the requirement that we avoid recognizable inconsistency seems little enough to ask in the name of rationality. It asks only that we avoid certain error. It turns out, however, that this is far too much to ask.

We agree with Foley's assessment that (PV) is too demanding. (WADA), however, seems to be a better candidate fundamental epistemic principle. As we will explain below, if S violates (WADA), then S's doxastic state *must* be defective—from both alethic and evidential points of view.

If an agent S satisfies (WADA)—i.e., if S's belief set is *non-dominated* in distance from vindication—then we say S is **coherent** (we'll also apply the term "coherent" to belief sets). To wit, our new coherence (*viz.*, non-dominance) requirement is

(NDB) Epistemically rational agents should (at any given time) be coherent.

Interestingly, (NDB) is strictly weaker than (CB). Moreover, (NDB) is weaker than (CB) in the right way, in light of the preface case (and other similar paradoxes of consistency). Our first two theorems help to explain why.

The first theorem states a necessary and sufficient condition for (*i.e.*, a characterization of) coherence: we call it *Negative* because it identifies certain objects, the *non*-existence of which is necessary and sufficient for coherence. The second theorem states a sufficient condition for coherence: we call it *Positive* because it states that in order to show that a certain belief set **B** is coherent, it's enough to construct a certain type of object.

Definition 1 (Witnessing Sets). **S** *is a **witnessing set** iff (a) at every world, at least half of the judgments*[11] *in* **S** *are inaccurate; and, (b) at some world, more than half of the judgments in* **S** *are inaccurate.*

If **S** is a witnessing set and no proper subset of it is a witnessing set, then **S** is a **minimal witnessing set**. Notice that if **S** is a witnessing set, then it must contain a minimal witnessing set. Theorem 1 shows that the name "witnessing set" is apt, since these entities provide a witness to incoherence.

Theorem 1 (Negative). **B** *is coherent if and only if no subset of* **B** *is a witnessing set.*

It is an immediate corollary of this first theorem that if **B** is logically consistent [*i.e*, if **B** satisfies (PV)], then **B** is coherent. After all, if **B** is logically consistent, then

---

[11] Throughout the paper, we rely on naïve counting. This is unproblematic since all of our algebras are finite.

there is a world w such that no judgments in **B** are inaccurate at w. However, while consistency guarantees coherence, the converse is not the case. That is, coherence does not guarantee consistency. This will be most perspicuous as a consequence of our second central theorem:

Definition 2. *A probability function* Pr **represents** *a belief set* **B** *iff for every* $p \in A$:

(i) **B** *contains* $B(p)$ *iff* $\Pr(p) > 1/2$.
(ii) **B** *contains* $D(p)$ iff $\Pr(p) < 1/2$.

Theorem 2 (Positive). **B** *is coherent if*[12] *there is a probability function* Pr *that represents* **B**.

To appreciate the significance of Theorem 2, it helps to think about a standard lottery case.[13] Consider a fair lottery with n tickets, exactly one of which is the winner. For each $j \leqslant n$ (for $n \geqslant 3$), let p_j be the proposition that the jth ticket is not the winning ticket. And, let q be the proposition that some ticket is the winner. Finally, let LOTTERY be the following belief set:

$$\left\{B(P_j)\,|\,1\leqslant j\leqslant n\right\}\cup\{B(q)\}.$$

LOTTERY is clearly coherent (just consider the probability function that assigns each ticket equal probability of winning), but it is not logically consistent. This explains why (NDB) is strictly weaker than (CB). Moreover, this example is a nice illustration of the fact that (NDB) is weaker than (CB) in a desirable way. More precisely, we can now show that (NDB) is entailed by both alethic considerations [(TB)/(CB)] and evidential considerations [(EB)].

While there is much disagreement about the precise content of (EB), there is widespread agreement that the following is a necessary condition for (EB).

Necessary Condition for Satisfying (EB). *S* satisfies (EB), *i.e.*, all of *S*'s judgments are *justified*, *only if:*

(R) There exists *some* probability function that probabilifies (*i.e.*, assigns probability greater than ½ to) each of *S*'s beliefs and dis-probabilifies (*i.e.*, assigns probability less than ½ to) each of *S*'s disbeliefs.

Many evidentialists agree that probabilification—relative to some probability function—is a necessary condition for justification. Admittedly, there is a lot of

---

[12] For counterexamples to the converse of Theorem 2, see (Easwaran & Fitelson 2013).
[13] We are *not endorsing* the belief set LOTTERY in this example as *epistemically rational*. Indeed, we think that the lottery paradox is not as compelling — as a counterexample to (CB) — as the preface paradox is. On this score, we agree with Pollock (1990) and Nelkin (2000). We are just using this lottery example to make a formal point about the logical relationship between (CB) and (NDB).

```
       (TB)                    (EB)
        │                       │
        ▼                      ╱
     (CB)/(PV)               ╱
          ╲                ╱
           ╲             ╱
            ▼          ▼
              (R)
               │
               ▼
          (NDB)/(WADA)
```

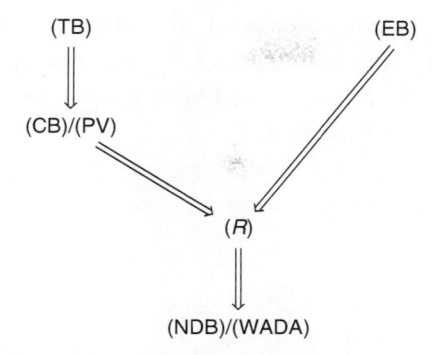

Figure 9.1 The logical relations between epistemic norms

disagreement about which probability function is implicated in (R).[14] But, because our Theorem 2 only requires the existence of some probability function that probabilifies S's beliefs and disprobabilifies S's disbeliefs, it is sufficient to ensure (on most evidentialist views) that (EB) entails (NDB). And, given our assumptions about prefaces (and perhaps even lotteries), this is precisely the entailment that fails for (CB). Thus, by grounding coherence for full beliefs in the same way Joyce grounds probabilism for credences, we are naturally led to a coherence requirement for full belief that is a plausible alternative to (CB). This gives us a principled way to reject (†), and to offer a new type of response to preface cases (and other similar paradoxes of consistency). Figure 9.1 depicts the logical relations between the norms discussed in this section.

In the remainder of the paper, we will explain how our new approach to individual coherence can undergird an interesting new conception of group coherence. This has important ramifications for judgment aggregation.

9.2. Consistency Preservation In Judgment Aggregation

9.2.1. *The standard doctrinal paradox*

Recent interest in Judgment Aggregation has been partly fueled by interest in a paradox concerning the aggregation of individual judgment into collective

---

[14] Internalists like Fumerton (1995) require that the function Pr(·) which undergirds (EB) should be "internally accessible" to the agent (in various ways). Externalists like Williamson (2000) allow for "inaccessible" evidential probabilities. And, subjective Bayesians like Joyce (2005) say that Pr(·) should reflect the agent's subjective degrees of belief (*viz.*, credences). Despite this disagreement, most evidentialists agree that (EB) entails (R), which is all we need for present purposes.

judgment (Kornhauser and Sager, 1986). The basic idea is quite simple: when groups aggregate their opinions on logically connected propositions there may be cases in which the majority rule (and indeed any supermajority short of unanimity), may fail to preserve consistency.

As an example, consider a case in which a group of three judges f $\{j_1, j_2, j_3\}$ makes the following judgments regarding three propositions $\{p, q, p \& q\}$.

	p	q	$p \& q$
j_1	D	B	D
j_2	B	D	D
j_3	B	B	B
majority	B	B	D

Despite the consistent judgments of the individual group members, the majority opinion is inconsistent. To see that the problem applies to any supermajority, one must simply generalize this pattern to larger sets of premises and larger group sizes.[15] In fact, this observation has been quite significantly generalized by thinking axiomatically about aggregation rules. A battery of impossibility results (List and Pettit, 2002; Pauly and van Hees, 2006; Dietrich, 2006; Dietrich and List, 2007a) has shown that many combinations of attractive properties are incompatible.

There is a fairly deep analogy between this paradox and the lottery paradox.[16] What is important for our current purposes is that analyzing the doctrinal paradox in terms of coherence turns out to be a fruitful endeavor (just as it is fruitful to analyze the lottery paradox in terms of coherence). If *coherence*, rather than *consistency* is our central normative concept, then we should investigate the possibility (or impossibility, as the case might be) of coherence-preservation in groups.

9.2.2. Aggregation Framework

Our aggregation framework is a slight generalization of the standard framework from List and Pettit (2002).[17]

Let $\mathcal{G}$ be a set of individuals (named 1, 2, ... n, with $n \geqslant 3$). Let Λ be a propositional language generated by a finite set of atomic sentences. An **agenda** $\mathcal{A}$ is a subset of Λ that is closed under negation. Let $\mathbf{B}_i$ be the **belief set** of individual i (on the

---

[15] Suppose for example that the acceptance threshold was 99%. Consider a case in which there are 101 relevant propositions, namely: $p_1, \ldots, p_{100}, (p_1 \& \ldots \& p_{100})$. Suppose that there are 101 judges: for all i between 1 and 100, j_i rejects p_i and accepts p_k for each $i \neq k$. Suppose finally that j_{101} accepts all of $p_1, \ldots, p_{100}$. Then the resulting 99%-supermajority opinion is: $\{p_1, \ldots, p_{100}, \sim (p_1 \& \ldots \& p_{100})\}$.

[16] As was first remarked by Levi (2004). See also Douven and Romeijn (2007); Chandler (2013).

[17] See also List and Puppe (2009), Grossi and Pigozzi (2012) and Mongin (2012) for recent surveys.

propositions in $\mathcal{A}$): $\mathbf{B}_i$ is an assignment of exactly one of belief (B) or disbelief (D) to every proposition in $\mathcal{A}$. A **profile** is a sequence $\vec{\mathbf{B}}$ of belief sets (one judgment set for each judge in $\mathcal{G}$). Let $\mathcal{B}$ be the set of all possible belief sets, and let $\vec{\mathcal{B}}$ be the set of all possible profiles. Any function $f : \vec{\mathcal{B}} \to \mathcal{B}$ can be called an **aggregation function**. It is interpreted as assigning a "group" belief set to any given profile.

The space of aggregation functions can be effectively investigated by laying down various properties. If f is defined on every possible profile, f is said to have **universal domain**.[18] Our definition of an aggregation function implicitly requires universal domain, and our claims below implicitly presuppose it. f is **unanimous** iff, whenever all judges agree on their judgment about a proposition, the aggregated judgment set agrees with them as well. f is **dictatorial** iff there is a judge i such that for all profiles the collective belief set always coincides with i's belief set. f is **independent** iff for each proposition p, the collective judgment depends only on the individual judgments on p. An independent f is **inversive** if a profile with the opposite pattern of judgments on p gives the opposite collective judgment. f is **systematic** if the pattern of dependence does not vary across propositions.[19]

Formally, f is **dictatorial** iff there is an $i \in \mathcal{G}$, such that for all $\vec{\mathbf{B}}$, $f(\vec{\mathbf{B}}) = \mathbf{B}_i$. Let $\vec{\mathbf{B}} \mid p$ the sequence of beliefs on p alone (as determined by $\vec{\mathbf{B}}$). f is **independent** iff for each $p \in \mathcal{A}$, there is a function $h_p : \{B,D\}^{\mathcal{G}} \to \{B,D\}$, s.t. $f(\vec{\mathbf{B}})(p) = B \Leftrightarrow h_p(\vec{\mathbf{B}} \mid p) = B$. Let $\vec{b}$ be a sequence of judgments from $\{B,D\}^{\mathcal{G}}$ and let $\vec{\mathbf{B}}^{-1}$ be the sequence of judgments with B and D reversed. f is **inversive** iff f is independent and for each $p \in \mathcal{A}, h_p(\vec{\mathbf{B}}) \neq h_p(\vec{\mathbf{B}}^{-1})$. f is **systematic** iff f is independent and for all $p, q \in \mathcal{A}, h_p = h_q$.

9.3. A Coherence-Based Perspective On the Doctrinal Paradox

Consider the Majority rule defined on odd-sized groups: for every proposition p in $\mathcal{A}$, $MAJ(\vec{\mathbf{B}})$ assigns whichever attitude to p more members of the group hold

---

[18] Our usage of "universal domain" differs from standard usage, which presupposes that the possible profiles are restricted to profiles of belief sets that are themselves consistent. See section 5.

[19] The inversive and systematic properties are logically independent. To see that inversive does not imply systematic, consider an aggregation rule that has one player as the dictator for some propositions and another player as the dictator for others. Although this is a strange rule for determining group beliefs, it is inversive, but not systematic. (It is inversive because reversing everyone's judgments includes reversing both dictators. It is not systematic because different dictatorships mean there is different dependence for different propositions.) To see that systematic does not imply inversive, consider an aggregation rule that says that the group believes every proposition in the agenda. This rule is systematic (since every proposition depends in the same, trivial, way on group beliefs) but not inversive (since no change to the group's beliefs reverses the group judgments).

in $\vec{\mathbf{B}}$. (This rule is evidently not defined for even-sized groups, since the two attitudes could possibly be held by the same number of members.) The standard doctrinal paradox stems from the observation that the Majority rule does not preserve consistency. That is to say, assuming that the individual judges submit consistent opinions, there is no guarantee that the group majority is consistent. In this section, we investigate how this result extends to our more permissive epistemic norm. We start by providing two reasons for optimism: in many ordinary contexts of aggregation, an analog of the doctrinal paradox for coherence simply doesn't arise, because in such contexts, aggregating by Majority produces coherent outcomes. Specifically, we argue that if either the judges are all consistent or the agenda has a certain kind of standard form, then Majority preserves coherence. We complement this argument with the observation that in the general case, there are some, rather complicated, failures of coherence preservation.

First, a general word is in order about the logic of the argument. Suppose that we have two normative constraints C_1 and C_2 such that C_1 is stronger than C_2. For example, these might be consistency and coherence, respectively. Suppose that we know that C_1 is not preserved by Majority. When investigating whether C_2 is preserved by Majority, we must account for two distinct effects. First, by weakening the normative constraint, we make it easier for the collective judgment to comply with the normative constraint itself. In the present setting, those cases in which Majority fails to preserve consistency turn out to be cases in which the majority opinion is coherent. The second effect is that by weakening the constraints to C_2, we must countenance new possible inputs to the aggregation process. Specifically, in the present setting, we must also consider what happens when we allow individuals to be coherent, but not consistent.

These two effects can be studied separately. Our first theorem shows that that, as long as the individuals that compose the group submit logically consistent attitudes, the group opinion is guaranteed to be coherent. (The proof in the Appendix shows that this follows immediately from Theorem 2.)

Theorem 3. *For every agenda $\mathcal{A}$, odd-sized group $\mathcal{G}$, and profile $\vec{\mathbf{B}}$, if all $\mathbf{B}_i$'s are consistent, then MAJ($\mathbf{B}$) is coherent.*

No incoherence can arise as long as the individuals submit perfectly consistent and complete judgments.

What about the general case? That is, what about the question whether our notion of rationality can be preserved by Majority for any *coherent* input profile? Here we distinguish two special cases.

We say that an agenda $\mathcal{A}$ is **simple** iff every minimal witnessing set of attitudes over the propositions in $\mathcal{A}$ assigns attitudes to exactly two propositions.[20]

Theorem 4. *Majority preserves coherence for simple agendas and odd-sized groups.*

To illustrate this theorem, note the following definition:

Definition 3. *An agenda $\mathcal{A}$ is truth-functional iff $\mathcal{A}$ can be partitioned in two subsets $\mathcal{A}^P$ and $\mathcal{A}^C$, such that:*

  (i) *no member of $\mathcal{A}$ is a tautology or a contradiction*
  (ii) *any inconsistent subset of $\mathcal{A}^P$ contains a proposition-negation pair (in other words, there are no logical dependencies among the sentences in $\mathcal{A}^P$ except for those involving proposition-negation pairs).*
  (iii) *$\mathcal{A}^P$ is closed under negation.*
  (iv) *$\mathcal{A}^C$ consists of a single proposition/negation pair.*
  (v) *any maximal consistent subset of $\mathcal{A}^P$ entails a member of $\mathcal{A}^C$.*

To illustrate, this definition characterizes agendas of the form:

Conjunctive: $\{p_1, \ldots, p_n, (p_1 \& \ldots \& p_n), \text{negations}\}$.
Disjunctive: $\{p_1, \ldots, p_n, (p_1 \vee \ldots \vee p_n), \text{negations}\}$.

In general, these are agendas that contain a set of "premises" and a "conclusion" that is some boolean compound of those premises, *e.g.*, the conjunctive agenda $\{p_1, \ldots, p_n, (p_1 \& \ldots \& p_n), \text{negations}\}$ is the union of the set $\{p_1, \ldots, p_n, \text{negations}\}$ (the *premises*) and the set $\{(p_1 \& \ldots \& p_n), \sim(p_1 \& \ldots \& p_n)\}$ (the *conclusion*).

Truth-functional agendas are an important and much-discussed class of agendas in Judgment Aggregation.[21]

Theorem 5. *Every truth-functional agenda is simple.*

Putting together theorems 4 and 5, we get:

Corollary 1. *Restricted to truth-functional agendas and odd-sized groups, Majority preserves coherence.*

It is a remarkable fact that such a large class of instances of the doctrinal paradox is eliminated when we move from consistency preservation to coherence preservation.[22]

---

[20] Our usage of "simple" deviates from traditional usage, where "simple" is often interpreted as "contains no minimally inconsistent subset of size greater than two" (Dietrich & List 2007b).

[21] In the early literature, almost all discussions of judgment aggregation were restricted to truth-functional agendas. More recently, broader classes of agendas have received some attention, e.g., the atomically closed agendas of Pauly and van Hees (2006), and the agenda used by Dietrich and List (2007a) to derive Arrow's theorem as a corollary of a result in judgment aggregation.

[22] Note that Corollary 1 can be combined with other preservation results to yield slightly stronger results. For example, List (2013) characterizes a weakening of consistency that he calls 2-consistency: a

However, the theory of judgment aggregation for coherent judgment sets is not as simple as these results might suggest. When we consider sufficiently elaborate agendas, it turns out that Majority does not preserve coherence. In fact, something a bit stronger is true: we can prove an impossibility result for coherence analogous to standard results that apply to consistency. That is to say, it turns out that a set of properties that are all satisfied by Majority (as well as by many other rules) are incompatible with (universal) coherence-preservation. The following definition characterizes one way in which an agenda can be "sufficiently elaborate".

Definition 4. *A belief set* **B** *is α-almost-coherent iff it is incoherent, but there are two distinct proposition-negation pairs {p, ~p} and {q, ~q} such that the belief set resulting from reversing judgments on either pair or both is coherent.*

A belief set **B** *is β-almost-coherent iff it is incoherent, but there are three distinct proposition-negation pairs {p, ~p}, {q, ~q}, and {r, ~r} such that reversing its judgments on any one of these pairs results in a coherent belief set.*

An agenda $\mathcal{A}$ *is* **complex** *iff there is a belief set* **B** *over* $\mathcal{A}$ *that is α-almost-coherent and there is a belief set* **B'** *over* $\mathcal{A}$ *that is β-almost-coherent.*

Theorem 6. *If the agenda* $\mathcal{A}$ *is complex, then every inversive, systematic, unanimous rule that preserves coherence on* $\mathcal{A}$ *is dictatorial.*

In the Appendix, we give an example of a belief set that is both α and β-almost-coherent. Our example involves an agenda with five proposition-negation pairs. Unsurprisingly (since it follows from Theorem 6) we show that on the agenda for this belief set there are coherent profiles such that their majoritarian aggregate is not coherent.

9.4. Related Work

We have investigated the preservation properties of a rationality constraint that is logically weaker than coherence. Naturally, much further work needs to be done to extend our approach. In this section we want to locate our analysis with respect to other studies that have also considered weaker rationality constraints.

One such study, and in fact one that is motivated in ways that are somewhat similar to ours, is List (2013). List advances a general distinction between *blatant* and *non-blatant* inconsistency. This distinction is formalized *via* the notion of

---

belief set B is 2-consistent iff it does not include a proposition-negation pair. It is evident that Majority preserves 2-consistency, so it is a simple consequence of Corollary 1 that Majority preserves *the combination* of coherence and 2-consistency.

k-consistency: a belief set **B** is k-consistent iff its smallest minimally inconsistent subset has size k. For example, compare two belief sets:

$\mathbf{B}_1$ assigns belief to every member of $\{p, q, \sim p\}$.
$\mathbf{B}_2$ assigns belief to every member of $\{p, q, \sim(p \& q)\}$

$\mathbf{B}_1$ is 2-inconsistent: its smallest minimally inconsistent subset has size 2 (it is the belief set that assigns belief to $\{p, \sim p\}$. By contrast, $\mathbf{B}_2$ is 3-inconsistent, but not 2-inconsistent. The result in List (2013) is that k-consistency is preserved by a supermajority with threshold $(k-1)/k$.

The important point, for our purposes, is that our notion of coherence is neither stronger nor weaker than any of List's notions of k-consistency.

Theorem 7. *For every k, there is a set of propositions that is k-consistent but not $k + 1$-consistent, such that an agent who believes all of them is coherent, and there is also a set of propositions that is k-consistent but not $k+1$-consistent, such that an agent who believes all of them is incoherent.*

Thus, these notions cross-cut each other.

It is however, elementarily possible to combine these notions of rationality to obtain stricter global norms (all of them weaker than consistency). For example, List's 2-consistency can be combined with our notion of *coherence* to produce a global rule that is evidence-sensitive but also rules out proposition-negation pairs.

In addition to List's work, there are studies, such as Dietrich's 2007 that explore generalized notions of consistency. Dietrich's aim is to extend the core results in the theory of judgment aggregation to a variety of non-classical logics. We stress a technical and a philosophical point: technically, our notion of *coherence* does not meet all the requirements that Dietrich imposes on his generalized notion of consistency. Philosophically, Dietrich's work allows us to point out that our notion is not based on a non-classical understanding of the semantic apparatus. It is based, rather, on a non-classical understanding of what it is for a belief set to be in compliance with epistemic norms.

9.5. Conclusion

We have defended a coherence norm for belief, according to which epistemically rational agents should adopt beliefs that avoid weak accuracy-domination. This coherence norm is strictly weaker than the norm of deductive consistency, but possesses a number of advantages over the consistency norm.

First, our coherence norm can be justified by alethic considerations, via a simple dominance argument. An analogous justification of the consistency norm would require an implausibly strong "possible vindication" premise, whose partial-belief analogue meets with general skepticism.

Second, our coherence norm is compatible with the evidential norm for belief, which states that epistemically rational agents should believe the propositions supported by their evidence. In the preface paradox, the evidential norm conflicts with deductive consistency. One common response is to give up on deductive consistency; this raises the question of what (if anything) to put in its place. Christensen suggests replacing it with an epistemology of partial belief, where partial beliefs are governed by the Kolmogorov axioms. If the Kolmogorov axioms are compatible with the evidential norm, then so is our coherence norm, since (as Theorem 2 states) every probability function can be represented by a coherent set of full beliefs.

Third, our coherence norm, unlike the deductive consistency norm, sets an attainable standard for collective rationality. It is well known that for a large class of agendas, Majority voting fails to preserve deductive consistency: even in a group whose members all have consistent opinions, there is no guarantee that the majority opinion will be consistent.

The move from consistency to coherence helps in two ways. First, if we keep the consistency requirement for individuals, but adopt a weaker coherence requirement for group beliefs, then beginning with permissible individual beliefs and taking a majority vote will always yield permissible group beliefs. In a group whose members all have consistent opinions, the majority opinion is guaranteed to be coherent (Theorem 3). Second, if we adopt the weaker coherence requirement for both individuals and groups, then beginning with permissible individual beliefs and taking a majority vote will still yield permissible group beliefs in an important class of cases. In particular, in a group whose members all have coherent opinions, the majority opinion is guaranteed to be coherent provided the group is odd-sized and the agenda is simple (Theorem 4). Results about simple agendas are of interest because all truth-functional agendas are simple (Theorem 5). Though the move from consistency to coherence is not a panacea for all voting paradoxes (see Theorem 6), it nonetheless represents significant progress.

We have shown that the coherence norm has useful implications for both individual and social epistemology. In both areas, we expect further investigation of coherence to yield further insight. In individual epistemology, there are unanswered questions about the relationship between partial beliefs and coherent full beliefs. What additional constraints must a coherent set of full beliefs satisfy in order to be represented by a probability function? Can these constraints be independently justified? In social epistemology, there are unanswered questions about the behavior of Majority on agendas that are neither simple nor complex, and about the behavior of other rules. Our early investigations into coherence are only the beginning of a potentially fruitful research program.

Appendix

PROOF OF THEOREM 1.

[B is coherent iff ($\Leftrightarrow$) it contains no witnessing set.]

($\Rightarrow$) We'll prove the contrapositive. Suppose that $S \subseteq B$ is a witnessing set. Let B′ agree with B on all judgments outside S and disagree with B on all judgments in S. By the definition of a witnessing set, B′ must weakly dominate B in distance from vindication [$d(B, B_w)$]. Thus, B is incoherent.

($\Leftarrow$) Again, we prove the contrapositive. Suppose that B is incoherent, *i.e.*, that there is some B′ that weakly dominates B in distance from vindication [$d(B, B_w)$]. Let S be the set of judgments on which B and B′ disagree. Then, S will be a witnessing set.

PROOF OF THEOREM 2.

[B is coherent if there is a probability function Pr that represents B.]

Let Pr be a probability function that represents B in sense of Definition 2. Consider the expected distance from vindication of a belief set—the sum of $Pr(w)d(B, B_w)$. Since $d(B, B_w)$ is a sum of components for each proposition (1 if B disagrees with w on the proposition and 0 if they agree), and since expectations are linear, the expected distance from vindication is the sum of the expectation of these components. The expectation of the component for disbelieving p is $Pr(p)$ while the expectation of the component for believing p is $1 - Pr(p)$. Thus, if $Pr(p) > 1/2$ then believing p is the attitude that uniquely minimizes the expectation, while if $Pr(p) < 1/2$ then disbelieving p is the attitude that uniquely minimizes the expectation. Thus, since Pr represents B, this means that B has strictly lower expected distance from vindication than any other belief set with respect to Pr. Suppose, for *reductio*, that some B′ (weakly) dominates B. Then, B′ must be no farther from vindication than B in any world, and thus B′ must have expected distance from vindication no greater than that of B. But B has strictly lower expected distance from vindication than any other belief set. Contradiction. Therefore, no B′ can dominate B, and so B must be coherent.

PROOF OF THEOREM 3.

[For every agenda $\mathcal{A}$, odd-sized group $\mathcal{G}$, and profile $\vec{B}$, if all B_i's are consistent, then $MAJ(B)$ is coherent.]

Since each judge is consistent, there must be some world in which the judge is accurate on every proposition in the agenda. Take one such world for each judge, and assign equal probability to each of these worlds (counting multiplicity, if the same world is repeated). Then any proposition that is accepted by the majority has probability greater than 1/2 and any proposition that is rejected by the majority has probability less than 1/2. Thus, the majority aggregate is representable by a probability function, and thus by Theorem 2, the majority aggregate is coherent.

PROOF OF THEOREM 4.

[Restricted to simple agendas and odd-sized groups, Majority preserves coherence.]

Let G be an odd-sized group and let $\mathcal{A}$ be a truth-functional agenda. Suppose (*by reductio*) that $\vec{\mathbf{B}}$ is a profile such that $MAJ(\vec{\mathbf{B}}) = \mathbf{E}$ where E is an incoherent set. This means that it must contain some minimal witnessing subset, which must have exactly two propositions. Each of these propositions must have the relevant attitude assigned by more than half of the judges. Thus, there must be some judge that assigns both attitudes. This judge therefore has a minimal witnessing subset of her attitudes, and is therefore incoherent.

PROOF OF THEOREM 5.

[Every truth-functional agenda is simple]

Let $\mathcal{A}$ be a truth-functional agenda. Let S be a minimal witnessing subset in $\mathcal{A}$. We break down the proof into three observations.

(i) S does not assign the same attitude to a proposition and its negation.

Proof: If it did, then in every world, these two attitudes would contribute one accurate and one inaccurate judgment. Thus, removing these two judgments would result in a belief set that has exactly one fewer accurate judgment and one fewer inaccurate judgment in every world than S. Since S was a witnessing set, this proper subset would be too, and thus S would not be minimal.

(ii) S must assign attitudes to exactly the same number of members of $\mathcal{A}^C$ and $\mathcal{A}^P$.

Proof: Since S doesn't assign the same attitude to a proposition and its negation, the attitudes S assigns within $\mathcal{A}^C$ and within $\mathcal{A}^P$ must each be consistent. This is because the only inconsistent subsets of either are proposition-negation pairs. Thus, there must be a world in which all S's judgments in $\mathcal{A}^C$ are accurate, and there must be a world in which all S's judgments in $\mathcal{A}^P$ are accurate. If either set constituted a majority of S, then the relevant world would show that S was not a witnessing set, and therefore the two parts must be the same size.

Note further that since $\mathcal{A}^C$ has exactly two propositions, this means that S must consist of either exactly two members of both $\mathcal{A}^P$ and of $\mathcal{A}^C$, or exactly one member of each.

(iii) S does not assign attitudes to exactly two members of $\mathcal{A}^C$ and exactly two members of $\mathcal{A}^P$.

Proof: The two members of $\mathcal{A}^C$ are a proposition-negation pair, and by the first observation, S has opposite judgments on them, so in every world they are either both accurate or both inaccurate. Neither is a tautology, so there must be some world w_1 in which these two judgments are both accurate. In every such world, both judgments S assigns to members of $\mathcal{A}^P$ must be inaccurate.

Because S is a witnessing set, there must also be some world w_2 in which a strict majority of S's judgments are inaccurate. In w_2, both judgments S assigns in $\mathcal{A}^C$ must be inaccurate, and at least one other judgment, say, the one to p_1, must also be inaccurate. But if c_1 is any member of $\mathcal{A}^C$, then there is no world where the judgments on p_1 and c_1 are both accurate. Since w_2 is a world in which both are inaccurate, $\{c_1, p_1\}$ is a witnessing set, which means that S was not minimal.

Thus, any minimal witnessing subset of such an agenda must assign attitudes to exactly one member of $\mathcal{A}^P$ and exactly one member of $\mathcal{A}^C$, so the agenda is simple.

PROOF OF THEOREM 6

[If an agenda has an α-almost-coherent belief set, and a β-almost-coherent belief set, then every inversive, systematic, unanimous rule that preserves coherence on this agenda is dictatorial.][23]

Fix an inversive, systematic, unanimous aggregation rule f that preserves coherence.

Let $\mathcal{G}$ be the set of judges. Say that $C \subseteq \mathcal{G}$ is a **winning coalition** for p, B iff for every $\vec{B} \in \{B, D\}^{\mathcal{G}}$ where C is exactly the set of judges that assign B to p, then $f(\vec{B})(p) = B$. Say that $C \subseteq \mathcal{G}$ is a winning coalition for p, D iff for every $\vec{B} \in \{B, D\}^{\mathcal{G}}$ where C is exactly the set of judges that assign D to p, then $f(\vec{B})(p) = D$.

By inversiveness, C is a winning coalition for p, B iff it is a winning coalition for p, D. By systematicity, C is a winning coalition for p, B iff it is a winning coalition for q, B. Thus, for an inversive, systematic aggregation rule, we can talk about C being a winning coalition *simpliciter*. By independence, if there is *some*

---

[23] This proof replicates in a Coherence setting a standard proof of Impossibility from the Judgment Aggregation literature. We adapted our proof from the proof of (Grossi and Pigozzi 2012).

$\vec{B} \in \{B, D\}^g$ where C is exactly the set of judges that agree with $f(\vec{B})$ on p, then C is a winning coalition.

Lemma 1: If C is not a winning coalition then its complement $-C$ is.

To see this, fix some $\vec{B}$ where all judges in C assign B to p and all judges in $-C$ assign D to p. If $f(\vec{B})(p) = B$ then C is a winning coalition, and otherwise $-C$ is.

Lemma 2: If C is a winning coalition, then so is any superset of C.

Assume that $C \subset C'$, and C is a winning coalition, but C' is not. By assumption, there is a belief assignment X on the agenda that is α-almost-coherent. That is, X is incoherent, and there are two distinct proposition-negation pairs $\{p, \sim p\}$ and $\{q, \sim q\}$ such that switching its judgments on either or both both gives a coherent belief assignment. Let every judge in C assign X with a reversal on $\{p, \sim p\}$. Let every judge in $C' - C$ assign X with reversal on both pairs. Let every judge outside of C' assign X with reversal on $\{q, \sim q\}$.

We show that the aggregate is X, and is thus incoherent. Every judgment in X other than those on p, $\sim p$, q, and $\sim q$ is shared by every judge, and thus by unanimity, is accepted by the aggregate. p and $\sim p$ have the reverse of X on every judge in C', but have the value given by X outside of C'. Since C' is not a winning coalition, its complement is, and thus the aggregate must agree with X on p and $\sim p$. q and $\sim q$ have the value from X on every judge in C, but not on any judge outside of C. Since C is a winning coalition, the aggregate has the value from X on q and $\sim q$. Thus, the aggregate is an extension of X, and thus must be incoherent, so our assumption that there could be a superset of a winning coalition that is not winning was false.

Lemma 3: The intersection of any two winning coalitions is a winning coalition.

Assume C and C' are winning coalitions but their intersection $C \cap C'$ is not. Let X be a β-almost-coherent belief assignment and consider three distinct proposition-negation pairs $\{p, \sim p\}$, $\{q, \sim q\}$, and $\{r, \sim r\}$ such that reversing X's judgment on any one of these pairs yields a coherent belief assignment. Let every judge in $C \cap C'$ assign X reversed on p and $\sim p$. Let every judge in $C' - C$ assign X reversed on q and $\sim q$. Let every judge outside C' assign X reversed on r and $\sim r$.

We show that the aggregate is X, and is thus incoherent. All judges agree with every judgment in X outside of p, q, r and their negations, and thus by unanimity, the aggregate does too. All judges outside of $C \cap C'$ agree with X's judgments on p and $\sim p$, while the judges in $C \cap C'$ disagree. Since $C \cap C'$ is not a winning coalition, its complement is, and thus X's judgments on p and $\sim p$ are shared by the aggregate. All judges outside of $C' - C$ agree with X's judgments on q and $\sim q$, while the judges in $C' - C$ disagree. But the complement of $C' - C$ is a superset of C, and is thus a winning coalition, by Lemma 2. Thus, X's judgments on q and $\sim q$ are shared by the aggregate as well. All judges in C' agree with X's judgments on r and $\sim r$. Since C' is a winning coalition, the aggregate does too. Thus, the aggregate includes all of X's judgments, so the aggregate must be incoherent, which contradicts the fact that f preserves coherence. Thus, our assumption that the intersection of two winning coalitions could fail to be a winning coalition was false.

Proof of theorem: By Lemma 1, for every singleton, either it or its complement is a winning coalition. If none of the singletons is a winning coalition, then every complement of a singleton is. But by Lemma 3, the intersection of any pair of winning coalitions is itself a winning coalition. But by repeated intersection of the complements of all singletons, we conclude that if no singleton is a winning coalition, then the empty set is, which is impossible. Thus, at least one singleton must be a winning coalition. So therefore, the aggregation rule must be a dictatorship, QED.

EXAMPLE

Here we want to provide an example of an agenda that satisfies the condition of Theorem 6. We also show that this agenda allows coherent input profiles with incoherent majoritarian aggregates.

Consider the boolean algebra over (at least) 11 worlds, $w_1, w_2, \ldots, w_{10}, w_{11}$.[24] Consider the agenda given by the following five propositions (and their negations—in what follows, we ignore mention of the negations, and assume that each judge makes consistent judgments on every proposition-negation pair):

$$A = \{w_1, w_2, w_3, w_4\}$$
$$B = \{w_1, w_5, w_6, w_7\}$$
$$C = \{w_2, w_5, w_8, w_9\}$$
$$D = \{w_3, w_6, w_8, w_{10}\}$$
$$E = \{w_4, w_7, w_9, w_{10}\}$$

The important thing is that for every pair of these propositions, there is exactly one world where both are true, and in any world where one of the propositions is true, exactly one other is as well.

On this agenda, note that the belief set $\langle B, B, B, B, B \rangle$ is incoherent—in every world it gets a majority of the propositions wrong (exactly three wrong in each of the worlds $w_1, \ldots, w_{10}$, and all wrong in all other worlds), so it is dominated by $\langle D, D, D, D, D \rangle$.

The belief set $\langle B, B, B, B, D \rangle$ is both α and β-almost-coherent. To show this, it suffices to show three things: that $\langle B, B, B, B, D \rangle$ is incoherent; that $\langle B, B, B, D, D \rangle$ is coherent (symmetry considerations mean that this also shows

---

[24] If you prefer to think of propositions sententially, then you can generate propositions with exactly this same logical structure by taking atoms p_1, p_2, p_3, p_4, and considering $w_1, \ldots, w_{16}$ as the 16 state descriptions (conjunctions of these four atomic sentences or their negations), and the propositions as each being a disjunction of four state descriptions.

that $\langle B,B,D,B,D\rangle, \langle B,D,B,B,D\rangle$, and $\langle D,B,B,B,D\rangle$ are coherent); and that $\langle B,B,D,D,D\rangle$ is coherent. Thus, the agenda satisfies the conditions of Theorem 6.

To see that $\langle B,B,B,B,D\rangle$ is incoherent, note that it is weakly dominated by $\langle D,D,D,D,D\rangle$. On worlds $w_1, w_2, w_3, w_5, w_6, w_8$, both belief sets have distance 2 from vindication. On worlds w_4, w_7, w_9, w_{10}, the former has distance 4 from vindication while the latter has distance 2 from vindication. On world w_{11}, the former has distance 4 from vindication while the latter has distance 0 from vindication.

Now we show that $\langle B,B,B,D,D\rangle$ is coherent. Consider the probability distribution that assigns probability 0 to any world in D or E and any world not in any of the five propositions, and probability 1/3 to each of the three remaining worlds. (In this case, w_1, w_2, w_3.) On this distribution, every proposition that is believed has probability strictly greater than 1/2 (in fact, they all have probability 2/3) and every proposition that is disbelieved has probability strictly less than 1/2 (in fact, both have probability 0). Thus, by Theorem 2, the assignment is coherent.

Finally, we show that $\langle B,B,D,D,D\rangle$ is coherent. Consider the probability distribution that assigns probability 1/3 to the unique world shared by the two propositions that are believed (in this case w_1), probability 1/9 to each of the six worlds that are in exactly one of those two propositions (in this case $w_2, w_3, w_4, w_5, w_6, w_7$), and probability 0 to all other worlds. On such a distribution, the two believed propositions have probability 2/3, and the three disbelieved propositions all have probability 2/9, and thus by Theorem 2, the belief set is coherent.

Therefore, this agenda satisfies the conditions of the theorem, and so the only aggregation function that is independent, inversive, systematic, and unanimous while preserving coherence is dictatorship.

In particular, we can see that Majority fails to preserve coherence. Just consider ten coherent judges who each have one permutation of $\langle B,B,B,D,D\rangle$. The majority judgment must be $\langle B,B,B,B,B\rangle$, which is incoherent.

Two final clarificatory notes on Theorem 6 are in order. First, "systematic" does not imply "inversive". To see this, consider the rule that says the group believes every proposition on the agenda. This rule is systematic, but not inversive. Second, systematicity is essential to the theorem—independence alone does not suffice. To see this, consider the following example.[25] Let $\mathcal{A}$ be (any) complex agenda. Now consider the agenda $\mathcal{A}^+ = \mathcal{A} \cup \{q, \neg q\}$, where q is some (non-tautological and non-contradictory) proposition that is logically unrelated to any of the propositions in $\mathcal{A}$. Then, $\mathcal{A}^+$ will also be complex. Now consider the following aggregation procedure: On the subagenda $\mathcal{A}$, individual 1 determines the collective

---

[25] We thank an anonymous referee for this example.

judgments, and on the subagenda $\{q, \neg q\}$, individual 2 determines the collective judgments. Although this aggregation procedure is dictatorial on each of these two subagendas, it is not dictatorial on the agenda $\mathcal{A}^+$ in its entirety, since there is no single dictator who determines the collective judgment for every proposition.

PROOF OF THEOREM 7

[For every k, there is a set of propositions that is k-consistent but not $k + 1$-consistent, such that an agent who believes all of them is coherent, and there is also a set of propositions that is k-consistent but not $k + 1$-consistent, such that an agent who believes all of them is incoherent.]

First, we will construct a set of $2k - 1$ propositions that is k-consistent but not $k + 1$-consistent. Since there are worlds in which a majority of the propositions are true, the set will be coherent. Let S be the set of all subsets of $\{1, \ldots, 2k - 1\}$ of size exactly k. For each s in S, let there be a distinct world w_s, and let this be all the worlds the make up the boolean algebra. Define a set of propositions $\{p_1, \ldots, p_{2k-1}\}$ as follows: the proposition p_i contains the world w_s iff $i \in s$. Then, for every set of k distinct propositions from this set, the indices form a set s, and the world w_s will make all of these propositions true, so the set is k-consistent. However, any collection of $k + 1$ propositions will contain at least one propositions from outside of s, and thus there is no world in which all of them are true, and so the set is not $k + 1$-consistent.

Similarly, we can construct a set of $2k + 1$ propositions that is k-consistent but not $k + 1$-consistent. Since there is no world where at least half of the propositions are true, the set will be incoherent. Let S be the set of all subsets of $\{1, \ldots, 2k + 1\}$ of size exactly k. For each s in S, let there be a distinct world w_s, and let this be all the worlds the make up the boolean algebra. Define a set of propositions $\{p_1, \ldots, p_{2k+1}\}$ as follows: the proposition p_i contains the world w_s iff $i \in s$. Then, for every set of k distinct propositions from this set, the indices form a set s, and the world w_s will make all of these propositions true, so the set is k-consistent. However, any collection of $k + 1$ propositions will contain at least one propositions from outside of s, and thus there is no world in which all of them are true, and so the set is not $k + 1$-consistent.

Acknowledgments

We have discussed various aspects of this project with a large number of individuals and groups over the last few years. While we cannot list all of these helpful individuals and groups here, we would like to single a few of them out. Thanks to an invitation by Jason Konek, we presented this material at the Philosophy Department at the University of Michigan, where we received very valuable feedback on the project. Nick Leonard, Gabriella Pigozzi, and an anonymous referee read various versions of this paper and gave us helpful notes. Finally, we'd like to thank Jennifer Lackey for the invitation which prompted this particular collaboration.

References

Chandler, J. (2013). Probability, acceptance and aggregation. *Erkenntnis* 78(1), 201–17.
Christensen, D. (2004). *Putting Logic in its Place*. Oxford: Oxford University Press.
Deza, M. and E. Deza (2009). *Encyclopedia of Distances*. Springer.
Dietrich, F. (2006). Judgment aggregation: (im)possibility theorems. *Journal of Economic Theory* 126(1), 286–98.
Dietrich, F. (2007). A generalised model of judgment aggregation. *Social Choice and Welfare* 28(4), 529–65.
Dietrich, F. and C. List (2007a). Arrow's theorem in judgment aggregation. *Social Choice and Welfare* 29(1), 19–33.
Dietrich, F. and C. List (2007b). Judgment aggregation with consistency alone. Online working paper http://eprints.lse.ac.uk/20110/.
Dietrich, F. and C. List (2008). Judgment aggregation without full rationality. *Social Choice and Welfare* 31(1), 15–39.
Douven, I. and J. Romeijn (2007). The discursive dilemma as a lottery paradox. *Economics and Philosophy* 23(3), 301–19.
Duddy, C. and A. Piggins (2012). A measure of distance between judgment sets. *Social Choice and Welfare* 39(4), 855–67.
Easwaran, K. (2012). Dr. Truthlove, or how i learned to stop worrying and love Bayesian probabilities. Unpublished manuscript.
Easwaran, K. and B. Fitelson (2012). An "evidentialist" worry about Joyce's argument for probabilism. *Dialectica* 66(3), 425–33.
Easwaran, K. and B. Fitelson (2013). Accuracy, coherence and evidence. To appear in *Oxford Studies in Epistemology* (Volume 5), T. Szabo Gendler & J. Hawthorne (Eds.), Oxford University Press.
Foley, R. (1992). *Working Without a Net*. Oxford: Oxford University Press.
Friedman, J. (2013). Suspended judgment. *Philosophical studies* 162(2), 165–81.
Fumerton, R. (1995). *Metaepistemology and Skepticism*. Rowman & Littlefield.
Grossi, D. and G. Pigozzi (2012). Introduction to judgment aggregation. In N. Bezhanishvili and V. Goranko (Eds.), *Lectures on Logic and Computation*, pp. 160–209. Springer.
Joyce, J. M. (1998). A nonpragmatic vindication of probabilism. *Philosophy of Science* 65(4), 575–603.
Joyce, J. M. (2005). How probabilities reflect evidence. *Philosophical Perspectives* 19(1), 153–78.

Joyce, J. M. (2009). Accuracy and coherence: Prospects for an alethic epistemology of partial belief. In F. Huber and C. Schmidt-Petri (Eds.), *Degrees of Belief*. Springer.

Kaplan, M. (2013). Coming to terms with our human fallibility: Christensen on the preface. *Philosophy and Phenomenological Research* 87(1), 1–35.

Klein, P. (1985). The virtues of inconsistency. *The Monist* 68(1), 105–35.

Kolodny, N. (2007). How does coherence matter? In *Proceedings of the Aristotelian Society*, Volume 107, pp. 229–63.

Kornhauser, L. A. and L. G. Sager (1986). Unpacking the court. *The Yale Law Journal* 96(1), 82–117.

Kyburg, H. E. (1970). Conjunctivitis. In M. Swain (Ed.), *Induction, acceptance and rational belief*, pp. 55–82. Reidel.

Levi, I. (2004). List and Pettit. *Synthese* 140(1), 237–42.

List, C. (2013). When to defer to supermajority testimony–and when not to. This volume.

List, C. and P. Pettit (2002). Aggregating sets of judgments: An impossibility result. *Economics and Philosophy* 18(1), 89–110.

List, C. and C. Puppe (2009). Judgment aggregation. In P. Anand, P. Pattanaik, and C. Puppe (Eds.), *The handbook of rational and social choice*, pp. 457–82. Oxford: Oxford University Press.

Miller, M. K. and D. Osherson (2009). Methods for distance-based judgment aggregation. *Social Choice and Welfare* 32(4), 575–601.

Mongin, P. (2012). The doctrinal paradox, the discursive dilemma, and logical aggregation theory. *Theory and decision* 73(3), 315–55.

Nelkin, D. K. (2000). The lottery paradox, knowledge, and rationality. *The Philosophical Review* 109(3), 373–409.

Pauly, M. and M. van Hees (2006). Logical constraints on judgment aggregation. *Journal of Philosophical Logic* 34(6), 569–85.

Pigozzi, G. (2006). Belief merging and the discursive dilemma: an argument-based account to paradoxes of judgment aggregation. *Synthese* 152(2), 285–98.

Pollock, J. L. (1990). *Nomic probability and the foundations of induction*. Oxford: Oxford University Press.

Ryan, S. (1991). The preface paradox. *Philosophical studies* 64(3), 293–307.

Ryan, S. (1996). The epistemic virtues of consistency. *Synthese* 109(2), 121–41.

Schervish, M., T. Seidenfeld, and J. Kadane (2009). Proper scoring rules, dominated forecasts, and coherence. *Decision Analysis* 6(4), 202–21.

Williamson, T. (2000). *Knowledge and Its Limits*. Oxford: Oxford University Press.

10

When to Defer to Supermajority Testimony—and When Not

Christian List

10.1. The Problem

Philip Pettit (2006) has argued that although it is sometimes rational to defer to majority testimony on perceptual matters—say, whether a car went through the traffic lights on the red—this is not generally the case with matters more deeply embedded in one's web of belief—say, whether abortion is wrong. A key problem is that deference to majority testimony may lead to inconsistent beliefs. For example, suppose one agent believes that p and q are both true, a second believes that p is true and q is false, and a third believes that p is false and q is true. Then p, q, and $not\text{-}(p\&q)$ are each believed by a majority, and thus deference to these majorities would lead to inconsistent beliefs. This is a version of the much-discussed 'discursive dilemma' or 'paradox of majoritarian judgment aggregation'(e.g., Pettit 2001, List and Pettit 2002, drawing on Kornhauser and Sager 1986).[1]

Pettit (2006) suggests that '[t]here is another...approach that will do better...This is not to allow just any majoritarian challenge to reverse a belief but to allow only a certain sort of supermajoritarian challenge to do so' (p. 184). As an illustration, he observes that, assuming consistent individual beliefs, there can never be supermajorities of 70 per cent believing each of p, q, and $not\text{-}(p\&q)$ to be

---

[1] Kornhauser and Sager's 'doctrinal paradox' consists in the fact that, in decisions on a conclusion whose truth-value depends on multiple premises (e.g., the conclusion might be that a defendant is liable for breach of contract, and the premises might be that there was a valid contract in place and that the defendant did a particular action), majority voting on the premises may lead to a different verdict than majority voting on the conclusion. The 'discursive dilemma' (e.g., Pettit 2001, List and Pettit 2002) consists in the fact that simultaneous proposition-by-proposition majority voting on multiple interconnected propositions (which need not be partitioned into premises and conclusions) may lead to inconsistent majority judgments.

Table 10.1 A Supermajoritarian Inconsistency

	p	q	r	not-(p&q&r)
Agent 1	False	True	True	True
Agent 2	True	False	True	True
Agent 3	True	True	False	True
Agent 4	True	True	True	False
Supermajority of 75%	True	True	True	True

true. If there were such supermajorities, the inconsistency would have to show up in the beliefs of at least one individual agent.

It is easy to see, however, that a 70 per cent supermajority requirement is insufficient to prevent an inconsistency between a larger number of propositions. In a group of four agents, for example, there can easily be 75 per cent supermajorities for each of *p, q, r,* and *not-(p&q&r)*, even when each agent holds individually consistent beliefs, such as when the first agent accepts all but the first of these four propositions, the second accepts all but the second, and so on, as shown in Table 10.1.

When does deference to supermajority testimony guarantee consistency, and when not? In this short paper, I sketch an answer to this question, drawing on formal results from the theory of judgment aggregation (particularly Dietrich and List 2007, generalizing List 2001, ch. 9; for related results, see Nehring and Puppe 2007).[2] Thus I follow Pettit (2006) in focusing on the consistency aspect of rationality (other aspects of rationality are beyond the scope of this paper).[3] I state necessary and sufficient conditions for achieving consistency through supermajoritarian deference and also for achieving something less than full consistency: namely what I call 'consistency of degree k', in short 'k-consistency'. This is the requirement that inconsistencies in an agent's beliefs, if there are any, should not be too blatant, where k is an integer number capturing the degree of 'blatancy' of the inconsistencies ruled out, in a sense to be made precise. My argument generalizes but also qualifies the observation that deference to supermajority testimony can sometimes be rational, at least on the consistency dimension.[4]

---

[2] One difference between the results in my earlier related works (List 2001 and Dietrich and List 2007) and the results in Nehring and Puppe (2007) is that the latter require completeness of judgments, while the former permit incomplete judgments (as I do in this paper). For review articles on judgment aggregation, see List and Puppe (2009) and List (2012).

[3] The somewhat broader title of this paper echoes the title of Pettit's paper (2006). At the end of this paper, I offer some brief remarks about some aspects of rationality other than consistency.

[4] For a more general treatment of the related problem of 'judgment transformation' (how agents can/should revise their judgments in light of the judgments of others) and a baseline impossibility

10.2. Minimally Inconsistent Sets and Supermajority Testimony

What are the simplest inconsistencies that can arise in an agent's belief set?[5] Call a set of propositions *minimally inconsistent* if it is inconsistent but all its proper subsets—obtained by removing at least one proposition from the set—are consistent.[6] For example, the sets {p, q, not-$(p\&q)$} and {p, q, r, not-$(p\&q\&r)$} are each minimally inconsistent: each of them becomes consistent as soon as we remove any one of its members. By contrast, the set {p, $p\&q$, not-p}, although inconsistent, is not minimally inconsistent: even if one of p or $p\&q$ is removed from it, it remains inconsistent. Any inconsistent set of propositions has at least one, and possibly many, minimally inconsistent subsets. It follows that any agent with inconsistent beliefs has at least one minimally inconsistent set of propositions among his or her beliefs. Conversely, any agent whose beliefs include no minimally inconsistent set of propositions is consistent throughout.

Under what conditions can deference to supermajority testimony lead an agent to believe a minimally inconsistent set of propositions?

---

theorem, see List (2011). It is worth addressing one potential objection to the present project of analysing the 'logic' of supermajority deference: why should we not simply let our response to any sort of testimony—whether majoritarian, supermajoritarian, or other—be guided by Bayesian conditionalization? In particular, the testimony in question may be interpreted as a piece of information, and Bayesian conditionalization may tell us how to update our beliefs in light of it. This Bayesian approach, however, has two problems from the present perspective. First, it tells us how to update credences (degrees of belief), not beliefs *simpliciter*, which, like Pettit, I am focusing on here. Second, Bayesian conditionalization becomes possible in the present context only once we make fairly precise assumptions about the testimony-generating process, including assumptions about the reliability of the reported beliefs and the nature of their mutual dependence or independence. (For further discussion, see also the last section of this paper.) By contrast, the present analysis of whether deference to supermajority testimony can yield consistent beliefs applies to beliefs *simpliciter* and requires no assumptions about the testimony-generating process. The cost is that this approach informs us only about one aspect of rationality, namely the consistency aspect, while being silent on other aspects that may be required for rationality *simpliciter*.

[5] For the purposes of this paper, I define a *belief set* as a set of propositions accepted by an agent. Thus the present focus is on beliefs *simpliciter* (i.e., a proposition is either believed or not), not on beliefs that come in degrees (as captured by credence or subjective probability functions). Crucially, belief sets need *not* be complete. (A belief set is *complete* if it contains a member of each proposition-negation pair from some relevant reference set of propositions under consideration.) Propositions are represented by sentences in a suitable logic, such as standard propositional or predicate logic. Generally, any logic satisfying some minimal conditions (including compactness), as defined in Dietrich (2007), is suitable. Apart from standard propositional and predicate logics, many modal, conditional, and deontic logics are examples of logics to which the present analysis applies.

[6] The significance of the notion of minimal inconsistency for problems of attitude aggregation was identified by Nehring and Puppe (e.g., 2007), who made extensive use of the notion of a 'critical family' of binary properties, which, translated into the language of propositions, is equivalent to the notion of a minimally inconsistent set of propositions.

WHEN TO DEFER TO SUPERMAJORITY TESTIMONY—AND WHEN NOT   243

Fact 1: It is possible for a minimally inconsistent set of k propositions to be each supported by a supermajority among agents with individually consistent beliefs if and only if the supermajority size is less than or equal to $^{k-1}/_k$.

To prove this fact, consider any minimally inconsistent set of k propositions. Call them $p_1, p_2, \ldots, p_k$. I first show that supermajorities of size $^{k-1}/_k$ (and by implication of smaller sizes) among agents with individually consistent beliefs can support each of these propositions. Take any set of agents divisible into k subsets of equal size. Suppose the agents in the first subset believe all of the k propositions except p_1, the agents in the second subset believe all except p_2, and so on. As every proper subset among $p_1, p_2, \ldots, p_k$ is consistent—in particular, every subset obtained by dropping precisely one of these propositions—any such agent holds consistent beliefs. But now each of $p_1, p_2, \ldots, p_k$—that is, each proposition in a minimally inconsistent set of size k—is supported by a supermajority of size $^{k-1}/_k$.

Conversely, I show that supermajorities of size greater than $^{k-1}/_k$ among agents with individually consistent beliefs can never support all of $p_1, p_2, \ldots, p_k$. Assume, for a contradiction, that there are k such supermajorities. For any two of these supermajorities, even if maximally distinct, the overlap must exceed $^{k-1}/_k - (1 - {^{k-1}/_k}) = {^{k-2}/_k}$. For any three, the overlap must exceed $^{k-2}/_k - (1 - {^{k-1}/_k}) = {^{k-3}/_k}$. Continuing, for all k supermajorities, the overlap must exceed $^{k-k}/_k = 0$. So the supermajorities must have a non-empty overlap, implying that at least one agent belongs to their intersection. But this would mean that this agent holds inconsistent beliefs, contradicting the assumption that all agents in question have individually consistent beliefs. This completes the proof.[7]

10.3. Ensuring Consistency

What, in light of Fact 1, could a rational policy of deference to supermajority testimony look like? Or at least, what could such a policy look like from the perspective of preventing inconsistency in our beliefs?

Suppose the aim is to arrive at fully consistent beliefs. Consider the entire set of propositions on which beliefs are to be formed or revised. (In the theory of judgment aggregation, this is called the *agenda*.) This set could, for example, contain all those propositions that occur somewhere in an agent's web of belief. Let k be the size of a largest minimally inconsistent set constructible from these propositions and their negations.[8] To illustrate, if the only propositions on which the agent

---

[7] A version of this argument was given in List (2001, ch. 9).

[8] Formally, the agenda is assumed to be closed under (single) negation and thus to contain proposition-negation pairs. The significance of the largest minimally inconsistent subset of the

forms or revises his or her beliefs are *p, if p then q*, and *q*, then the largest minimally inconsistent set constructible from these propositions and their negations would be {*p, if p then q, not-q*}, and thus *k* would be 3. In the earlier example, where the relevant propositions were *p, q, r*, and *not-(p&q&r)*, *k* is 4. If the set of propositions is larger and more complex, *k* can of course be significantly larger.

Fact 1 immediately implies that the policy of adopting all and only those beliefs held by a supermajority of size greater than $^{k-1}/_k$ can never lead to an inconsistency. If it did, the resulting inconsistent belief set would have to include a minimally inconsistent set of propositions; but that set would contain at most *k* propositions (as *k* is the size of the largest minimally inconsistent set constructible from the given propositions and their negations), and Fact 1 implies that no such set can be supported by supermajorities of size greater than $^{k-1}/_k$ among agents with individually consistent beliefs. Thus the following holds (Dietrich and List 2007, generalizing List 2001):[9]

Fact 2: Let *k* be the size of a largest minimally inconsistent set of propositions constructible from the propositions on which beliefs are to be formed or revised and their negations. The set of propositions that are each supported by a supermajority of size greater than $^{k-1}/_k$ among agents with individually consistent beliefs is consistent.

However, for any supermajority size below unanimity, the set of propositions supported by supermajorities of that size is not guaranteed to be *deductively closed*: the propositions receiving the required supermajority support may entail other propositions that fail to receive such support (Dietrich and List 2007; see also Nehring 2005). This means that deferring to supermajority testimony on propositions on which there is the required supermajority agreement while suspending belief on all other propositions (within the set on which beliefs are to be formed or revised) may not be a rational policy: it may make the agent vulnerable to 'lottery-like' paradoxes: the agent may believe several propositions but fail to believe some of their implications, even among the relevant propositions. (The classical lottery paradox consists in the possibility that an agent may believe of every single one among a million lottery tickets that this particular ticket will not win, while also believing that one of the million tickets will win.) In the present context, this problem

---

agenda for the possibility of consistent attitude aggregation was also identified by Nehring and Puppe (e.g., 2007), albeit in a property-based rather than propositional-logic-based framework.

[9] Related but not fully equivalent results (relying on a combinatorial notion called the 'intersection property') can be found in Nehring and Puppe's work on binary attitude aggregation (e.g., 2007). As noted above, their relevant results require—unlike here—that belief sets be complete, i.e., for every proposition-negation pair under consideration, the agent has to accept either the proposition or its negation. In the present case, following List (2001, ch. 9) and Dietrich and List (2007), incompleteness is permitted: the agent may have no belief on some proposition-negation pairs.

can generally be avoided only if the supermajority threshold is raised to unanimity, a condition that ensures a deductively closed set of supported propositions. Empirically, however, unanimous agreement is rare, and so a policy of unanimitarian deference would seldom lead us to acquire new beliefs.

Independently of the issue of deductive closure, another consideration may also push us in the direction of a unanimity threshold. As the set of propositions on which beliefs are to be formed or revised increases in size and complexity, the value of k—the size of the largest minimally inconsistent set constructible from these propositions and their negations—typically increases as well, and thus the supermajority threshold required to ensure consistency approaches unanimity.

10.4. Avoiding Blatant Inconsistencies

Achieving full consistency in one's beliefs may not always be feasible. Indeed, it is perhaps unrealistic to expect the beliefs of a normal human agent to be consistent. On the other hand, we do expect those beliefs to be free at least from the most blatant inconsistencies. When is an inconsistency blatant? An agent who believes a single proposition that is self-contradictory, such as $p\&(not\text{-}p)$, is clearly blatantly inconsistent. An agent who simultaneously believes a proposition and its negation, such as p and also $not\text{-}p$, is also fairly blatantly inconsistent, even if each of p and $not\text{-}p$ is not contradictory by itself. An agent who believes three propositions which are in contradiction, such as p, *if p then q*, and $not\text{-}q$, is still rather blatantly inconsistent, but not as much as one who believes a self-contradictory proposition or a proposition-negation pair. An agent with inconsistent beliefs across five propositions, such as four logically independent conjuncts and the negation of their conjunction, is still inconsistent, but intuitively less so than any one of the earlier agents.

Now suppose that, although my large set of beliefs is inconsistent in its entirety, it turns out that every combination of 1588 or fewer propositions among my beliefs is consistent, and the smallest set over which I hold inconsistent beliefs contains 1589 propositions. Should my beliefs still be described as blatantly inconsistent? Intuitively, the inconsistency here is much less blatant than in any of the earlier cases.

My proposal is to measure the blatancy of an agent's inconsistency by the size of the smallest minimally inconsistent set of propositions believed by the agent. The smaller this size, the more blatant the agent's inconsistency. To be sure, this is a rather simple and crude measure, but I illustrate its usefulness in a moment. In the examples just given, the values of the measure are 1, 2, 3, 5, and 1589, respectively, capturing the intuitive ranking of how blatant the inconsistencies in question are.

Just as the blatancy of an agent's inconsistency can be measured by the size of the smallest minimally inconsistent set of propositions among the agent's beliefs, so the degree of consistency of the agent can be measured in a closely related way. Call an agent whose belief set is free from any minimally inconsistent subset of k or fewer propositions *consistent of degree k*, or in short k-*consistent*. For example, an agent who believes no self-contradictory proposition is 1-consistent. An agent who, in addition, believes no proposition-negation pair (and no inconsistent set of similar complexity) is 2-consistent. One who further does not believe any inconsistent set of the form $\{p, \textit{if p then q, not-q}\}$ is 3-consistent. And so on. In the contrived example of my less-than-fully-consistent beliefs, I would be 1588-consistent. Full consistency, finally, is the special case of k-consistency for an infinite value of k.

Perhaps the best a human agent can ever hope to achieve is k-consistency for a reasonably large value of k. What could a policy of deference to supermajority testimony look like if the aim were to achieve k-consistency for some finite value of k? The following corollary of the proof of Fact 1 answers this question.

Fact 3: For any value of k, the set of propositions that are each supported by a supermajority of size greater than $^{k-1}/_k$ among agents with individually consistent (or merely k-consistent) beliefs is k-consistent.

To prove this fact, fix some value of k and assume, for a contradiction, that some set of propositions that are each supported by a supermajority of size greater than $^{k-1}/_k$ among agents with individually consistent (or k-consistent) beliefs violates k-consistency. This set will then have at least one minimally inconsistent subset of k or fewer propositions. Consider the k or fewer supermajorities of size greater than $^{k-1}/_k$ supporting those propositions. The proof of Fact 1 shows that these supermajorities must have a non-empty intersection, implying that at least one agent belongs to all of them. By implication, this agent must support a minimally inconsistent set of k or fewer propositions, which contradicts his or her individual consistency (or k-consistency). This completes the proof.

Of course, if the underlying set of propositions on which beliefs are to be formed or revised has no minimally inconsistent subsets of size greater than k, then k-consistency implies full consistency. In this case, Fact 3 reduces to Fact 2. Otherwise, Fact 3 is more general.

Fact 3 suggests that, while full consistency may often be hard to achieve through deference to supermajority testimony short of unanimity, supermajoritarian deference may nonetheless be a good route to k-consistency for a suitable value of k. And this remains true even if the agents constituting the supermajorities in question are themselves merely k-consistent. Thus, for any value of k, deference to supermajorities of size greater than $^{k-1}/_k$ preserves k-consistency.

In summary, the larger the supermajority threshold we require for the acquisition of a belief, the less blatant the inconsistencies we are liable to run into.

10.5. Coherence and Correspondence

For a sufficiently high threshold, deference to supermajority testimony may yield consistent beliefs; and for lower thresholds, it may yield beliefs that are not too blatantly inconsistent. In both cases, other beliefs, on which there is no sufficient supermajority agreement, may need to be revised accordingly.

Does this make supermajoritarian deference rational? My focus has been on 'coherence' considerations: supermajority testimony is less prone to inconsistency than majority testimony. But 'coherence' is only one aspect of rationality and may not be sufficient for rationality *simpliciter*. A different aspect, on which my analysis has been silent, is 'evidential well-supportedness', which, in turn, is motivated by 'correspondence' considerations. Does supermajority testimony in support of a proposition provide good evidence for the truth of that proposition?

There is one situation in which the answer to this question is positive, as in the simple-majority case discussed by Pettit (2006). This is the situation in which agents meet the (very restrictive) conditions of Condorcet's jury theorem. That is, they each have an *independent* and *better-than-random* chance of making a correct judgment on each proposition in question (e.g., Grofman, Owen and Feld 1983). The probability of a correct majority judgment on such a proposition will then converge to certainty with increasing group size. Further, using Bayesian reasoning, it can be shown that the conditional probability of the proposition being true, given that it is supported by a majority (and, *a fortiori*, the conditional probability given supermajority support), will approach certainty as well (see, e.g., List 2004). Under these Condorcetian conditions, deference to supermajority testimony may be epistemically rational *simpliciter*, over and above yielding consistent beliefs.

In general, however, agents need not meet these demanding conditions on all propositions, let alone on matters deeply embedded in their webs of belief (see also Bovens and Rabinowicz 2006 and List 2006, Section VI). For example, as a simple consequence of the laws of probability, an agent cannot generally be as reliable at detecting the truth of a conjunction as he or she is at detecting the truth of each conjunct. The agent may have a probability of 0.7 of detecting the truth of p and also a probability of 0.7 of detecting the truth of q, but—if his or her judgments on p and q are independent from one another—only a probability of 0.49 of the detecting the truth of $p\&q$. Thus, even if the agent meets Condorcet's conditions (particularly better-than-random reliability) on each of p and q, he or she may not meet them on their conjunction. Agents who are highly reliable on 'simple' matters (such as p and q taken separately) can still be less reliable on 'composite' or 'derivative' matters (such as $p\&q$). Since the belief set of any agent (expert, witness, and so on) consists of 'simple' as well as 'derivative' propositions, we cannot assume that the Condorcetian conditions will be satisfied across the board. As a result, there is no guarantee that the majority, or supermajority, will be reliable on all propositions. Deference to majority or supermajority testimony may not be epistemically rational, even if such testimony is internally consistent.

An analysis of when supermajority testimony—over and above being consistent—is a good indicator of the truth of the relevant propositions is beyond the scope of this short paper (for some relevant results, see Feddersen and Pesendorfer 1998 and List 2004). But it seems wise to exercise caution in deferring to such testimony. Before you take on a set of beliefs because there are supermajorities supporting them, make sure these beliefs are not only internally consistent—which they may well be—but also likely to be correct.

Acknowledgements

This is a revised version of a paper that was first circulated in October 2006. I am grateful to Franz Dietrich, Philip Pettit, and Wlodek Rabinowicz for discussions and feedback, and to the anonymous referees of this paper and the editor of the present volume for very helpful comments.

References

Bovens, L. and W. Rabinowicz. 2006. "Democratic Answers to Complex Questions—An Epistemic Perspective." *Synthese 150*: 131–53.
Dietrich, F. 2007. "A generalised model of judgment aggregation." *Social Choice and Welfare* 28(4): 529–65.
Dietrich, F. and C. List. 2007. "Judgment Aggregation by Quota Rules: Majority Voting Generalized." *Journal of Theoretical Politics 19*(4): 391–424.
Fedderson, T. and W. Pesendorfer. 1998. "Convicting the Innocent: The Inferiority of Unanimous Jury Verdicts under Strategic Voting." *American Political Science Review* 92: 23–35.
Grofman, B. G., G. Owen and S. L. Feld. 1983. "Thirteen theorems in search of the truth." *Theory and Decision 15*: 261–78.
Kornhauser, L. A. and L. G. Sager. 1986. "Unpacking the Court." Yale Law Journal 96(1): 82–117.
List, C. 2001. Mission Impossible? The Problem of Democratic Aggregation in the Face of Arrow's Theorem. DPhil-thesis, University of Oxford.
List, C. 2004. "On the Significance of the Absolute Margin." *British Journal for the Philosophy of Science 55*: 521–44.

List, C. 2006. "The Discursive Dilemma and Public Reason." *Ethics* 116(2): 362–402.
List, C. 2011. "Group communication and the transformation of judgments: an impossibility result." *Journal of Political Philosophy* 19(1): 1–27.
List, C. 2012. "The theory of judgment aggregation: An introductory review." *Synthese* 187(1): 179–207.
List, C. and P. Pettit. 2002. "Aggregating Sets of Judgments: An Impossibility Result." *Economics and Philosophy* 18: 89–110.
List, C., and C. Puppe (2009) Judgment aggregation: a survey. In P. Anand, C. Puppe and P. Pattanaik (eds.), *Oxford Handbook of Rational and Social Choice*. Oxford (Oxford University Press).
Nehring, K. 2005. The impossibility of a Paretian rational. Working paper, University of California, Davis.
Nehring, K. and C. Puppe. 2007. "The structure of strategy-proof social choice. Part I: General characterization and possibility results on median spaces." *Journal of Economic Theory* 135(1): 269–305.
Pettit, P. 2001. "Deliberative Democracy and the Discursive Dilemma." *Philosophical Issues* (supplement to *Nous*) 11 (2001): 268–99.
Pettit, P. 2006. "When to defer to majority testimony—and when not." *Analysis* 66: 179–87.

Index

Adler, Jonathan E. 72 n. 11, 75 n. 15
agency 5, 178 n. 11, 98–109
   Stoic account 122, 129–32, 135, 138
agents 7, 21, 23–4, 26, 30–1, 38, 99–104, 106,
   108–9, 115–17, 133, 146, 169, 202–3, 217–18,
   220–3, 225 n. 14, 231–2, 239, 242–50
   group 5, 12, 14, 23–4, 30, 37–8, 46 n. 5, 88,
      97–9, 109–20, 125, 203
aggregation 4, 6, 13, 17–19, 22–7, 29–36, 46,
   65, 82, 88, 119, 221, 225–31, 235, 237–9,
   242–6
Albericus de Rosciate 115
Annas, Julia 123 n. 1–2, 125 n. 5, 129–32, 134
   n. 24, 137 n. 27
Antony, Louise 91 n. 32
aptness 167, 169–70, 174, 176–7
Aristotle 125, 137
assertion 86–7, 89, 107, 148 n. 5, 169–70, 173–4,
   177–80, 183–4
Audi, Robert 70, 72, 75 n. 15, 78 n. 21, 86

Baldus de Ubaldis 115
Ballantyne, Nathan 153 n. 11, 160 n. 14, 162
Banissy, Michael J. 43 n. 1
Bartolus of Sasseferrato 115
belief 3, 5–7, 12–14, 16, 18–20, 22–37, 54–5,
   65–6, 70–81, 84, 104–5, 107–8, 122, 125–6,
   128, 133–6, 140, 142–9, 151–62, 167,
   169–86, 189–96, 198–202, 205, 207–10,
   217–27, 230–8, 242–50
   collective 1–6, 11–14, 16, 18, 20, 22–38, 44,
      46–8, 58 n. 13, 64–8, 110–11, 122, 126–9,
      132, 134, 136, 140, 189–211, 227, 232
Bergmann, Michael 75 n. 14
Bird, Alexander 4, 11, 50–1, 57
Block, Ned 100
BonJour, Laurence 75 n. 14–15
Bouvier, Alban 190 n. 3, 211 n. 67
Bovens, Luc 249
Bradley, Richard 34
Bratman, Michael 11, 116 n. 12
Brenna, Jason 147 n. 3
Briggs, Rachael 6, 120 n. 15
Brown, Matthew J. 49 n. 7, 51 n. 9, 62
Burge, Tyler 72, 75 n. 15

Cariani, Fabrizio 6, 82, 91 n. 32
Canning, Joseph P. 115
Chalmers, David 145

Chandler, Jake 226 n. 16
Chisholm, Roderick M. 75 n. 15
Christensen, David 5, 17 n. 4, 145 n. 1, 147 n. 3,
   149 n. 6, 151 n. 9, 157 n. 13, 217–20, 232
Cicero 135 n. 25
Clark, Andy 50 n. 8
Clark, Austen 190 n. 3
closure 146–7, 152–3, 155–6, 159–60, 221 n. 8,
   247
Coady, C.A.J. 66 n. 5, 70–1, 86
Cohen, L. Jonathan 190–6, 199, 201, 207–10
Cohen, Stewart 28
coherence 6, 103, 110–1, 115, 119, 217–32,
   234–5, 237–8, 249 *see also* incoherence
Comesaña, Juan 21, 32 n. 15
Condorcet Jury Theorem 30
competence 6, 30–1, 34, 71, 77–8 n. 19, 167–76,
   178, 187
conciliationism 5, 142–5, 148–9, 151, 154,
   157, 161
credence 149, 178–9, 182–3, 218–20, 222,
   225, 244

deductive consistency 6, 217, 219, 231–2
DeRose, Keith 28
desire 102–5, 107–8, 113, 191, 194
Deza, Elena 221 n. 9
Deza, Michel Marie 221 n. 9
Dietrich, Franz 65, 221 n. 7, 226, 229 n. 20–1,
   231, 243–4, 246, 250
discursive dilemma 46, 118–19, 242 *see also*
   doctrinal paradox
divergence arguments 2–3
doctrinal paradox 6, 225–9, 242 n. 1 *see also*
   discursive dilemma
dominance 222–3, 231
Douven, Igor 226 n. 16
Duddy, Conal 221 n. 9
Dummett, Michael 72 n. 11
Durkheim, Émile 54–5

Easwaran, Kenny 6, 217 n. 1–2, 219 n. 5, 221
   n. 7, 224 n. 12
Elga, Adam 145 n. 1, 151 n. 9
Elgin, Catherine Z. 70, 86
Empiricus, Sextus 129 n. 14
Engel, Pascal 190–1
Epictetus 130 n. 20, 132 n. 23, 137
Eschmann, T. 115

eudaemonia 123
evidentialism 3, 32
experts 29, 33–5, 46–8, 88, 130, 139, 155, 158–9, 176

fallibility 142, 145, 151–3, 161–2
Faulkner, Paul 72 n. 11
Feld, Scott L. 30 n. 14, 249
Feldman, Richard 15
Fine, Kit 12
Fitelson, Branden 6, 217 n. 1–2, 219 n. 5, 224 n. 12
Foley, Richard 217 n. 2, 222–3
Frances, Bryan 148 n. 5, 151 n. 9
Fricker, Elizabeth 66 n. 5, 70, 75 n. 15, 86
Fricker, Miranda 140 n. 30
Friedman, Jane 221 n. 7
Fumerton, Richard 147 n. 3, 225 n. 14

Gellius 132 n. 23, 135 n. 26
Giere, Ron 48–50, 58, 62
Gilbert, Margaret 6, 11, 13 n. 2, 43–4, 47–8 n. 6, 51, 53, 58 n. 13, 64 n. 1, 68 n. 6, 91 n. 31, 116 n. 12, 126–8, 190–1, 194–203, 205–11
Goldberg, Sanford 21, 23–4 91 n. 32, 147–8
Goldman, Alvin I. 4, 21–2, 26, 29, 32, 34, 37 n. 18, 38, 64 n. 1, 75 n. 14–16, 76, 79 n. 25, 91 n. 32, 190 n. 4
Goodin, Robert E. 31
Graham, Peter J. 71 n. 9
Grantham, Ross 117
Grofman, Bernard 30 n. 14, 34, 249
Grossi, Davide 226 n. 17, 235 n. 23
grounding 12, 14, 20
Grube, G.M.A. 193 n. 16

Hakli, Raul 196 n. 28, 201 n. 41, 205–6, 209 n. 64, 211 n. 67
Hardwig, John 49, 72 n. 11, 74 n. 12
Hawthorne, John 75 n. 15
Heider, Fritz 106
Hobbes, Thomas 117–18, 120
Hutchins, Edwin 45, 49–50, 52, 55–6

incoherence 103, 223, 228 *see also* coherence
Inwood, Brad 123

Jackson, Frank 100–1
James, Aaron 211 n. 67
joint acceptance 3, 13 n. 2
Joyce, James 219–20, 222, 225 n. 14
judgment 6, 11, 13, 17, 25, 27, 31–2, 34 n. 16, 65–7, 69, 81–3, 88, 97, 103–4, 115, 117–19, 130, 133, 151–4, 156, 161, 167–70, 173, 175–6, 178–9, 181–2, 184, 218, 220–1, 223–31, 233–9, 242–3, 245, 249

justification 14–15, 19–21, 23–30, 33, 36, 38, 49, 66 n. 5, 72 n. 11, 74–6, 148, 159, 169–70, 174, 224
collective 1–4, 11–13, 15, 17–30

Kanai, Ryota 43 n. 1
Kaplan, Mark 217 n. 2
Kawall, Jason 126 n. 6
Kitcher, Philip 51
Klein, Peter 217 n. 2
Knorr-Cetina, Karin 47–8, 49 n. 7, 56, 58–9
knowledge 1, 4, 6, 15, 24, 27–8, 50–1, 55–6, 57, 60, 64, 66, 68–9, 71–81, 83–6, 89, 107, 124, 133, 146, 167, 169–70, 172–8, 182–7
collective 1–2, 4, 42, 44–8, 50, 52–3, 57–8, 61–2, 71–3, 127 n. 7, 189, 195 n. 22, 198 n. 34
scientific 4, 42, 48, 50, 57, 62
Kolmogorov axiom 232
Kolodny, Niko 217–19
Konek, Jason 240
Kornblith, Hilary 21, 91 n. 32, 145 n. 1, 147, 151
Kornhauser, Lewis 200 n. 37, 226, 242
Kuhn, Thomas 48 n. 6
Kyburg, Henry 217 n. 2

Lackey, Jennifer 4, 11, 15, 33, 39 n. 19, 66 n. 5, 71, 74–5, 77–8, 86, 120, 126 n. 7, 140 n. 32, 148–50, 162, 179 n. 12, 211 n. 67, 240, 250
Leonard, Nick 240
Levi, Isaac 226 n. 16
Lewis, David 195 n. 22
List, Christian 6–7, 11–14, 17 n. 4, 19, 25, 31, 34 n. 16, 65, 69, 82 n. 28, 88–9, 98, 100–1, 109–10, 116 n. 12, 118–20, 126 n. 7, 200 n. 37, 221 n. 7, 226, 229–31, 242–6, 249
Long, A.A. 124, 130–2, 135 n. 25–6
Lyons, Jack 21

McDowell, John 72 n. 11, 75 n. 15
McGeer, Victoria 102–3
McIntosh, Chad 97 n. 1
Magnus, P.D. 51
Mathiesen, Kay 11, 190 n. 3, 201 n. 42
Meijers, A.W.M 196 n. 28, 202 n. 46
memory 19, 22–3, 38, 72, 170, 176–7, 180–4
Menzies, Peter 101
Merton, Robert K. 50
Mill, John Stuart 142–3, 151–3, 157, 161–2
Miller, Boaz 211 n. 67
Miller, Michael K. 221 n. 9
Mongin, Philippe 226 n. 17

Nelkin, Dana K. 224 n. 13
Nehring, Klaus D. 243–4, 246
non-reductionism 4, 66, 68–70, 73, 77, 79–81, 83, 88, 90

non-summativism 2–5, 64, 66–9, 80, 88, 196
norms 43–4, 55, 169, 181, 217–18, 225, 231
Nozick, Robert 75 n. 14, 77 n. 18, 79 n. 23

Osherson, Daniel 221 n. 7
Owen, Guillermo 30 n. 14, 249
Owens, David 72 n. 11

Pauly, Marc 65 n. 4, 226, 229 n. 21
Peacocke, Christopher 100
Pettit, Philip 5–6, 11–14, 17 n. 4, 19, 25, 34 n. 16, 43–4, 46, 58, 65 n. 4, 66–7, 81–2, 89 n. 30, 100–5, 109–10, 114 n. 11, 116 n. 12, 118–19, 126 n. 7, 190 n. 3, 200 n. 37, 226, 242–4, 249–50
Piggins, Ashley 221 n. 9
Pigozzi, Gabriella 221 n. 9, 226 n. 17, 235 n. 23, 240
Pilchman, Daniel 6, 211 n. 67
Plantinga, Alvin 72 n. 11, 75 n. 14, 77 n. 18
Plato 192–3, 210
Plutarch 131 n. 21
Polak, Benjamin 119
Pollock, John 75 n. 14, 217 n. 2, 224 n. 13
Popper, Karl 58
pragmatic encroachment 6, 167, 169, 176–7, 180
preface paradox 6, 218, 220 n. 7, 224 n. 13, 232
Priest, Maura 193 n. 17, 200 n. 38
Pritchard, Duncan 77 n. 18, 79 n. 24
Puppe, Clemens 226 n. 17, 243–4, 246 n. 8–9

Quinton, Anthony 11, 64–5, 194–5, 199

Rabinowicz, Wlodek 249–50
reductionism 4–5, 64–6, 78, 80, 90
Reed, Baron 75 n. 14–15, 91 n. 32
Reeve, C.D.C. 193 n. 16
rejectionism 201–11
reliabilism 3–4, 19, 21–6, 28–9, 32–3, 35–8
reliability 6, 17, 21–6, 29–37, 69–70, 73, 77–81, 83–5, 87, 90, 99, 101, 146, 162, 168–77, 180–1, 183–4, 244, 249
Reynolds, Steven L. 72
Romeijn, Jan-Willem 226 n. 16
Ross, James 71 n. 9, 72 n. 11
Rotondo, Andrew 162
Ryan, Sharon 217 n. 2

Sager, Laurence 200 n. 37, 226, 242
Schaffer, Jonathan 12
Schervish, Mark 222 n. 10
Schmitt, Frederick F. 3, 11, 15, 19, 21, 35 n. 17, 39 n. 19, 43–4, 67, 72 n. 11, 190 n. 3
Schweikard, David 116 n. 12

science 42–3, 47–53, 55–7, 60–2, 155
Searle, John 11, 102 n. 3
Sedley, David 130–2, 135 n. 25–6
Sherman, Nancy 125 n. 5
Siakel, Daniel 211 n. 67
Simmel, Marianne 106
Skinner, B.F. 117
skopos 5, 122–8, 137, 140,
Smith, Holly 35 n. 17, 39 n. 19
Smith, Michael 105
Sosa, Ernest 5–6, 75 n. 15, 77 n. 18, 79 n. 24–5, 91 n. 32, 145, 178
Spener, Maja 149–50, 162
Stevenson, Leslie 192 n. 14
Stoic 5, 122–5, 127–9, 131–40
summativism 2–4, 12, 35, 64–7, 80, 194–6, 199–200, 208
Sundell, Tim 91 n. 32
supermajority 6–7, 65, 82, 226, 231, 242–50
supervenience 12, 14, 58, 60
Surowiecki, James 87
Swift, Henry 162

telos 5, 122–8, 137–40
testimony 1, 3–7, 15, 19, 23–4, 64–81, 83–90, 177, 182, 184, 242–6, 248–50
    deflationary account of 4–5, 66, 69, 80–1, 83–7, 90–1
    majority 6, 242, 249–50
    supermajority 6–7, 243–6, 248–50
Thompson, Christopher 34
Tollefsen, Deborah 11, 65 n. 3, 68–9, 81, 89, 126–7, 190 n. 3, 196 n. 28, 201 n. 40, 208–9
transmission 14–15, 18–20, 23–4, 26, 29 n. 12, 38, 72, 79
Trefethen, Amanda 211 n. 67
Tuomela, Raimo 11, 43, 47–8, 53, 58, 68 n. 6, 116 n. 12, 190 n. 3, 192 n. 13, 196 n. 28
Turri, John 91 n. 32

van Hees, Martin 65 n. 4, 226, 226 n. 21
virtues 5, 82, 122–8, 133, 135–8, 140, 219

Weatherson, Brian 151 n. 9
Welbourne, Michael 72 n. 11
White, Heath 125 n. 5
Williams, Michael 75 n. 15
Williamson, Timothy 72 n. 11, 77 n. 18, 79 n. 24, 170 n. 4, 225 n. 14
Woolf, C.N.S. 115
Wray, K. Brad 11, 127–9, 132–5, 190 n. 3, 196 n. 28–29, 202, 211 n. 67
Wright, Crispin 14 n. 3
Wright, Sarah 5, 138 n. 29

Printed and bound by CPI Group (UK) Ltd, Croydon, CR0 4YY